FORTY ANTI-CATHOLIC LIES

DR. GERARD M. VERSCHUUREN

FORTY
ANTI-CATHOLIC
LIES

A MYTH-BUSTING
APOLOGIST SETS THE
RECORD STRAIGHT

SOPHIA INSTITUTE PRESS
MANCHESTER, NEW HAMPSHIRE

Sophia Institute Press
Box 5284, Manchester, NH 03108
1-800-888-9344
www.SophiaInstitute.com

Sophia Institute Press® is a registered trademark of Sophia Institute.

Library of Congress Cataloging-in-Publication Data

Names: Verschuuren, G. M. N. (Geert M. N.), author.
Title: Forty anti-Catholic lies : a myth-busting apologist sets the record
straight / by Gerard M. Verschuuren, Ph.D.
Description: Manchester, New Hampshire : Sophia Institute Press, 2018. |
Includes index.
Identifiers: LCCN 2018013702 | ISBN 9781622825240 (pbk. : alk. paper)
Subjects: LCSH: Catholic Church—Apologetic works.
Classification: LCC BX1752 .V47 2018 | DDC 282—dc23 LC record available
at https://lccn.loc.gov/2018013702

6th Printing

CONTENTS

PART 3: CATHOLICISM AND ITS UNIQUENESS

PART 4: CATHOLICISM AND OTHER RELIGIONS

PART 5: CATHOLICISM AND ITS HISTORY

PART 6: CATHOLICISM AND SCIENCE

PART 7: CATHOLICISM AND SOCIETY

PREFACE

If you are a Catholic, you should know your Catholic Faith. If you are not a Catholic but have an opinion about the Catholic Faith, you should know what the Catholic Faith really is, so you don't spread misinformation about what Catholics believe.

Unfortunately, there is much misinformation in our culture about Catholicism. It has been spread through books, newspapers, television, the Internet, and other mass media. Some say it is fabricated information based on an antireligious bias, and specifically an anti-Catholic prejudice in media and academia. Whatever the underlying motive, there is definitely a propaganda war going on against the Catholic Church.

Nowadays, anti-Catholic rhetoric is often disguised. Many "liberals" and "progressives" do not oppose Catholics because they are Catholics — that could be seen as discrimination — but because Catholics are believed to have certain beliefs "out of line" with mainstream thinking. Those alleged beliefs, however, are often caricatures and misrepresentations of the real beliefs Catholics hold.

What do Catholics really believe? Asking any Catholic is not always the best way to find out, for some Catholics may not even know the basics of their own Faith, or they may already have been affected by the misinformation that keeps bombarding all of us. As Albert Einstein put it, "It is easier to split atoms than prejudices." So we need to go beyond just scratching the surface.

Let's try to set the facts straight in this book. In a rather arbitrary order, we will discuss some more popular myths and fabrications about Catholics. You can read them consecutively or use the table of contents to search for specific topics. In each case, we will try to separate real Catholic beliefs from fabricated beliefs about the Catholic Faith, so you can learn from them yourself or prepare yourself better for discussions with those who attack your Faith. Our goal is religious correctness rather than political correctness.

In this book, I speak of "lies" about the Catholic Church. Although a "lie" is usually defined as a false statement made with deliberate intent to deceive, I do not mean that all people who believe in these lies necessarily have a deliberate intent to deceive others about Catholicism. They are sometimes only misinformed and lack the correct knowledge—in which case their "lie" is only an inaccurate or false statement. To better inform them, I wrote this book. For those who use these lies intentionally to smear the Catholic Church, I can only hope and pray that this book may change their intentions.

I often use the term "Catholics" instead of the term "the Catholic Church." Let this not deceive you. I do not mean that Catholics form a single unified bloc; there are always disagreements, and even dissenters. But in general, Catholics as a group are more homogenous than Protestants, because Catholics have much in common that sets them apart from other Christians. The main reason for this is that the Catholic Church makes it her mission to keep Catholics united in doctrine and in morals. How much this is possible is up to you to decide when reading this book.

FORTY ANTI-CATHOLIC LIES

PART I

CATHOLICISM AND THE BIBLE

I

CATHOLICS ARE FORBIDDEN TO READ THE BIBLE

THE LIE

The Catholic Church ignores, opposes, hides, and even sometimes destroys the Bible in order to keep it from the people. Catholics are not allowed to read the Bible on their own. In fact, that's part of what got Martin Luther in trouble when he translated the Bible into German so everyone could read it.

The personal reading, understanding, and interpreting of Scripture was, and still is, considered a very serious threat to the authority of the Catholic Church. She does not want Catholics to read the Bible out of fear that her doctrines will be found out to be false. As a result, most Catholics live a life of *sine Scriptura* (*without* Scripture), whereas most Protestants live a life of *sola Scriptura*" (Scripture *alone*).

THE TRUTH

According to a recent Rasmussen poll, 25 percent of Evangelical Protestants read the Bible daily, as do 20 percent of other Protestants, while daily Bible-reading is done by only 7 percent of Catholics. The poll also showed that 44 percent of Catholics "rarely or never" read the Bible, whereas this is true of only 7 percent of Evangelicals and 13 percent of other Protestants. No wonder Catholics usually have trouble in reciting whole phrases from the Bible or locating them in the Bible. They even have a hard time looking up a specific book in the Bible.

Although it is true that Catholics do not always read the Scriptures, they always *hear* the Scriptures, for you can't go to Mass without hearing Scripture readings over and over again. There are several reasons Catholics did not, and still do not, read Scripture as often as Protestants do.

The first reason is that, for many centuries, the faithful were not educated enough to be able to read at all. Most people were, at best, only functionally literate. This explains why the Church used stained-glass windows and art to tell Bible stories. Obviously, Bible reading requires readers—which were for centuries in short supply. Besides, due to invading vandals such as Huns, Visigoths, and Vikings during the "Dark Ages," the infrastructure of Europe had been devastated, and education had been hampered (see chapter 28). This also affected Bible reading. Had it not been for the Catholic Church hiding all her Bibles and her textbooks from the rampaging and pillaging of these vandals, however, all schools of learning would have died during these "Dark Ages." On the other hand, it is still amazing to see that some saints from this "dark" period in history were able to read the Bible even in Hebrew: St. Jerome, St. Paula, St. Isidore of Seville, St. Gall, St. Alcuin, and St. Rabanus, to name just a few.

The second reason Catholics did not *read* the Bible was that copies of the Bible were hard to come by before the printing press was invented by Johannes Gutenberg in 1436. Before that time, hardly anyone owned a "Bible." During most of the Middle Ages, each Bible was written by hand. So, prior to 1436, the idea of everybody having a Bible was out of the question, even if one was able to read.

Each Bible had to be copied by hand, and it took many years for a monk working behind the walls of a monastery, called a *scriptorium*, to do this. Each Bible was made on sheep's hide (vellum), so it took 250 sheep and thousands of hours to make each Bible. This explains why copies of the Bible were chained to the walls of churches during this period—not to prevent people from reading them, but so that people could not steal them, or take them home to read, or take them away from others. So it is true that the Church chained Bibles to the walls in the Middle Ages, but for the same reason the telephone company used to chain its phone books to phone booths: to prevent people from taking them away.

A third reason for not reading the Scriptures was the lack of Bibles in the vernacular. In the fifth century, when St. Jerome translated the Bible from the original languages into Latin, Latin was the language of the people. His Bible is therefore called the Vulgate, the "people's version." Some claim that using Latin was a shrewd way for the Catholic Church to prevent people from reading the Bible. Nothing is further from the truth. The Latin Vulgate was always available to anyone who wanted to read it. True, not everyone could read Latin because for centuries there were no public schools and literacy was not that common, especially not among the peasants. But those who had been educated could read Latin. Latin was the common language of Europe for centuries; scholars and scientists published everything in Latin so that more people could read it. But yes, even if you were literate, you had to know Latin to be able to read Scripture.

This is not as strange as it may sound. Even when Jews—often called the "People of the Book"—wanted to read their Book, the

Bible, they were expected to make the effort to learn Hebrew, at least until the nineteenth century. Although there was a Greek translation of the Old Testament, the Septuagint, that version had been adopted by the Christians, so the Jews basically abandoned it. From then on, any Jew who wanted to read the Bible had to learn Hebrew. In a similar way, Catholics who wanted to read the Bible were expected to make the effort to learn Latin.

The fourth reason Catholics did not read Scripture was that *vernacular* Bible versions were rare for a while, because Greek and Latin were still "living" languages. But soon vernacular Bibles would come along. Although many think that these did not exist until the sixteenth century, there were some much earlier examples in the Catholic Church. In seventh-century Britain, before English was even a language, Caedmon, a monk of Whitby, paraphrased most of the Bible into the common tongue. During the early eighth century, St. Bede the Venerable also translated parts of the Bible into the language of the common British people. Another example is the mission of Sts. Cyril and Methodius to the Slavic people in Moravia during the ninth century. These two saints are famous for introducing the Slavonic liturgy, after St. Cyril developed an alphabet for the Old Slavonic language, the precursor of the Russian "Cyrillic" alphabet. So, in 885, St. Methodius translated the entire Bible into this language.

And the list could go on and on. Prior to the publication of Luther's Bible in German, there had been more than twenty versions of the whole Bible translated into various German dialects—done by Catholics, of all people. In Italy there were more than forty editions of the Bible before the first Protestant version appeared, beginning at Venice in 1471; and twenty-five of these were in the Italian language before 1500, with the explicit permission of Rome.

Catholics are forbidden to read the Bible

The fifth reason most Catholics did not read the Bible is that the rise of vernacular Bible versions, made easier by the invention of the printing press, created new problems. The 180 Bibles produced by Johannes Gutenberg in 1455, printed and then illuminated by hand, took a year to produce—roughly the time a monastery scriptorium took to produce a single copy. Although that was an awfully small press run, the output would multiply fast—but so would the problems that would come with it. With the invention of printing, there was a communications explosion, and one suddenly saw lots of people making very poor and heretical translations of the Bible and popularizing them throughout Christendom. As usual, good inventions may have bad side effects.

Obviously, creating a vernacular version requires translation—and translation means interpretation. St. Peter says about the epistles of St. Paul, "There are some things in them hard to understand, which the ignorant and unstable twist to their own destruction, as they do the other Scriptures" (2 Pet. 3:16). Even Martin Luther realized that there are as many theologies as there are heads. How right he was: Soon there would be more than three hundred Protestant denominations, each having its own distinct beliefs about the interpretation of Scripture. Many of these interpretations conflicted with each other, yet every one of them claimed divine inspiration. Nowadays, we can even see a rise of what George Weigel calls "entrepreneurial Christianity—founding your own church." No wonder the Catholic Church tried to stop this fragmentation.

This problem had surfaced already long before Luther. As early as the twelfth century, there was a movement of people called the Albigensians (or Cathars). Until such time, the Church had been happy to translate the Bible into the vernacular tongue, but now she saw the authority of the Bible abused by cult leaders who preyed on the ignorance, or the latent extremism, of the people. In 1129, at the Council of Narbonne, in direct response to the abuses of the Albigensians and related heresies, the Bible was forbidden to all, except priests, bishops, and others in religious vocations. The people would hear the Bible in church anyway, but at least not through questionable translations.

Similar reactions happened when later Bible translations emerged—translations by people such as John Wycliffe and William Tyndale, which contained erroneous or questionable translations as well as anti-Catholic footnotes. St. Thomas More commented that searching for errors in the Tyndale Bible was like searching for water in the sea. Even King Henry VIII, in 1531, condemned the Tyndale Bible as a corruption of Scripture. So it should not surprise us that it became illegal in Anglican England and the American colonies to print the Bible in English. The Crown claimed a copyright on the King James Version (KJV), and printing of that version was a privilege accorded exclusively to the king's printers and the universities of Oxford and Cambridge. So the Catholic Church was not alone in matters like these.

Now we should be able to respond better to some issues raised by the anti-Catholic rhetoric mentioned at the beginning of this chapter. First, did the Catholic Church have a problem with the Bible? Quite the opposite! If the Church were really against the Bible, why did her monks work so diligently through the centuries making copies of it? Catholics had the best and the brightest of biblical scholars long before modern times—just consider Origen, Tertullian, St. Augustine, St. John Chrysostom, St. Jerome, and St. Thomas Aquinas, to mention a few.

Besides, the first book ever printed was a Catholic Bible, printed by Johannes Gutenberg. Even the first printed Bible in English was published by British Catholics exiled to France at the colleges of Douay and Rheims. They published the New Testament in 1582 and the Old Testament in 1610. This Douay-Rheims Bible was a rather literal translation of the Latin Vulgate and went through several revisions. It was completed in 1610, one year before the King James Version was published. The Catholic New Testament translation, published in 1582, was one of the reliable sources used by the KJV translators.

Second, did the Church forbid Catholics to read the Bible? What she did ban was not the Bible itself but unauthorized translations of it, because they were a source of confusion for the faithful and often spread anti-Catholic propaganda through their translations and footnotes.

The idea that the Bible was on the list of forbidden books is a plain fabrication. In 1564, Pius IV promulgated in his constitution *Dominici gregis,* the *Index of Forbidden Books* (see chapter 36). According to its third rule, the Bible may be read in the vernacular by pious and learned individuals, according to the judgment of the bishop, as a help to the better understanding of the Vulgate. The stipulation is clear and prevents uneducated minds from being swayed by corrupted translations.

Third, did the Catholic Church burn Bibles? Yes, she did sometimes burn Bibles translated in the vernacular. The Church did not burn Bibles to keep Scripture away from people, though; instead she burned Bibles — that is, poorly translated bibles — to protect her flock. Does this action make the Church anti-Bible? Of course not. If it did, then the Protestants of this period were also anti-Bible. In 1522, John Calvin, the leading Protestant Reformer, had as many copies as could be found of the Servetus Bible burned, since Calvin did not approve of it. In those days it was common practice on both sides to burn unapproved books (see chapter 36).

The Catholic Church cherishes the Bible as one of its most precious gifts. But another precious gift is her sacraments (see chapter 5). Some Catholics are of the opinion that, to save their souls, it is more important to participate in the sacraments than to read the Bible. But even then, the Bible is part of all sacraments. During Mass, for instance, Catholics read or hear more from the Bible than most Protestants do during their services. Nowadays, the Church has a four-year cycle of three or four Bible readings during the first half of the Mass. As a consequence, Catholics who go to church are regularly exposed to a wider range of biblical texts than are most Protestants, who usually hear their ministers preach on a small selection of their own favorite passages. Interestingly enough, the first Bible to have chapters and numbered verses was produced by the Catholic archbishop of Canterbury, Stephen Langton.

All of this is in line with what Vatican II says in its constitution *Dei Verbum*: "Easy access to Sacred Scripture should be provided for all the Christian faithful." The *Catechism of the Catholic Church* (133) explicitly quotes St. Jerome, the translator of the first official Latin Bible, where he says, "Ignorance of Scripture is ignorance of Christ."

CONCLUSION

Catholics are *not* forbidden to read the Bible. The Catholic Church encouraged the translation of the Bible into Latin, and later into vernacular languages, so more people could read the Bible. Catholics do not live a life without Scripture. Catholics listen to four Bible readings every Sunday, and many even every weekday. And no, the Bible was never placed on the *Index of Forbidden Books*. These are lies, mere fabrications. The truth is much more intricate than these fabrications suggest.

2

CATHOLICS ADDED BOOKS TO THE BIBLE

THE LIE

Catholics manipulated the books of the Bible to their own choosing. They invented books that they then added to their own Bible. Books that Catholics added to the *Old* Testament of the Bible are the books of Tobit, Judith, Baruch, 1 and 2 Maccabees, and Ecclesiasticus (also known as Sirach, not to be confused with Ecclesiastes). "Catholic" books you cannot find in some Protestant *New* Testaments are the Letter to the Hebrews, the Letter of James, and the book of Revelation. This is a clear corruption by the Catholic Church of the Word of God.

THE TRUTH

In fact, the story is more complicated. To get things straight, we need to delve into some history. Let's start with the Old Testament. When the Hebrew Bible was translated into Greek — to accommodate the Jews in the Diaspora, outside Palestine, who were no longer fluent in Hebrew — the Septuagint was born and finally finished in 132 B.C. This translation contained books that were very popular among Jews but would later be rejected by the rising faction of Pharisees. These additional books included Tobit, Judith, Sirach, and Maccabees. Together they are often referred to as *deuterocanonical* books.

But then, near the end of the first century A.D., after Jerusalem had been demolished by the Romans, the leading rabbis at the time determined at the town of Jamnia which books should be considered part of the rabbinical Hebrew Bible from then on. These books were from now on considered *canonical*—part of the authorized *canon*. Texts current among the Pharisees at the time became normative for the Jewish tradition to come. Some books from the Septuagint did not make it through this rabbinical censorship. The books of the Maccabees, for instance, used to be highly popular among both Jews and Christians, but were banned from the rabbinical canon because the dynasty that had come forth from the Maccabees had turned pagan. So they were censored. Ironically, the still popular Jewish feast of Hanukkah traces its origin back to the rejected books of the Maccabees.

The Christians of the first and second centuries did not follow the new rabbinical canon. St. Paul, for instance, died before that canon was established, so he routinely referred to the Septuagint and its canon, which included books that would later be removed by the Pharisees. Besides, Christians would read their Old Testament in Greek (the Septuagint) and very soon in Latin. There were various Latin translations until around 400, when St. Jerome undertook an official, papal translation into Latin, known as the Vulgate. It would become the official Bible of the Catholic Church for quite a while and was based on all the books found in the Septuagint.

But the question remains: What should be included in the Bible? As to the Old Testament, the Church had to ask herself whether the Hebrew Scriptures should be part of the Christian canon. The answer of the early Christian Church was a definite yes. All of them? Whereas the Jews did not accept books such as Maccabees in their canon, Christians did, because those had played an important role in their own circles—they were used in their liturgies, for instance. It was not Scripture that could decide this; it was the "living Church" of the first centuries, which Catholics call *Tradition*. So the outcome was rather predictable: the Septuagint should be the standard!

But what about the canon of the New Testament? Before the idea of a canon of New Testament Scripture had been formulated, the Church had already developed her own concept of what was canonical and orthodox. The Scriptures of the Old Testament needed a canon of New Testament interpretation—a living interpretation by means of the Faith handed down from the apostles, which was the *Tradition* of the apostles and their successors. Scripture is not an entity in itself. It is a product of the Church and her tradition—guided by apostolic succession (see chapter 3). We are not, as Pope Benedict XVI once noted, a people of the Book—like Jews and Muslims—but a people of the Word that was "in the beginning" and became flesh.

Consider the alternative: If the Church does not determine the correct canon, who or what should? If the Church does not determine the correct canon, we could easily end up with multiple denominations, which would keep splitting into smaller and smaller fractions, each creating its own Bible canon, leading to a very fragmented Christianity. It is not up to each Christian to determine which books are canonical and orthodox, and therefore should be included in Scripture. The Bible is a book that came from the very heart of the Church; the apostles authored and the Church authorized the New

Testament. So, it is the Church that has authority over Scripture; individuals do not.

And this is what happened. The early Church decided to omit a few Gospels—for instance, the Gospel of Peter plus all the gospels of "gnostic" origin—because they went against her tradition and were not used in her liturgies. Soon more detailed common guidelines were developed. In 367, the archbishop of Alexandria, St. Athanasius, published a listing of orthodox, canonical books, identical to the one we find in our current Catholic New Testament. They can also be found in the Vulgate.

Things changed dramatically when the Protestant Reformers entered the scene, however. When they decided to go back to the prime sources of the Old Testament, they went back to the Hebrew canon of Jamnia in A.D. 70. So the books that occur in both the Septuagint and the Vulgate but are missing in the official rabbinical canon of A.D. 70 were called *deuterocanonical* (i.e., belonging to the second canon) and given the label *Apocrypha* by the Reformers. They discarded these deuterocanonical books because in certain instances these books contain decidedly Catholic doctrine, as in the case of 2 Maccabees 12:42–46, which clearly supports the doctrine of prayers for the dead, which could be seen as support for a Purgatory (see chapter 6).

In Martin Luther's translation, the Apocrypha are still part of the text, placed between the Old and the New Testaments. They were also included in the Protestant King James version of 1611 but were rejected by the Puritans as not being of "divine inspiration." The Puritans did not seem to realize that their version was based on a historical coincidence that had suppressed books not in compliance with rabbinic orthodoxy established in A.D. 70. Besides, we should ask ourselves why the decisions of a

Jewish council held more than thirty years after the Resurrection of Christ would be binding on the Christian community.

Something similar happened to the Protestant canon of the New Testament. The canon that had been used in the Church for more than a millennium was abruptly changed by the Reformers. For his own Bible, Martin Luther would reject some of the books that had long been part of the Catholic canon—books such as the Letter to the Hebrews, the letters of St. James and St. Jude, and the book of Revelation. In 1826, the influential Bible Society of London even refused to include them in their new Bible edition.

Luther's reasons for rejecting them varied. The book of Revelation, for instance, he found just too bizarre: "A revelation should be revealing," he said. When he first translated and published the New Testament, he thought that the book of Revelation should not have the same status or authority as the four Gospels and the letters of Paul or Peter. And so he put it at the end, didn't number it, and didn't put "Saint" in front of John's name. He thought it was an edifying book, but not of the same status as other books. But then he changed his mind, because Revelation allowed him to make one of his central points, which was that the papacy had to be the antichrist mentioned in Revelation (see chapter 7).

His reason for rejecting the Letter to the Hebrews was of a different nature. The letter speaks extensively about the high priesthood of Jesus, whereas it was Luther's goal to abolish the priesthood as found in the Catholic Church (see chapter 9). So Luther's doctrines were not based on the Bible; rather, his Bible was defined by his own doctrines.

Something similar can be said about his rejection of the Letter of James. St. James says, "What does it profit, my brethren, if a man says he has faith but has not works?" (2:14), but this line basically contradicts Luther's *sola fides* doctrine (only faith, not works; see chapter 8). Because James's letter went against this doctrine, Luther rejected its place in the Bible. What is actually happening here is again that, instead of using a certain scriptural interpretation to form a set of doctrines, Luther used a set of doctrines to authorize his selection of canonical books. That comes close to self-serving circular reasoning.

CONCLUSION

Catholics did not add books to the Bible, but Protestants did remove some — thus violating their own rule, as the very doctrine of *sola Scriptura* prohibits anyone from changing anything in the Bible, whether by adding or deleting parts. As to the question "Which Bible?" the answer is not left up to individuals, but to the Church, which "owns" the Bible.

3

CATHOLICS THINK THE
BIBLE IS NOT ENOUGH

THE LIE

Catholics not only add their own books to the Bible, but they also add their own Catholic interpretation to the Bible. They ignore the fact that Scripture alone determines what we should believe in Christianity. Besides, they accept as doctrine teachings or beliefs that are not explicitly mentioned in the Bible.

Catholics violate Luther's doctrine of *sola Scriptura* (Scripture alone), which makes it very clear that Scripture is the supreme authority in all matters of doctrine and practice. The doctrine of *sola Scriptura* maintains that individual believers need only the Bible as a rule of faith and that they can obtain a true interpretation of a given Scripture passage simply by comparing it with what the rest of the Bible teaches.

THE TRUTH

Catholics have a rather different view; they claim that we need Tradition in addition to Scripture. The idea that Scripture is our only authority in matters of faith is deceiving.

Before we can prove that Tradition is needed as well, we need to ask: What is wrong with the idea of *sola Scriptura?* The problem with the rule—or doctrine, if you will—of "Scripture alone" is that it does not and cannot work on its own. There are several reasons for this. Let's discuss them briefly.

The first reason is very straightforward: the doctrine of *sola Scriptura* is nowhere to be found in Scripture. As the theologian Joel S. Peters puts it, "There is not one verse anywhere in the Bible in which it is taught, and it therefore becomes a self-refuting doctrine." Besides, it's impossible to claim that Scripture is inspired and true because Scripture says so. That would be like declaring defendants in court innocent because the defendants themselves say they are. As Tim Staples puts it, "The Protestant appeal to the sole authority of Scripture to defend *Sola Scriptura* is a textbook example of circular reasoning. One cannot prove the inspiration of Scripture, or any text, from the text itself. The Book of Mormon, the Hindu Vedas, the Qur'an, the writings of Mary Baker Eddy, and many other books claim inspiration, but this does not make them inspired." A claim to inspiration is not a guarantee of inspiration. All sect leaders claim inspiration. It is the Church's task to separate the inspired wheat from the uninspired chaff.

The second reason is that the *sola Scriptura* doctrine requires Protestants to show, based on Scripture alone, which books belong in Scripture. But this is something impossible because there is no canon list to be found in Scripture (see chapter 2). Since the Bible did not come with an inspired table of contents, the doctrine of *sola Scriptura* creates its own inconsistency: we must assume we know with certainty which books belong in the Bible based on the doctrine of "Scripture alone." As Joel Peters put it, "The unadulterated fact is that one cannot know unless there is an authority outside the Bible which can tell him." In other words, a book's presence in the Bible cannot be that which initially made it biblical, for it was not initially in the Bible; on the contrary, the early Church deemed certain books to be divinely inspired and therefore included them in the Bible, thereby making them biblical.

The third reason is that Scripture cannot become a standard of orthodoxy until Scripture is complete, so that we can know what is supposed to be in it. If we want to prove everything from Scripture alone, we need a canon of Scripture to begin with. In fact, we cannot even begin to use *sola Scriptura* before we have identified what the Scriptures are. It was not until the Synod of Rome (382), under Pope Damasus I, and the Councils of Hippo (393) and Carthage (397) that we find a definitive list of canonical books, and each of these councils acknowledged the very same list of books. Up to that point, the New Testament's specific books were not explicitly established. So, in every Bible, there is a very important page not inspired by the Holy Spirit—and that is its table of contents.

Reason 4 is a consequence of the previous argument. How could the earliest Christians have lived by "Scripture alone," when they had only the Hebrew Scriptures but no Scriptures about Jesus yet? Were they perhaps not "real" Christians? The doctrine of *sola Scriptura* could never have worked for them. During his journeys around the Mediterranean, St. Paul did not walk around with a copy of the New Testament in his pocket—for there was no New Testament yet.

The fifth reason is that the Church is not the product of Scripture. It's the other way around: Scripture is the product of the Church. The New Testament did not exist for a while, although the Church was very much alive. When Paul died in the year 67, most parts of the New Testament did not exist yet. The Gospel of Mark was probably finished by the year 70, the Gospel of Matthew around 80, the Gospel of Luke around 85, and the Gospel of John around 90 to 100. In other words, for most of the first century of the Church's existence, there was no New Testament. The New Testament was in the process of being created in the heart of the Church.

Reason 6 can be rather brief, yet very revealing. The doctrine of *sola Scriptura* prohibits adding anything to or deleting anything from the Bible. But, as a matter of fact, not only do Catholics accuse Protestants of removing books, but Protestants accuse Catholics of adding books to the Bible. Apparently, there must be something other than "Scripture alone" that makes them do so. "Scripture alone" is not enough to explain their actions.

Reason 7 is based on the fact that the texts of Scripture are open to various interpretations. Hence, Scripture cannot be interpreted by itself. As St. Thomas Aquinas said, "[It] is the task of the good interpreter to look, not at the words, but at the meaning." In the Acts of the Apostles, Philip ran to the Ethiopian eunuch in his chariot, "and heard him reading Isaiah the prophet and said, 'Do you understand what you are reading?' He replied, 'How can I, unless someone guides me?'" (8:30–31). Even Jesus Himself often demonstrated how the scribes and Pharisees used wrong interpretations, and hence He corrected them by properly interpreting Scripture, thus demonstrating that the Scriptures do not interpret themselves. Besides, if the doctrine of *sola Scriptura* were true, it would be expected that all Protestants would be in agreement with each other in terms of doctrine, as the Bible could not simultaneously teach contradictory beliefs.

The eighth reason is based on the fact that there are thousands of biblical manuscripts in existence; these manuscripts contain numerous variations of the text; one writer estimates that there are more than two hundred thousand variations. These facts leave Protestants in the position of not knowing whether they possess what the biblical authors originally wrote. Thanks to biblical research and archaeological discoveries, modern Bible versions may have a certain superiority to older Bible versions. On the other hand, Bibles based on the Latin Vulgate of St. Jerome (fourth century) — in English, this is the Catholic Douay-Rheims Bible — are based on original texts that have since perished. In other words, these older, traditional versions bypass sixteen centuries of possible textual corruption. This means that although modern Protestants may have in some respects a "better" or more accurate Bible than their forebears, in other respects they may have a "poorer" or less accurate Bible.

An interesting case in this regard is the difference between the Catholic and Protestant versions of Matthew 6:9–13 — of what Catholics usually call the Our Father and what Protestants typically refer to as the Lord's Prayer. Both sides can pray together almost in unison during ecumenical events until they reach the end of the prayer. After "Deliver us from evil," Protestants always add an extra line, "For thine is the kingdom, the power, and the glory, for ever and ever." Protestant Bible translations have this extra line in Matthew 6:13, but Catholic Bibles do not, because St. Jerome did not mention this line in his Vulgate translation. Jerome, and many other biblical scholars through the centuries were of the opinion that, to the best of their abilities in researching the oldest copies of Matthew, this extra line was added by some pious translator to some very old translation of Matthew, but it was not there in the beginning. Therefore, it is not considered part of the Bible. No Christian wants to be at the mercy of translations and copies of the original made by people who had their own personal reasons for changing things. Not all sources are of the same quality; sometimes older texts are more reliable than newer versions.

Here is reason 9: if there are many legitimate possible interpretations of Scripture, by definition there is no ultimate interpretation; and if there is no ultimate interpretation, then a person cannot know whether his interpretation is objectively true. The bottom line is this: if any given denomination claims that its own interpretation is correct above those of the other denominations, it has effectively set itself up as a final authority. Joel Peters concludes from this that, for Protestants, "the problem here is that such an act violates *Sola Scriptura*: setting up an authority outside Scripture."

The tenth reason is of a historical nature. The doctrine of *sola Scriptura* did not exist before John Wycliffe (a forerunner of Protestantism) mentioned it in the fourteenth century, and it did not become widespread until Martin Luther came along in the sixteenth century. Where did this idea ultimately come from? The claim that the Bible teaches this doctrine is nothing more than a repeated effort to project this belief back into the pages of Scripture. Luther was ultimately saying that the final authority in matters of faith is Martin Luther. Imagine, says Joel Peters, "millions upon millions of Christians who lived prior to the 14th century would have been left without a final authority, left to flounder spiritually, unless by chance they had access to a hand-copied Bible."

Based on all of these reasons, we must come to the conclusion that there is more to Christian faith than Scripture alone. This more is called *Tradition* in the Catholic Church. There must be something before and beyond Scripture that creates Scripture, determines what belongs to it, and interprets it. Scripture didn't just fall from Heaven. Protestants have tried very persistently to reject the role of Tradition, but that is a hard case to make, as we will discuss a bit further.

Scripture is a product of Tradition—the Tradition of the early Church, in particular, the apostolic succession, connecting all later generations with the first generation of apostles, and thus in a direct line with Jesus Christ Himself. We find all of this already at the very beginning of the Church. We know, for instance, that when St. Clement I succeeded St. Peter as his third successor, he sent a letter from Rome to disruptors in the Church of Corinth. Clement's taking the initiative to instruct and discipline a distant Catholic community demonstrates the influence of the bishop of Rome in the early Church. And when St. Ignatius of Antioch (ca. 37–107) was on his way to Rome to be martyred, he sent letters to seven communities, exhorting them to submit to the authority of their bishops. He was the first one to use the word "catholic" for the whole Church. Scripture alone tends to divide the Church, but Scripture combined with Tradition unites the Church. No wonder Pope John Paul II called the Catholic Church an expert in unity.

Apparently, Tradition was very much alive from the very beginning. This truth has been expressed in various ways by later illustrious members of the Church. St. Thomas More states, "The Church was gathered and the faith was believed before any part of the New Testament was put in writing." And, much more recently, Archbishop Fulton Sheen said something similar: "When finally the Gospels were written, they recorded a tradition; they did not create it. It was already there."

Scripture also tells us that not all of the things that Jesus said and did were written down. St. Paul says, "Stand firm and hold to the traditions which you were taught by us, either by word of mouth or by letter" (2 Thess. 2:15). He obviously speaks about two kinds of tradition: preaching and writing. All of the Word of God was at one time passed on orally, which is Sacred Tradition. Later on, some of Sacred Tradition was written down in Scripture, which became Written Tradition. Nowhere do we see our Lord commissioning his apostles to evangelize the world by creating manuscripts in His name. The emphasis is always on preaching the gospel, not on writing, printing, and distributing it.

Joel Peters summarizes this as follows: "The doctrine of *Sola Scriptura* overlooks—or at least grossly underemphasizes—the fact that the Church came before the Bible, and not the other way around. It was the Church, in effect, which wrote the Bible under the inspiration of the Holy Spirit: the Israelites as the Old Testament Church (or 'pre-Catholics') and the early Catholics as the New Testament Church."

It is ironic that the very same Protestants who normally mock Tradition in favor of Scripture do use a Bible based on a tradition: they use the Bible that the Reformers handed on to them. Even the doctrine of *sola Scriptura* itself has become a Protestant "tradition" that popped up rather recently and abruptly in the sixteenth century. In fact, there is no Scripture without Tradition. Protestants would like to get rid of Tradition, but they cannot live without it. The *Catechism* puts it in a nutshell: "Sacred Tradition and Sacred Scripture make up a single sacred deposit of the Word of God" (97). The Catholic Church is the living continuation of the Tradition in which the Scriptures were born.

CONCLUSION

It is not only Scripture that is crucial in Christianity. There is also something else needed. In the Catholic Church, it's called

Tradition. Tradition produced Scripture, safeguards it, and interprets it. Scripture is a vital authority in Christianity, but it cannot be so without Tradition, for Scripture alone cannot determine how to read and interpret Scripture. It is actually hard, if not impossible, to defend *sola Scriptura* in a coherent way. So, the Catholic Church does not manipulate Scripture with her Tradition, but she realizes that Scripture without Tradition comes close to an empty shell.

4

CATHOLICS MANIPULATED THE TEN COMMANDMENTS

THE LIE

The Catholic Church believes that her authority stands above the Word of God and that she can change even God's Ten Commandments as desired. This is very clear, for instance, when Catholics justify their use of religious statues by deleting the Second Commandment—"You shall not make an idol." By doing so, Catholics intentionally try to hide an important commandment. They also split the Tenth Commandment into two to get back to Ten Commandments. But the Catholic Church does not have the right to change what God Himself has instituted.

THE TRUTH

The truth is that Catholics simply group the commandments differently than most Protestants. In Exodus 20:2–17, which gives the Ten Commandments, there are actually *fourteen* imperative statements. To arrive at Ten Commandments, some statements have to be grouped together, and there is more than one way of doing so.

Why *Ten* Commandments?, you might ask. Jews place five commandments on each tablet or table, as if they represent the five fingers on each hand, whereas Catholics follow St. Augustine, who placed three Commandments on the first tablet and seven on the second. Either split is based on the idea that the first tablet has "love God" commands, and the second one "love neighbor" commands — which is a nice thought, as long as we do not lose sight of the fact that all ten commands are simultaneously ten ways to love God and ten ways to love our neighbor. They go hand in hand, as the *Catechism* notes: "The two tables shed light on one another; they form an organic unity.... One cannot honor another person without blessing God his Creator. One cannot adore God without loving all men, his creatures" (2069).

Interestingly and quite surprisingly, Rabbi Gamaliel, who was the Jewish Law teacher of St. Paul, mentions that "the Sages say *ten* on one tablet and *ten* on the other." That may have very well been the case, because the commandments establish a covenant between God and His people; so it is possible that both tablets were complete replicas of one another — one for each "party" in the Covenant. This can be compared to diplomatic treaties of ancient Egypt, in which a copy was made for both parties.

So how did the numbering of the Ten Commandments come about? Catholics follow the division of the commandments going back to St. Augustine. It is also that of the Lutheran confession. The Greek Fathers worked out a slightly different division, which is found in the Orthodox Churches but also in Calvinist communities. This explains why there are some discrepancies between the various Christian denominations. The *Catechism* simply states, "The division and numbering of the Commandments have varied in the course of history" (2066).

Catholics manipulated the Ten Commandments

As to the First Commandment, the historic Jewish numbering of the Ten Commandments has always grouped together the imperatives "You shall have no other gods before me" and "You shall not make for yourself a graven image" (Exod. 20:3, 4). The reason is that, in the ancient world, polytheism and idolatry were always connected—idolatry being the outward expression of polytheism. But the Calvinists and the Orthodox Church decided differently and split them into two commands: "You shall have no other gods" and "You shall not make an idol"—the latter one often used against Catholics.

As to the Third Commandment, Jews, Catholics, and Protestants typically summarize the Sabbath commandment as, "Remember the Sabbath to keep it holy," though the commandment's actual text takes four verses (Exod. 20:8–11). In this case, we are merely dealing with a numbering issue.

As to the Ninth and Tenth Commandments, St. Augustine separated the commandment in Exodus 20:17 into two: "You shall not covet your neighbor's wife" and "You shall not covet your neighbor's goods." First of all, he didn't want to place the neighbor's wife on the same level as the neighbor's goods. Second, Augustine knew too well how destructive sexuality can be, so he made sure there is a Ninth Commandment, separate from the Tenth. Unfortunately, this gave the Catholic Church the blemish of being mostly—or even only, according to some—focused on sexual sins. I know of a priest who did routinely speak about sins against the Sixth and Ninth Commandments, so he was commonly known as "Six by Nine." Most Protestants wouldn't get that numerical jibe.

Where did the Ten Commandments come from? The best and shortest answer is: directly from God. But as to how they got to us, the Bible is more ambivalent. According to Deuteronomy, it was God who personally wrote them on the two tablets of stone, with his own finger and in a special handwriting (Deut. 5:22; 10:2–4). The book of Exodus, however, has a different, more down-to-earth version: it was Moses himself who wrote down on the two tablets of stone everything God had told him on the mountain (Exod. 24:4; 34:27). Jeremiah goes even one step further when he says that God will write his law upon the hearts of people, rather than on tablets of stone. But no matter how they got to us, they do come from God.

In essence, the Decalogue (Greek for the Ten Commandments) is a dialogue in the covenant between God (I) and man (you). All Commandments are stated in the first person — *"I am the Lord"* — and addressed by God to another person — *"You shall …"* Therefore, in the words of the *Catechism*, "God makes his will known to each person in particular, at the same time as he makes it known to the whole people" (2063). So, in essence, the Decalogue brings our religious and social lives into unity. The Decalogue stands for the "ten words" that connect God to man and man to God. They are ten words of wisdom — a manual of how to treat one another as one people under God. This was well put by Pope Benedict XVI in his book *Jesus of Nazareth* (pt. I, 146) where he says, "that we give God his just due and, in so doing, discover the criterion for what is justly due among men."

The other day, I found in my mailbox a brochure for nutrients that proclaimed in big letters: "instant happiness delivered at home." We all know better, I hope. Happiness is not for sale! God has a much better prescription for happiness: two tablets a day — that is, the two tablets holding the Ten Commandments. They are not ten suggestions, not even ten options, but Ten Commandments. They are not nutritional supplements but "nutritional essentials."

CONCLUSION

Catholics did *not* manipulate the Ten Commandments. If there is any manipulation involved, then all denominations have done so, or none have, but not just the Catholic Church. The Church had good reason to separate and number the commandments the way she did, free from any suspicious motives.

5

CATHOLICS INVENTED
NEW SACRAMENTS

THE LIE

Catholics added four or five sacraments to the two or three sacraments we find in the Bible. The Council of Trent in 1563 made it binding Church tradition for Catholics to believe that the New Covenant has "seven Sacraments instituted by Christ." Hardly any Christian disputes that Baptism and the Eucharist were instituted by Christ, and perhaps Penance, but to declare the same for the other four sacraments is a claim impossible to justify.

The Catholic Church is a master in using her magic wand of "tradition" to invent and add her own sacraments, but the traditional "proof" texts cannot bear the weight of evidence they are credited with. They are examples of selectively chosen texts, taken out of context, to confirm her own Catholic position.

THE TRUTH

This discussion is similar to the one about who or what determines the list of books in Scripture: Who or what determines the list of sacraments? In the case of Scripture, we discovered, the

Tradition of the Church has to be invoked (see chapter 3). For the sacraments, something similar may have to be done. A Scriptural basis for the sacraments is indeed important, but one needs to remember that the New Testament is not a how-to manual of the sacraments and liturgy. When the Holy Spirit descended upon the apostles at Pentecost, the purpose was to give birth to the Church, not to deliver a manuscript. Therefore, in addition, we need to look at Tradition, because that's where the "manuals" of the sacraments and liturgy were developed. An important source for this Tradition is the *Didache* [pronounced *did*-a-kee or *did*-a-kay]. It is the oldest known written catechism, composed not later than the year 90 and perhaps as early as 60. It deals extensively with the practices of the early Church.

The basic question is this: Which sacramental actions is the Church empowered to perform? Here is what the *Catechism* has to say about them: "The sacraments are efficacious signs of grace, instituted by Christ and entrusted to the Church, by which divine life is dispensed to us. The visible rites by which the sacraments are celebrated signify and make present the graces proper to each sacrament. They bear fruit in those who receive them with the required dispositions" (1131). Protestants have a different conception about sacraments. For most of them, baptism, communion, ministry, marriage, and so forth are simply signs and symbols of faith. Protestants would call them merely a sign and a witness — sort of a reminder to stay committed to Jesus.

The Catholic Church, on the other hand, teaches that while God gives grace to us without outward symbols, He has also chosen to give grace to us through visible symbols: the seven sacraments. While Catholics agree that the sacraments are a sign and a witness, they also believe, more importantly, that they truly are vehicles of the power of Christ in and of themselves. They also give efficacious grace. In other words, when I am baptized, I truly am washed of all sin at that moment. When I am receiving the Eucharist in Communion, I truly am partaking of the Body of Christ (see chapter 17). When a couple gets married, there is a huge grace that pours out on them just by the action of getting married. When a priest is ordained, a power flows upon him that gives him the ability to forgive sins and celebrate the Eucharist (see chapter 9).

CatholicBridge.com uses the analogy of a light switch to illustrate how Catholics believe the sacraments work:

> If I walk into a room and flick on a switch that is on the wall, it is not my human will that creates light in the room. This is obvious if I flick the switch and the bulb is burnt out. In that case, I have the will to create light in the room but no light comes on. When I flick a light switch there is an incredible amount of complex activity that happens on the other side of the wall, and also at a central power plant. It is not my human will that creates the light; it is my willingness to tap into the complex series of events that creates the miracle of light in my room. On the other hand, if I do not hit the light switch nothing will happen and I will sit in the dark.

Seen in this light, the Catholic Church distinguishes seven sacraments: Baptism, Confirmation, the Eucharist, Penance (or Confession), Anointing of the Sick, Holy Orders, and Matrimony. Let's discuss them individually.

* * *

Baptism is the least controversial sacrament in Christianity. It is widely acknowledged, because it has a strong scriptural basis, although there is discussion about when it should be administered. It is undisputed because Jesus Himself was baptized by John the Baptist in the Jordan River. Besides, it was an important sacrament in the Acts of the Apostles. Philip the deacon, for instance, preached in Samaria, made conversions, and conferred Baptism. Or when St. Paul came to Ephesus, he found disciples who had received only John's Baptism, so therefore "they were baptized in the name of the Lord Jesus" (see Acts 19:1–6).

Protestants like to stress that it is essential for "sacraments" that they were specifically implemented in the Bible or that they were personally instituted by Jesus, but such claims are often hard to make. For example, nowhere in the Bible do we read that the apostles were baptized, nor that Jesus Himself had baptized them. But again, the New Testament is not a how-to manual of the sacraments. Only the Church can tell us—but did not always do so in the earliest documents—which sacraments were used and how. Yet, for most of Christianity, Baptism did "pass the test." The fact that the Bible doesn't mention specifically how baptism was done in the early Church is most likely because the New Testament was written for people who had already been baptized.

Baptism can be done at any age, but as to the best time for Baptism, the *Catechism* says, "The sheer gratuitousness of the grace of salvation is particularly manifest in infant Baptism. The Church and the parents would deny a child the priceless grace of becoming a child of God were they not to confer Baptism shortly after birth" (1250). Then it adds, "The practice of infant Baptism is an immemorial tradition of the Church. There is explicit testimony to this practice from the second century on, and it is quite possible that, from the beginning of the apostolic preaching, when whole 'households' received baptism, infants may also have been baptized" (1252). In Acts 16:15, Lydia and

Catholics invented new sacraments

her entire household were baptized. In short, if Baptism confers grace, why wait for it?

Bishop Polycarp, himself a disciple of the apostle John, stated at his martyrdom (A.D. 168) that he had been in the "service of Christ" for eighty-six years. Other recorded dates from Polycarp's life make it likely that eighty-six years was his age from birth as well. We may conclude from this that his parents were already Christians, or at least were converted quite soon after his birth. If his parents were pagans at his birth, he would have been baptized with the "house" at their conversion. Hippolytus of Rome wrote around 215, "Baptize first the children, and if they can speak for themselves let them do so. Otherwise, let their parents or other relatives speak for them." Apparently, early Christian writings indicate that Christians as early as the second century maintained infant Baptism.

* * *

The *Eucharist* is also widely acknowledged in most branches of Christianity, although its importance and interpretation may vary (see chapter 17). A large part of St. Paul's First Letter to the Corinthians is devoted to the Eucharist. Paul starts out his pastoral teaching on the Eucharist with this "The cup of blessing which we bless, is it not a participation in the blood of Christ? The bread which we break, is it not a participation in the body of Christ?" (1 Cor. 10:16). The New Covenant Liturgy is a progression of the Old Covenant Passover Liturgy: "For Christ, our paschal lamb, has been sacrificed. Let us, therefore, celebrate the festival" (1 Cor. 5:7–8). So there is no mention of a glorified prayer session without the Eucharistic Banquet—that is, as St. Paul says, without the "participation in the [body and] blood of Christ."

* * *

With *Penance* we have reached the point where the difference between Catholic and Protestant doctrine begins to widen, especially when it comes to private confession. The *Catechism* tells us:

> During the first centuries, the reconciliation of Christians who had committed particularly grave sins after their Baptism (for example, idolatry, murder, or adultery) was tied to a very rigorous discipline, according to which penitents had to do public penance for their public sins, often for years, before receiving reconciliation.... During the seventh century, Irish missionaries, inspired by the Eastern monastic tradition, took to continental Europe the "private" practice of penance, which does not require public and prolonged completion of penitential works before reconciliation with the Church.... It allowed the forgiveness of grave sins and venial sins to be integrated into one sacramental celebration. In its main lines, this is the form of penance that the Church has practiced down to our day. (CCC 1447) (see chapter 41)

Nevertheless, the Catholic Church maintains that the authority to forgive sins was in principle "instituted" by Christ, because the earliest Christian communities forgave sins from the very beginning while specifically invoking the authority of Jesus Christ: "If you forgive the sins of any, they are forgiven them; if you retain the sins of any, they are retained" (John 20:23). "And if he has committed sins, he will be forgiven" (James 5:15). Christ told the apostles to follow His example: "As the Father has sent me, even so I send you" (John 20:21). What Jesus did, they were to do. Just as the apostles were to carry Christ's message to the whole world, so they were to carry His forgiveness: "Truly, I say to you, whatever you bind on earth shall be bound in heaven, and whatever you loose on earth shall be loosed in heaven" (Matt. 18:18).

It is hard, however, for many Protestants to accept the fact that a priest can forgive someone's sins. Yet we see St. Paul forgiving someone in the name and person of Christ: "Any one whom you forgive, I also forgive. What I have forgiven, if I have forgiven anything, has been for your sake *in the presence of Christ*" (2 Cor. 2:10, emphasis added). That's how the priest can forgive the repentant believer—acting on Christ's behalf, "in the person of Christ" or "in the presence of Christ," as the Bible says.

The *Catechism* (986) summarizes this: "By Christ's will, the Church possesses the power to forgive the sins of the baptized and exercises it through bishops and priests normally in the sacrament of Penance" (986). It explains further, "When he celebrates the sacrament of Penance, the priest is fulfilling the ministry of the Good Shepherd who seeks the lost sheep, of the Good Samaritan who binds up wounds, of the Father who awaits the prodigal son and welcomes him on his return, and of the just and impartial judge whose judgment is both just and merciful" (1465). From this follows, "Confession to a priest is an essential part of the sacrament of Penance" (1456).

* * *

Confirmation: Most Protestants deny that we have here an independent sacrament instituted by Jesus. Yet there are very strong indications that Confirmation did play a role in the early Church. The Acts of the Apostles, for instance, have preserved two very significant episodes regarding Confirmation. "Now when the apostles in Jerusalem heard that Samaria had accepted the word of God, they sent them Peter and John, who went down and prayed for them, that they might receive the holy Spirit, for it had not yet fallen upon any of them; they had only been baptized in the name of the Lord Jesus. Then they laid hands on them and they received the Holy Spirit" (Acts 8:14–17). Also, when St. Paul came to Ephesus, he found disciples "[who had] not even heard that there is a Holy Spirit." They had received only John's Baptism. Upon hearing of the Redeemer, "they were baptized in the name of the Lord Jesus; and when Paul laid his hands upon them, the Holy Spirit came upon them, and they began to speak in tongues and to prophesy" (Acts 19:2, 5–6).

These texts point out that after the Baptism of water came a second rite—the imposition of hands—by which the newly baptized received the Holy Spirit. This second rite was reserved to the apostles; in Samaria, Peter and John imposed hands on the new believers who had been baptized by a deacon; at Ephesus, it was Paul who imposed hands. Thus, the initiation that had begun with Baptism was completed with the gift of the Holy Spirit.

* * *

Is *Anointing of the Sick* perhaps another invention of the Catholic Church? Protestants usually think there is no basis for Christ's having personally instituted an anointing of the sick, but this sacrament didn't just fall out of the sky. We find some clear indications in the Gospels. Matthew's Gospel foreshadows the anointing of the sick: "These twelve Jesus sent out, charging them ... 'Heal the sick, raise the dead, cleanse lepers, cast out demons'" (10:5, 8). Then there is the Gospel of Mark, reporting how Jesus "called to him the twelve, and began to send them out two by two, and gave them authority over the unclean spirits.... And they cast out many demons, and anointed with oil many that were sick and healed them" (6:7, 13). Then, after His death and Resurrection, Jesus showed the apostles the "sign" to help the sick: "These signs will accompany those who believe: … they will lay their hands on the sick, and they will recover" (Mark 16:17–18).

However, while a healing ministry did exist in the life of Jesus and in the early Church, there was as yet no set form for a sacrament of healing. Paul's letter to the Corinthians mentions a charismatic gift of healing, but James infers a more ecclesiastical form of healing ministry: "Is anyone sick among you? Let him bring in the priests of the church and let them pray over him, anointing him with oil in the name of the Lord, and the prayer of faith will save the sick person, and the Lord will raise him up. If he has committed any sins, he will be forgiven" (5:14–15).

The first time the Anointing of the Sick is mentioned as a fixed liturgy is at the end of the first century in the so-called Teachings of the Twelve Apostles, the *Didache*. At the end of the second century it is mentioned, again only incidentally, by St. Irenaeus. The *Catechism* summarizes this as follows:

> From ancient times in the liturgical traditions of both East and West, we have testimonies to the practice of anointing of the sick with blessed oil. Over the centuries the Anointing of the Sick was conferred more and more exclusively on those at the point of death. Because of this it received the name "Extreme Unction." Notwithstanding this evolution, the liturgy has never failed to beg the Lord that the sick person may recover his health if it would be conducive to his salvation. (1512)

* * *

Holy Orders: Protestants believe that there is no such sacrament. This issue is discussed sextensively in another chapter (see chapter

9), but let us merely stress here that in the Letter to the Hebrews, Jesus is called the "High Priest," who made, by His sacrificial atonement on Calvary, the Jewish priesthood and its prescribed ritual sacrifices redundant. Given the fact that the only priesthood recognized by the first Christians, being pious Jews, was that of the Temple, their own "priests" carried out tasks that had very little relevance to the tasks that the Jewish priests used to exercise in the Temple. Therefore, they made use of other names that described more accurately their functions in these first Christian communities—including the title *presbyteros*, which means "elder" but could very well be translated as "priest" nowadays. The translation "elder" is actually strange, since Timothy was called an "elder," although he was not an "older man" at all, but one to whom Paul exhorted, "Let no one despise your youth" (1 Tim. 4:12).

Besides, there are Bible passages that seem to indicate that these "elders" or "priests" played a special role in the early Church —a role that was assigned by the laying on of hands, similar to the way we see prophets in the Old Testament passing on power to their successors by the laying on of hands and anointing. In 1 Timothy 4:14, Paul says to Timothy, "Do not neglect the gift you have, which was conferred on you through the prophetic word with the imposition of hands of the presbyterate [the Christian, not Jewish priesthood]." In 2 Timothy 1:6, he says, "Hence I re-mind you to rekindle the gift of God that is within you through the laying on of my hands." And then in 2 Timothy 2:2, "And what you have heard from me before many witnesses entrust to faithful men who will be able to teach others also."

* * *

Is the sacrament of *Matrimony* another Catholic invention? A key text in this discussion is Ephesians 5:32–33, where Paul says about marriage, "This is a great *mystery*, and I mean in reference to Christ and the church; however, let each one of you love his wife as himself, and let the wife see that she respects her husband" (emphasis added). The Greek word *mysterion*—which is used to this day for the sacraments in Eastern Christianity—was translated in the Vulgate as *sacramentum*, a word that denoted the oath of loyalty sworn by soldiers to their earthly lord, the emperor. It was applied by Tertullian around 200 to the Christian mysteries, by which man adhered to God. Protestants now claim that the sacramentality of Matrimony goes back to the fact that *mysterium* was mistranslated as *sacrament*.

Obviously, it is not Matrimony itself that is in discussion here. Marriage is the one institution that no one seems to challenge. The Letter to the Hebrews puts it very clearly, "Let marriage be held in honor among all, and let the marriage bed be undefiled; for God will judge the immoral and adulterous" (13:4). St. Paul says, "A wife is bound to her husband as long as he lives" (1 Cor. 7:39). In Ephesians 5:22–25 St. Paul sets up an analogy between husbands and wives and Christ and His Church. Some people, especially men, might think this means husbands get to "lord it over" their wives. But as Randall Smith puts it, "When a husband says to his wife, 'I am supposed to be like Christ to you,' she should promptly take off her socks and stick out her feet to be washed."

But does this make it a sacrament—a visible sign of the invisible reality of grace? Taking the lead of St. Augustine, the medieval Christian Church developed the *sacramental* understanding of Matrimony by including Marriage in the select seven to which the term "sacrament" was applied. The first more official declaration about Marriage as a sacrament was made much later, at the 1184 Council of Verona. Marriage was now seen as a sanctification of the Christian couple. The bride and groom confer the sacrament on one another, so the Church's representative, typically a priest or a deacon, is simply a witness to the sacrament.

Does Marriage have a strong foundation in Scripture? As an institution it certainly does, but not literally as a sacrament. Yet, its sacramental understanding is definitely in line with Church tradition and practice: a visible sign of an important invisible reality in life.

CONCLUSION

Catholics did *not* add newly invented sacraments to the few sacraments that non-Catholic Christians acknowledge. All seven sacraments of the Catholic Church have a foundation in Scripture and in the early practices of the Church. Besides, we need to acknowledge that the New Testament is not a how-to manual of the sacraments. For more information about the practices of the early Church we also need to look somewhere else.

6

CATHOLICS INVENTED PURGATORY

THE LIE

Purgatory is an invention made up by Catholics during the Middle Ages. It is an illegitimate invention for several reasons. First, it is found nowhere in the Bible. Second, it is a denial of the sufficiency of Christ's sacrifice. It represents what some describe as "a second-chance theology that is abominable." And third, it was created as a "Catholic money maker," for without purgatory, the Church would have gone broke.

THE TRUTH

Purgatory is certainly a Catholic concept, but in no way a Catholic invention. At the beginning of the Reformation, there was still some hesitation, especially on Luther's part, about whether the Catholic doctrine of Purgatory should be retained, but as the breach widened, the denial of Purgatory by the Protestant Reformers became virtually universal. Nevertheless, modern Protestants, while they still avoid the name Purgatory, now sometimes speak of "the middle state." (By the way, Orthodox Christians speak in terms of a *theosis*, a journey of transformation.)

What is Purgatory in Catholic doctrine? It is a place or condition of temporal punishment for those who depart this life in God's grace. The *Catechism* says about Purgatory: "All who die in God's grace and friendship, but still imperfectly purified ... undergo purification, so as to achieve the holiness necessary to enter the joy of heaven" (1030). What does this mean?

I think this is best explained by an example the late and legendary Mother Angelica of EWTN uses: If a prostitute had a profound conversion and decided to enter Mother Angelica's convent, a one-day transition would definitely be too short a period for such a person to make the transition—actually a massive shock—in spite of all her good intentions. Indeed, for most of us, the transition from a life on earth to a life in Heaven would be equally dramatic, so shocking that we would need some extra preparation time, as nothing unclean can enter the presence of God, according to Revelation 21:27.

No wonder the Catholic Church has always stressed the importance of Purgatory, where we can see in all clarity who we were and where we came from before we can enter the eternal glory of God. The late Fr. Benedict Groeschel expressed this well: "Purgatory is not a temporary Hell, but a preliminary Heaven." We need a "preliminary" Heaven, because holiness is certainly not something that happens overnight.

As Andres Ortiz puts it, "The Bible does not mention the exact word 'purgatory,' but instead it makes reference to a place which can be understood as what is referred to as Purgatory." However, the fact that there is no such term doesn't mean the end of Purgatory—for, as he puts it, "One might as well even deny that there is something called the Bible because no such name is found in the Bible." Although the name itself does not create the place, the place must exist first, before we can give it a real name.

Catholics invented Purgatory

Well, does Purgatory exist, so we can name it that way? We find several indications in both the Old and New Testaments that Purgatory does exist. One of the three strongest lines of the New Testament can be found in Revelation 21:27, where it says, "But nothing unclean shall enter [Heaven]." The second one is in 1 Corinthians 3:14–15: "If the work which any man has built on the foundation survives, he will receive a reward. If any man's *work* is burned up, *he* will suffer loss, though he himself will be saved, but only as through fire" (emphasis added). As Tim Staples put it: "The truth is: both the works of the individual and the individual will go through the cleansing 'fire' described by St. Paul in order that 'he' might finally be saved and enter into the joy of the Lord." What is being referred to can't possibly be Heaven because there are imperfections that need to be "burned up"; it cannot be Hell either, because souls are being saved. So what is it then? The answer is: Purgatory!

The third line can be found in Matthew 5:25–26, in the midst of the famous Sermon on the Mount, in which our Lord teaches about Heaven (v. 20) and Hell (vv. 29–30), in a context that presents "the Kingdom of Heaven" as the ultimate goal (see vv. 3–12). Here, Jesus ends one of His parables with the following statement: "[If you] be put in prison, truly, I say to you, you will never get out until you have paid the last penny." Now, we know that in Heaven no last penny needs to be paid, and from Hell there is no liberation at all; hence, this reference must apply to a third place—Purgatory.

We find also references to Purgatory in early Christianity. Graffiti in the catacombs of the first three centuries mentions prayers for the dead. Some of the earliest Christian writings also refer to the Christian practice of praying for the dead. St. Augustine's mother asked her son to remember her soul in his Masses.

St. Ambrose said about the deceased, "We have loved them during life; let us not abandon them until we have conducted them by our prayers into the house of the Lord." Such prayers would make no sense if these early Christians thought the souls of the dead were already in Hell or in Heaven, for they could no longer benefit from prayers. Besides, Luke 16:22 speaks of "Abraham's bosom," and 1 Peter 3:19 says that after his death and before his resurrection, Christ "went and preached to the spirits in prison," telling them that Heaven would now be opened to them.

Obviously, the existence of Purgatory assumes that there is a Heaven and a Hell. Because we are free human beings (see chapter 6), we will be held accountable for our choices in life. In every life, we make good as well as bad choices. Evil is a matter of bad choices; and bad choices affect not only our own lives but also those of others. That is what a final judgment is about. If there is no *instant* repayment for good or bad actions and choices, there must be a *final* repayment in the final stage of life. We need and deserve to be judged, if the good God is also a just God. Good actions are to be rewarded with Heaven, bad ones with Hell. As St. Augustine says, God "did not will to save us *without* us." God does not judge us on our feelings and emotions—for those are sometimes beyond our control—but He does judge us on our free choices in life.

From this follows rather conclusively that the ultimate consequence of human freedom is the existence of an eternal Heaven as well as an eternal Hell. For sure, no sane person wants Hell to exist; no sane person wants evil to exist, but evil does exist. If there is evil and if there is eternity, then there can be Hell. Hell is just evil eternalized. Heaven welcomes all people—but so does Hell. C. S. Lewis called Hell "the greatest monument to human freedom." The *Catechism* puts it this way: "Our freedom has the power to make choices for ever, with no turning back" (1861). Unless there is a Purgatory, those who don't make it directly to Heaven would be necessarily bound for Hell.

A final judgment is the answer to many questions we might have had in life. What about all those people who have experienced so little joy in their lives or who had received the "wrong genes"? What about all those victims of genocide, gas chambers, torture, terrorism, wars, drugs? What about all those people who cannot be called back to life again to receive a bit more warmth and love? What about those neglected by their spouses or their parents or their children? So many people had hoped for something good in life but received so much evil and suffering instead. What are we to do with all these people and with those who caused this?

Put differently, there are too many "debit" accounts that still need to be settled—not so much those little accounts that one might like to settle with one's next-door neighbors, but rather those enormous accounts that caused sorrow, tears, afflictions, and disasters to millions of people. The fact that we speak in terms of "accounts that need to be settled" implies already that our minds can go up "into the sky" to take a mental bird's-eye view of the world. So why would we not be able also to go up "into Heaven" to see everything from an even higher perspective—God's point of view, if you will? If there were no final judgment, those accounts would remain unsettled. In a godless world, in a world without a final destination, there is no hope that those issues will ever be addressed. Yet, the earth is crying out for justice—God's justice!

But is there not God's forgiveness also? you might ask. Yes, there is, but not unconditionally. Pope Benedict XVI once put it this way: Unconditional forgiveness—the abolition of

Hell—would be a kind of "cheap grace" to which the German Protestant theologian Dietrich Bonhoeffer rightly objected in the face of the appalling evil encountered in Nazi Germany in his day. If God did not will to save us *without* us, then there must be salvation as well as damnation (see chapter 6). The afterlife would be a period of repayment—for the good things done as well as the bad things done. As C. S. Lewis put it, those "who did most for the present world were just those who thought most of the next."

Fortunately, says the Catholic Church, there is also something in between Heaven and Hell, some kind of "middle state," or Purgatory—otherwise those who did not make it into Heaven had only one option left, Hell. Purgatory is a place or state where human imperfection is corrected in the "fire of purification" before entering God's Heaven, where "nothing unclean shall enter." This is counter to the cheap optimism that prevails nowadays in the minds of many, holding that the life of practically everyone automatically and immediately ends up in a state of eternal bliss.

CONCLUSION

Catholics did *not* invent Purgatory. It is not a Catholic invention that came from nowhere. It does have a basis in Scripture; it does not take anything away from Jesus' sacrificial death on the Cross; and it is certainly not a moneymaker. All accusations to the contrary are lies and fabrications.

PART 2

CATHOLICISM AND ITS CONTROVERSIES

7

CATHOLICS ARE LED BY
THE ANTICHRIST

THE LIE

Catholics consider the pope to be Christ's vicar, which means his "substitute." In Greek, "antichrist" simply means "in the place of Christ." Thus, by very definition, the pope *is* the antichrist, period. The seat of his residence would be in Rome, which is built upon seven hills. In Revelation 17:1 it is confirmed that this refers to the antichrist, and in verse 9 his seat is identified: "The seven heads are seven hills on which the woman is seated" (Rev. 17:9). Undoubtedly, Catholics are being led by the antichrist.

THE TRUTH

Who really is the antichrist in the Bible? The prefix "anti" has *two* meanings: "against" or "instead of." Some see the antichrist as someone or something who is *against* Christ, coming from *outside* the Church—for instance, Nero, Hitler, Communism, or ISIS. Others see the antichrist as someone or something who acts *instead* of Christ, coming from inside Christianity—for example, heretics, liars or deceivers, false shepherds, or antipopes. So the question is: Should we look inside the Church for a divider in the name of Christ, a heretic who denies Christ's divinity, or rather outside the Church for a surrogate Christ, an enemy of Christ?

The Bible seems to make the same distinction. On the one hand, especially in the Letters of St. John, the antichrist comes from *inside* the Church: "Who is the liar but he that denies that Jesus is the Christ? This is the antichrist, he who denies the Father and the Son" (1 John 2:22). Also, "Every spirit which does not confess Jesus is not of God. This is the spirit of antichrist, of which you heard that it was coming and now it is in the world already" (1 John 4:3). Or, "For many deceivers have gone out into the world, men who will not acknowledge the coming of Jesus Christ in the flesh; such a one is the deceiver and the antichrist" (2 John 7). All of this refers to the earliest *heresies* in the Church.

On the other hand, especially in the book of Revelation, the antichrist seems to come from *outside* the Church. Although the word "antichrist" does not occur in Revelation, there are certain parallels. Some point to the "beast" of 11:7, some to the "red dragon" of chapter 12, others to the beast "having seven heads and ten horns" of chapter 13, and many scholars identify the antichrist with the beast that had "two horns, like a lamb" and spoke "as a dragon" (13:11), or with the whore of Babylon sitting upon a scarlet beast, full of names of blasphemy, "having seven heads and ten horns" (13:1), or finally, with Satan "loosed out of his prison," and seducing the nations (20:7). Many see this as a reference to Roman emperors such as Nero, who gave themselves divinity and persecuted Christ's followers. The early Christian Fathers identified the antichrist more specifically as a government official—a king coming to power in the Roman Empire.

Catholics are led by the antichrist

We read in the *Didache* (A.D. 70), "Then shall the deceiver of the world appear, pretending to be the Son of God." St. Polycarp (ca. 69–155) warned the Philippians that everyone who preaches false doctrine is an antichrist. St. Hippolytus (170–235) put it this way: "Christ is a lion, so Antichrist is also a lion. Christ is a king, so Antichrist is also a king. The Savior was manifested as a lamb, so he too in like manner will appear as a lamb without; within he is a wolf."

It was, in particular, St. Robert Bellarmine (1542–1621) who promoted the view of a personal antichrist to come just before the end of the world. Soon this became a common perception among Christians. The *Catechism* speaks of a final trial of the Church "in the form of a religious deception offering men an apparent solution to their problems at the price of apostasy from the truth" (675). The supreme deception is that of the antichrist. John Henry Cardinal Newman speaks in similar terms: "The coming of Christ will be immediately preceded by a very awful and unparalleled outbreak of evil, called by St. Paul an Apostasy, a falling away, in the midst of which a certain terrible Man of Sin and Child of Perdition, the special and singular enemy of Christ, or Antichrist, will appear."

So what is the connection then between the pope and the antichrist? The idea that the Roman Catholic pope is the antichrist has been part of anti-Catholic rhetoric since the Reformation. Luther stated it repeatedly. For example: "This teaching [of the supremacy of the pope] shows forcefully that the pope is the very antichrist, who has exalted himself above, and opposed himself against, Christ." The Lutheran *Book of Concord* says something similar: "The pope is the real Antichrist who has raised himself over and set himself against Christ." The biblical basis of this can be found in 2 Thessalonians 2:4, which speaks of the one "who opposes and exalts himself above every so-called god and object of worship, so as to seat himself in the temple of God, claiming that he is a god."

Well, the antichrist seats himself as the head of this false church of Roman Catholics.

What are we to make of these Protestant claims? When calling the pope the antichrist, the most likely interpretation of most Protestants is that a pope claims to be and to act *instead* of Christ. However, popes never do make such a claim; they always refer to Christ Himself. When has any pope required worship of himself, as God, instead of Christ? The pope cannot be the antichrist. For him to deny that Christ has come in the flesh would undercut the basis of his position — being the Vicar of Christ. Besides, the Catholic Church historically is seated at the Lateran and the Vatican, on Vatican Hill, where St. Peter was crucified, and these locations are certainly not on or near Rome's seven hills, mentioned in the book of Revelation.

Antichrists will not be so called — otherwise they would have no followers; instead they come disguised. As 1 John 2:19 puts it, "They went out from us, but they were not of us." They will tempt Christians with the same three temptations with which Christ was tempted. They will set up a counterchurch that will have all the notes and characteristics of the real Church, but in reverse and emptied of its divine content, without any reference to Jesus, her founder.

Could the Catholic Church be this counterchurch? The pope as the antichrist has been part of anti-Catholic rhetoric since the Reformation, when it was needed to justify the Protestant Reformers' desire to leave the Catholic Church and renounce many of her teachings. As a matter of fact, it would nicely serve as a convenient explanation for their Church-exodus. It gave them reason to believe that the Catholic Church was the result of the "Great Apostasy" of 2 Thessalonians 2:3 and that the date of the founding of the Catholic Church was not in the first century, but in the fourth century, when Emperor Constantine made it the official religion of the Roman Empire—which makes for another link to the antichrist.

This stand also gave Protestants reason to reject the pope's authority to teach, with or without the consent of individual members of the Church. Yet the pope's authority in matters of faith cannot be dismissed that easily. After all, Jesus did not ask for a vote when He decided to give Himself up to die on the Cross—His disciples would have voted against it! The Church is not a democracy with voting rights or an egalitarian congregation of equal members. She is the guardian of Christ's "legacy." Members of the Church, including her theologians, may think they are part of the *teaching* Church, but they belong to the *believing* Church.

The teaching office of the Church consists only of the bishops in union with the pope. Christ promised to protect the teachings of the Church when He said, "He who hears you hears me, and he who rejects you rejects me, and he who rejects me rejects him who sent me" (Luke 10:16). So rejecting the pope is rejecting Jesus Himself. St. Paul warns us that some people seek teachers "to suit their own likings, and will turn away from listening to the truth and wander into myths" (2 Tim. 4:3–4). In contrast, the Magisterium is the Church's teaching office, established by Jesus Christ to "guard what has been entrusted" (1 Tim. 6:20) and to keep her members inside the flock—whether her members like it or not.

Does it make sense to connect this teaching Magisterium with the antichrist? It is hard to believe that the very custodian of the Christian heritage could be the antichrist. St. Peter failed personally many times in life, but he was infallible in passing on what Jesus had told him. The same can be said about his successors: they are known to have failed in their personal lives, but in matters of doctrine they were and are infallible. Besides, the notion that the antichrist would be a pope (or, apparently, all popes, according to the confused ramblings of some) was never once mentioned by a single writer in the early Church. And what's more, Christ's admonition that no one knows the day or the hour (Matt. 25:13) must logically extend also to this: no one knows the precise identity beforehand of the antichrist.

CONCLUSION

Catholics are *not* led by the antichrist. The pope cannot be identified with the antichrist, and the Vatican can certainly not be connected with Rome's seven hills, mentioned in the book of Revelation. When Protestants, Mormons, and Jehovah's Witnesses speak of the "Great Apostasy" (2 Thess. 2:3)—a collapse of truth in the Catholic Church—they are actually creating a "Great Myth." The Reformation was not a recovery of what had been lost, but a radical departure from what had always been in Christianity.

8

CATHOLICS THINK SALVATION CAN BE EARNED

THE LIE

Catholics believe that salvation comes from what *we* do ourselves—it is something we can *earn* by working hard. So they believe we can just *buy* our way into Heaven. This is clearly in contrast with what the Bible says: No one can force his way into Heaven. It all depends on God's grace.

THE TRUTH

Because there is sin in the world—as a consequence of the Fall in Paradise—we have to face the question of how sinful people could ever be saved. Why is this a serious question? If it is true that we are all sinners, no one should or could be saved. Yet the Bible speaks also of salvation. How can that be if we are all sinners? Is God perhaps two-faced?

In the Bible, God reveals Himself not only as a God of *love* but also as a God of *justice*. Love and justice are divine attributes that are essential to God—without them, God would not be God. God is both love and justice; He is both loving and just.

So when God is just, He is also loving, and when He is loving, He is also just—similar to the way parents should deal with their children.

Obviously, there is a certain tension between God's love and justice when it comes to His relationship with sinful people. That's where the concept of *mercy* comes in. That's why it is important to mention God's mercy as well. But mercy talk could easily obscure that we must first acknowledge that we can do what is wrong. As Fr. James Schall, S.J., puts it, "Mercy without judgment bypasses free will." On the one hand, *justice* might require that sinful people should not be saved, so there would at best be salvation only for some, perhaps not even one person. On the other hand, *love* might require that sinful people are forgiven their sins so all can be saved, which would entail salvation for many, if not all. Hence, it should not come as a surprise that this "tension" has stirred quite a debate in Christianity.

The issue of salvation has a long history in which the Catholic Church had to defend her longstanding theology against various opposing claims and interpretations. It is an age-old contentious controversy that has its roots in a perceived antagonism between God and man. It has led to questions such as: Does salvation come from what *we* do or from what *God* does? Is salvation something we can *earn* or something we must *receive*? Does salvation come from our *works* or from God's *grace*? Can we buy our way into Heaven, or must God invite us into Heaven? The keyword in all these questions is the word *or*—suggesting that a choice has to be made and that only one choice is correct.

As with many other theological debates, extreme either-or positions put God and man in a power battle. The underlying assumption is that whatever we give to God, we must take away from man; that whatever we give to man, we are to take away from God. However, God and man can never be in competition with each other—that would be a complete misunderstanding of God's omnipotence, for God and man are on entirely distinct levels.

It is a false dilemma. To think differently creates false opposites, contrasts, or disagreements. Yet the reasoning behind it seems rather attractive or even compelling: if God is *all-powerful*, then He can choose freely who will be saved and who will be damned, so it doesn't matter what we do on our own. As a consequence, by putting human freedom against God's sovereignty, certain groups of Christians have made this issue into an either-or dilemma: either God wins and we lose all, or we lose and God wins all.

Before anything else, there is God's grace. God's part comes first: without grace we can't do anything—if only because we are creatures who can only exist thanks to our Creator; without creation there could not possibly be any creatures, for we are contingent beings who can only receive our being. Everything is grace, and without it, we would fail. Without God we could not do anything—we could not even exist! We could not love if we were not loved by God first. Grace, which literally means "gift," is not something received in return for anything given from our side—it is free and unmerited. So when we say that our salvation depends on what *we* do ourselves, we should realize that salvation ultimately comes from God's grace, not from our doings. Even when we do "good works," on our side, they are always a fruit of grace, coming from God's side first. Jesus emphasizes this with the imagery of the vine. "I am the vine, you are the branches.... Apart from me you can do nothing" (John 15:5). Although good fruits require constant care on our part, the power to grow can come only from God.

But there is also another side to all of this—the human part. Branches need to be cultivated to bear good fruit, so they require constant care and hard work on *our* side too. We need to do our part, our works, to let God's grace work. God's grace does not take away any responsibilities on our side. Although we do not earn salvation—for it is a gift—we do have the choice to accept or reject that gift through our works. What we do on our side does not take anything away from what God does in His sovereignty. We are free either to cooperate with God's grace or not to cooperate. But God's grace is not a once-and-for-all deal; it must be preserved, nourished, and cherished—which is the task of a lifetime. In other words, God's grace is captivating but not irresistible. God's plan does include the possibility that we could throw away the gift we have been given. We do have that "power."

Obviously, the Catholic Faith rejects false dilemmas. It rejects putting our work in opposition to God's grace. These two are not in competition with each other, but they grow in union. St. Ignatius of Loyola used to put this in the following terms: work as if everything depends on you, but trust as if everything depends on God. Applied to the theological notion of salvation, this would entail that God provides sufficient grace for everyone to be saved, but whether it is *efficient* and put into effect (efficacious) depends on us. Aquinas says, "Grace changes the will without forcing it." God offers salvation to all, but this may not automatically produce salvation for all.

This "balanced" Catholic view about grace and works has often been rejected by other Christian denominations. They wonder whether human beings are really free to reject God's grace. In their view, God's grace is irresistible; otherwise God's sovereignty would be in danger. But again, that puts God and us in a power battle. God gave us the freedom to decide whether we accept grace and do good, or whether we reject it and do evil. If Adam and Eve could fall from grace, certainly all of us, their descendants, can fall from grace as well. If God's grace were irresistible, Adam and Eve could never have rejected it.

Let us use an analogy to explain rationally how an almighty God can give us freedom. A sovereign king can pass a law that makes him no longer sovereign—which is somehow what God did for the world. God sets limits to His omnipotence by setting no bounds to human freedom. When it comes to our salvation, we are certainly at God's mercy, but He has also chosen to be at *our* mercy. Otherwise, we would be nothing more than puppets on the world scene. Instead, God lets the actors on the world stage be free actors, who may not act the way the Author of the play would like them to act. God *wills* perfection in us but *allows* imperfection. Unlike dictators, who take human freedom away from us, God made us in His image and thus He created us, not as marionettes, but as beings endowed with freedom as well. Since God made us after His own image, we cannot just be marionettes or automata. Because we are rational beings, made in God's image, we have been created with free will and are master over our acts—the right to choose is ours.

Even thanking God for our lives and for His grace is a matter of free will. Chesterton said once that, if the world is determined, it makes no sense to say thank you to the waiter for bringing the mustard. To give thanks implies that something that did happen need not have happened. We can either do certain things or not do them—do them this way or that way. It makes no sense to praise or blame people for their deeds if what they did had to happen anyway apart from any agency of theirs.

Yet God would never force people against their will to come to Him. That is not Godlike, and not biblical. That's why the

Church welcomes *all* peoples. But she does more than that—after all, Hell does the same—for she also brings them into unity, into the unity of the truth. All members of the Church become one, because all profess the same faith.

Yet, it may sound strange or even offensive to some that the sovereign, all-powerful God of Christianity made Himself dependent on us—for instance, on Mary's *fiat,* so that with her *fiat,* God's Son could be born in her womb. Nevertheless, that is the way God works. The only way God wanted to redeem humanity was by means of the free yes of a human being, Mary. God's power is tied to the unenforceable yes of a human being, of the future Mother of God, and of human beings like you and me. Did Mary "earn" her salvation to become Queen of Heaven? Yes, in a way, she did (see chapter 12). And something similar could be said about all the saints—and hopefully about us, too, at the end of life.

CONCLUSION

Catholics do *not* think that salvation can be earned. They know that they cannot just *buy* their way into Heaven and they cannot earn salvation merely by working hard. Salvation is something we must *receive.* No one can force his way into Heaven. It all depends on God's grace. No matter how hard we try, God must *invite* us into Heaven first! But whether we arrive there also depends on how we live our lives. So, salvation depends *also* on what we do ourselves.

9

CATHOLICS INVENTED PRIESTS

THE LIE

The Catholic Church was infiltrated by pagans after Catholicism became the official religion of the Roman Empire in 312. Pagan Roman priests rushed to get new jobs as priests in the new official religion. So the actual founder of Roman Catholicism is not Jesus but the Roman emperor Constantine.

That's when the early Church changed its presbyters into priests, borrowing much of their significance from pagan religions. There is no basis in Scripture for the priesthood. What the Catholic Church teaches is a pseudo-priesthood: a "hierarchical priesthood" (of bishops and priests) separate from the common "priestly" function of the "community of believers" at large.

THE TRUTH

Those claiming that the priesthood was invented later in Christianity should acknowledge that this claim itself was also invented — although much later, some fourteen centuries later, during the Protestant Reformation. This revolutionary development created a romantic, distorted view of grassroots churches in early Christianity: radically egalitarian and charismatic, not authoritarian or hierarchical, gathered around a table rather than an altar—basically the model found in Congregational churches.

Contrary to this idealized, or rather ideological, view by the Protestant Reformation, the early Church was not just an amalgam of diverse groups who met in private houses to share meals in memory of Jesus. Far from that! Not only was the liturgy of the early Church rather unified, structured, and settled—as appears from early documents, such as the *Didache* (ca. 70)—but so was the management and organization of the early Christian communities, according to the writings of the early Church Fathers. The Protestant Reformers may have wished to go "back to the sources," but they, in fact, initiated a "break with the sources." Interestingly enough, many former Protestant ministers who recently converted to Catholicism did so after reading the writings of the early Church Fathers. This opened their eyes as to how "Catholic" the early Church was, even in her earliest stages.

Did the early Church have priests as we understand them today? Or are we indeed dealing here with another later development—a Catholic invention, as some say? True, the Letter to the Hebrews in particular draws a clear distinction between the Jewish priesthood and the high priesthood of Christ; it teaches that the sacrificial atonement by Jesus Christ on Calvary has made the Jewish priesthood and its prescribed ritual sacrifices obsolete and redundant. The time of priests in the temple is over. Thus, for Christians, Christ Himself is the only High Priest, and Christians have no priesthood independent or distinct from participation in the priesthood of Christ, the head of the Church.

If Jesus is indeed the new High Priest, we might wonder whether we still need other priests. At first sight, the Bible seems to say we don't, because the New Testament people of God are called a "royal priesthood" (1 Pet. 2:9), invited to exercise Christ's mission as priest, prophet, and king—similar to the way the Old Testament people of God were called "a kingdom of priests" (Exod. 19:6). But that may not be the end of the story. Just as the Jewish "kingdom of priests" still had a special group of priests, so also the Christian "royal priesthood" has an order of men specially called to serve as priests. As the apologist James Akin puts it, "We have Jesus as our great, high priest at the top, and there is the universal priesthood of all New Testament believers at the bottom. But the Bible indicates there is also a middle, ministerial priesthood that is ordained to serve the Church full-time."

Catholics certainly agree that all true Christians are priests. They call this the "common or universal priesthood." But at the Last Supper Jesus invited His apostles to a very special role in His ministry. The Church calls this the "ministerial or ordained priesthood." Today when people talk about a priest, they are generally talking about this special kind of "ministerial priest." Even most Protestants intuitively understand the distinction between the "common priesthood" (people in the pews) and the "ministerial priesthood" (the person serving the congregation). Otherwise they would not go through the process of training, certifying, and in some cases ordaining pastors.

This poses the question: What is it that makes a minister or pastor a priest? To find out whether there is really talk of "priests" in the early Church, we need to stress what is essential for being a priest.

The answer is: to make *sacrifices*. In fact, the language of offering and of sacrifice does pervade the entire New Testament, especially in the writings of St. Paul (e.g., Phil. 2:17; 4:18; Rom. 15:16). Jesus offered Himself as a sacrifice for us, becoming our

High Priest, but He also commanded His apostles to "do this in memory of me"—to re-present the sacrifice He had presented at Calvary. What else could these men be re-presenting, if not a sacrifice?

Well, just as Jesus presided over the Last Supper, the re-presentation of this must also be presided over: there must be someone to speak and offer the sacrifice, someone to operate in the place of Christ. When Jesus gave them the command—and with the command, the power—to do what He had just done, He made His apostles priests. Thus, Jesus instituted the ministerial priesthood.

Why then are they not called "priests" in the New Testament? Indeed, the ordained ministers of the New Covenant are rather called apostles, bishops, and presbyters, but never priests (*hiereus* in Greek). Nowhere in the New Testament does anyone but Christ receive the title *hiereus* in Greek translations. Why not? First of all, we should not expect this noun to be used as a title for New Covenant ministers, for that same term was used for the more numerous Jewish and even pagan priests of the first century (cf. Luke 1:8–9; Acts 14:13)—that is, until the Temple was demolished by the Romans in A.D. 70. Yet Paul did use the word "priestly" once when he said, "because of the grace given me by God to be a minister of Christ Jesus to the Gentiles in the *priestly* service [*hierourgounta*] of the gospel of God" (Rom. 15:15–16, emphasis added).

Second, the only priesthood the first disciples, being pious Jews, were familiar with was that of the Temple. However, the tasks that Christian "priests" carried out had very little relevance to the tasks that the Jewish priests would exercise in the Temple. Therefore, they made use of other names that described better their new functions in these first Christian communities—names such as *apostle,* which means "sent," *episcopos,* which means "overseer," *presbyteros,* which is often translated as "elder."

Third, the issue is largely a matter of terminology and translation. Joseph T. Richardson gives the following analysis of the problem. In many recent Bible translations, there is indeed no mention at all of "priests," which leads Protestant readers in particular to presume that the Catholic priesthood has no basis in Scripture and stems only from "traditions of men." However, Hebrew ministers of the Old Testament came to be called "priests" in English translations, and in fact there is no other or better word in English that can adequately be applied to them. Likewise, when the Christian Bible was translated into Latin, the ministers of the *Old* Covenant (*hiereis*) were translated as *sacerdotes,* literally those who make holy gifts—a word used in Latin for priests in the Roman and Greek religion. So the word "priests" was properly used in that context.

But this was different in the *New* Testament translations, where *presbyteros* was translated as "presbyters" or "elders"—to avoid confusion with priests in the Temple—although the word "presbyter" is most likely the origin of the English word "priest." So this makes one wonder: Why was "presbyter" translated not as "priest" but as "elder"? It is odd that modern Bible translations do use the word "priest" in the Old Testament—in which it has no historical or etymological root—but not in the New Testament—from which the word actually derives. Richardson is right: there is some inconsistency here. That's why he asks, "Why is it that the Old Testament priesthood is translated with that word in English today, and not the New Testament priesthood?"

Because of this translation issue, Protestant Christians are left to question why the New Testament ministry is even called a "priesthood." Then Richardson points out that Timothy, the recipient of Paul's epistles, by all appearances was an "elder" or overseer—and yet Timothy was not an "older man" at all, but one to whom Paul exhorted, "Let no one despise your youth" (1 Tim. 4:12). Richardson concludes, "The office of presbyter, then, was not exclusively limited to 'older men,' and came to mean more than the literal meaning of the word in Greek; and that word continued to be used, even when a younger man held the office." This certainly pleads for calling them "priests."

Richardson also points out that even Wycliffe, a proto-Protestant who made his own English translation of the Bible, understood the ministers of the New Testament to be rightfully called "priests," and the Latin word "presbyter" he translated to be the root of the English word "priest." He also translated the ministers of the Old Testament—*sacerdotes* in Latin—as "priests" in English. Likewise, William Tyndale, who made the first of the new English Bibles of the Reformation, said, "Now whether ye call them elders or priests, it is to me all one." The heirs to Tyndale's translation, including the King James Bible and every major English translation since, have translated the word *presbyteros* as "elder." Richardson concludes, "There is certainly an element of reaction and even rebellion in some Protestant translations, particularly in more recent ones: a conscious rejection of the idea of a New Testament ministerial priesthood."

We have at least one more question left: Are priests to be ordained? Timothy, as well as Titus and other early bishops, certainly carried out their ministry of ordaining priests, and the result is what we have today in the Catholic Church: a sacramental priesthood with a chain of ordinations running straight back to the first century. When the apostles appointed Matthias to replace Judas (Acts 1:15–23), it was clearly to an office, one vested with special responsibility and authority. And because bishops were considered successors to the apostles, they were filling an office with unique powers and responsibilities.

These powers and responsibilities were passed on "by the laying on of hands." In 1 Timothy 4:14, St. Paul explains how he must fulfill his ministry and then tells Timothy: "Do not neglect the gift you have, which was given you by prophetic utterance when the council of presbyters [priests] laid their hands upon you." This gift of the Holy Spirit, through the laying on of hands in ordination, was something Paul instructed Timothy to pass on in the future. Part of his duty as a bishop was to ordain presbyters [priests] in different congregations. 1 Timothy 5:21–22 puts it in these terms: "In the presence of God and of Christ Jesus and of the elect angels I charge you to keep these rules without favor, doing nothing from partiality. Do not be hasty in the laying on of hands, nor participate in another man's sins; keep yourself pure." In other words, pass it on, but make sure it ultimately comes from the High Priest, Jesus Christ. St. Thomas Aquinas puts it this way: "Only Christ is the true priest, the others being only his ministers." Thus, Catholic clergy share in the one, unique priesthood of Christ.

Since Christ is the High Priest [*archiereus*] in the Letter to the Hebrews, all men who, through the sacrament of Holy Orders, have become priests participate in Christ's priesthood; they act in the person of Christ, the Head of His Body, the Church. The Catholic priesthood, therefore, is a share in the priesthood of Christ and traces its historical origins to the twelve apostles appointed by Christ. Those apostles in turn selected other men to succeed them as the bishops (*episkopoi*, "overseers") of the Christian communities, with whom were associated presbyters (*presbyteroi*, "priests") and deacons (*diakonoi*, "servants"). As communities multiplied and grew in size, the bishops appointed more

and more "presbyters" [priests] to preside at the Eucharist in place
of the bishop in the multiple communities in each region. Today,
the rank of presbyter is typically what one thinks of as a priest,
although technically both a bishop and a presbyter are priests in
the sense that they share in Christ's ministerial priesthood and
offer sacrifice to God in the person of Christ. Therefore, we should
consider their authority *hierarchical*, a word that also comes from
the Greek word for priest [*hiereus*].

The letters of St. Ignatius of Antioch, written in the first de-
cade of the second century, testify to this. Over and over he advises
the churches in Smyrna, Rome, and so forth, about ecclesial authority. He tells the Christians in Ephesus, for instance, to "obey
the bishop and the presbytery with an undivided mind" and directs
the believers in Smyrna to "follow the bishop, even as Jesus Christ
does the Father, and the presbytery as you would the apostles; and
reverence the deacons, as being the institution of God." Ignatius
concluded from this, "Let that be considered a valid Eucharist
which is celebrated by the bishop, or by one whom he appoints."
As the *Catechism* puts it, "The ordained priesthood guarantees that
it really is Christ who acts in the sacraments through the Holy
Spirit for the Church" (1120). Without priests, there would no
longer be a Eucharist.

In other words, when people gather for Mass, they are not
only in the cenacle of the Last Supper, but also at Mount Calvary.
Without Calvary, there would have been no Last Supper, no
sacrifice. Protestants who oppose the traditional understanding
of the Eucharist tend to get hung up on temporal and chronological aspects — calling it "science fiction" to suggest that Jesus
could give His body up for us "before going to Calvary." But in
fact, the table of the Last Supper is also an altar on which the
Lamb of God has been slaughtered. This is what the priest does

during every Mass: he offers sacrifice to the Father in the person of Christ. That's why the *presbyter* is not just an "elder" but a "priest"—actually an ordained priest.

CONCLUSION

Catholics did *not* invent priests. Although a Catholic priest is no longer the kind of priest who made sacrifices in the Jewish Temple, priesthood is at the core of Jesus' role in the salvation history of the Bible. It is certainly not a pagan invention but is in line with Jesus being the High Priest and commissioning others to stand in for Him. So the "elders" of the New Testament are really priests. One could well argue that the word *elder* is more of an invention than the word *priest* in Christianity.

10

CATHOLICS WRONGLY CALL THEIR PRIESTS "FATHER"

THE LIE

When Catholics address priests as "Father," they are engaging in an unbiblical practice that Jesus forbade: "Call no man your father on earth, for you have one Father, who is in heaven" (Matt. 23:9). Also, the scandals in which some Catholic priests have been involved are proof that we should never call them "Father."

Besides, the title "Father" that priests ask for expresses some form of religious superiority, whereas in Christ we are all supposed to be equal. As St. Paul said in his letter to the Galatians, "There is neither Jew nor Greek, there is neither slave nor free person, there is not male and female; for you are all one in Christ Jesus" (3:28). In a similar vein, there is neither priest nor layperson in Christianity — we are all one in Christ.

THE TRUTH

What Jesus says in Matthew 23:9 — "And call no man your father on earth, for you have one Father, who is in Heaven" — can

77

easily be misinterpreted. Notice that His command makes no distinction between spiritual fathers, which is what priests are to Catholics, and biological fathers. In other words, if you interpret this passage to say, literally, that no man is to be called "father," you cannot distinguish between calling a priest "Father" and calling the man who is married to your mother "Father." Does this mean we should call Dad our "male parent" instead? Of course not! When God gave us the commandment "Honor your father and mother," it is hard to believe He really meant "Honor me and your mother." As a matter of fact, the concept of God's role as Father would be meaningless if we obliterated the concept of earthly fatherhood.

So, Matthew 23:9 does not really forbid us to call people other than God "father." You might say, though, that this may be true of biological or legal fathers, but how could the title "Father" also be used beyond that range? It surely can and has been used beyond the biological realm. Typically, the title is used as a sign of respect to those with whom we have a special relationship. For example, Elisha cries, "My father, my father!" to Elijah as the latter is carried up to Heaven in a whirlwind (2 Kings 2:12). Later, Elisha himself is called a father by the king of Israel (2 Kings 6:21). Also, the New Testament speaks of calling one's ancestors "father," as when Stephen refers to "our father Abraham" (Acts 7:2), or when Paul speaks of "our father Isaac" (see Rom. 9:10). St. Paul also refers to himself as a spiritual father, saying, "I became your father in Christ Jesus through the gospel" (1 Cor. 4:15). He also regularly refers to his helpers as his children and sons; for instance: "But Timothy's worth you know, how as a son with a father he has served with me in the gospel" (Phil. 2:22), and "I appeal to you for my child, Onesimus, whose father I have become in my imprisonment" (Philem. 1:10).

Catholics wrongly call their priests "father"

Apparently, there is nothing wrong with calling our priests "fathers," for they are our "spiritual fathers." When Protestants deem this to be wrong, they should realize that they often call their ministers "Pastor," which means "shepherd." However, in John 10:16 Jesus said: "So there shall be one flock, one shepherd." Are Protestants wrong then in calling their minister "Pastor"? All that Jesus is doing in Matthew 23:9—and in the line before it—is to show the scribes and Pharisees how sinful and proud they were for not looking humbly to God as the source of all authority and fatherhood and teaching and pastoring, and instead setting themselves up as father figures, pastors, and teachers with "ultimate" authority instead of "derived" authority.

How did the title "Father" develop in the Catholic Church? Until about the year 400, a bishop was called "father" (papa). St. Ignatius of Antioch, for instance, expressed this explicitly when he wrote: "Let everyone revere ... the bishop as the image of the Father." The title of "papa" was soon restricted solely to addressing the bishop of Rome, the successor of St. Peter, and in English was rendered "pope." Shortly after, St. Benedict (480–547) assigned the title to spiritual confessors, since they were the guardians of souls. Moreover, the word "abbot," denoting the leader in faith of the monastic community, is derived from the word *abba*, the Aramaic word for "father," but in the very familiar sense of "daddy." Later, in the Middle Ages, the term "father" was also used to address the Franciscans and Dominicans, since by their preaching, teaching, and charitable works they cared for the spiritual and physical needs of all of God's children. This also became the custom in parishes, where Catholics are under a priest's spiritual care. So the word "Father" (Fr.) for a priest may actually be more appropriate than the word "Reverend" (Rev.), which is more common in Protestant churches. Catholics only revere their priests because they are "fathers" to their flock.

Priests, in turn, follow the apostles' biblical example by sometimes referring to members of their flock as "my son" or "my daughter" or "my child." Just as a father must nourish, instruct, challenge, correct, forgive, listen to, and sustain his children, so must a priest do the same for his spiritual children. So the title "Father" is actually much more humbling than "Reverend," as it comes with a grave responsibility. The emphasis is more on dedication and concern on the part of the father than on respect and reverence on the part of the children.

Unfortunately, this immediately raises the question, "Aren't there also unworthy priests who have caused scandals?" Of course there are, as much so as there are policemen, school teachers, and elected representatives in civic office who have caused scandals. But does the fact that there are unworthy priests blemish their priesthood? In a sense, it certainly does, but it does not "undo" their priesthood. Let's see why not.

St. Augustine addressed a similar issue in his dispute with the Donatists. Donatism was the heresy that claimed that the effectiveness of the sacraments depends on the moral character of the minister. In other words, if a minister involved in a serious enough sin were to baptize a person, that baptism would be considered invalid (see chapter 5). St. Augustine pointed out that the problem with Donatism is that no person is morally pure. The effectiveness of the administration of sacraments does not cease to be effective when the sinfulness of the minister is in question—think, for instance, of someone like Graham Greene's "whiskey priest." God is the one who works in and through them, and God is not restricted by the moral state of the administrant. The point is that the Church is holy, but her members are not. She is not holy because of the people who bear a certain title—instead, it is her sacraments and her message that make her holy. The same with priests: They are not holy on their own account, but when they administer the sacraments, they act on behalf of Christ, who is holy.

Obviously, priesthood is of a "permanent" nature. Like the sacrament of Baptism, it can never be erased: baptized Christians can cease to practice their Faith, and even publicly deny Christ, but they can never undo their Baptism. Priestly ordination works in the same manner. The Council of Trent (1545–1563) says, "If anyone says a priest can ever become a layman again, let him be anathema." As the common saying goes, "Once a priest, always a priest"—or as the psalm puts it, "You are a priest for ever" (Ps. 110:4). The 1983 *Code of Canon Law* reaffirms this teaching of the Council of Trent.

Apparently, when some people refer to a priest who has "left" the priesthood as a "former priest" or "ex-priest," they are outside the consistent teaching of the Catholic Church. A priest cannot be "annulled," but he can be laicized. That is, he can be released from the rights, duties, and responsibilities that are connected to the clerical state. Practically speaking, this would mean that a priest no longer functions outwardly as a priest. To the outside world he would appear to be a layman, working at an ordinary job, and living the regular life of the laity. When a priest is released from the clerical state, he is still technically a priest, but he may no longer exercise the power of orders. However, if a laicized priest were to say Mass, it would be a *valid* Mass, since he never loses the ability to celebrate the Eucharist—but it would be *illicit*.

Where does this leave us? Surely, being a priest is not an easy task. We are not just talking here about the practical, day-to-day duties a priest has for his flock, but more in particular about the emotional and spiritual burdens priests carry. Probably the following prayer expresses this best:

> Keep them, I pray, dearest Lord, keep them, for they
>   are Thine—
> Thy priests whose lives burn out before Thy conse-
>   crated shrine.
> Keep them, for they are in the world, though from
>   the world apart.
> When earthly pleasures tempt, allure—shelter them
>   in Thy heart.
> Keep them, and comfort them in hours of loneliness
>   and pain,
> When all their life of sacrifice for souls seems but in
>   vain.
> Keep them, and O remember Lord, they have no one
>   but Thee.
> Yet they have only human hearts, with human frailty.
> Keep them as spotless as the Host that daily they
>   caress.
> Their every thought and word and deed, deign, dear-
>   est Lord, to bless.

CONCLUSION

Nowhere in the Bible are we forbidden to call people other than God "father." Although we are all "one in Christ," there are still different gifts and callings in the Church—"varieties of service, but the same Lord," says St. Paul (1 Cor. 12:5)—such as the gift of healing, the gift of prophecy, the gift of discernment of spirits, and we might add, the gift of being a priest. Although the body has many parts, one part cannot say to another part, "I do not need you." We need priests to administer the sacraments and to act on behalf of Christ, in whom we are all one.

II

CATHOLICS HAVE AN EASY
WAY OUT: CONFESSION

THE LIE

The Catholic Church invented Confession so that Catholics who violate the moral code can just run back to a priest in a confessional every once in a while and live happily ever after. With the so-called Last Sacrament, a priest can even wipe out all their sins at once and thus secure for them a road leading straight into Heaven.

Catholics can do the evilest things in life, but they have nothing to worry about. All they have to do is go to Confession and start with a clean slate again—all is forgotten and forgiven. But how can a priest forgive sins? Either only God can or everyone can!

THE TRUTH

Part of this myth is simply a misunderstanding of the position of the priest. Catholics do not confess their sins to a priest "instead of to God," but directly to God *through* a priest, appointed by our Lord as an official stand-in for Christ (in Latin, *alter Christus*).

The *Catechism* makes this very clear: "Only God forgives sins (cf. Mark 2:7). Since he is the Son of God, Jesus says of himself, 'The Son of man has authority on earth to forgive sins' and exercises this divine power: 'Your sins are forgiven' (Mark 2:5, 10; Luke 7:48)" (1441). The *Catechism* explains this further, "Christ has willed that in her prayer and life and action his whole Church should be the sign and instrument of the forgiveness and reconciliation that he acquired for us at the price of his blood" (1442).

Since he would not always be with the Church physically and visibly, Christ delegated this power to other men so that the Church would be able to offer forgiveness to future generations. He gave this as a transmissible power to the apostles so it could be passed on to their successors, the bishops, and eventually to each priest. There is a great song by the Evangelical Christian rock band Audio Adrenaline that says, "I want to be your hands; I want to be your feet." Catholics have no problem with the fact that Jesus has ordained some to act on His behalf in the material world. We must keep in mind that the priest is not the one who forgives—the forgiveness comes from Jesus. Before every confession, the priest calls upon Jesus to come. He is simply performing a "service" for Jesus and in the name of Jesus. There is always a definite connection to Jesus.

There is a "horizontal" connection that stretches forward in time: from apostle to bishop to bishop to bishop—called *apostolic succession*. But there is also a "vertical" connection that stretches downward in the hierarchy: from Christ to pope to bishop to priest. Each priest is indirectly connected with the first priests, the apostles, and thus with Christ. In essence, there is an unbroken line of bishops laying hands on priests—a line that can be traced back directly to the Last Supper of Jesus with His twelve apostles. These twelve would next lay hands on priests who later were appointed bishops so they could lay hands on new priests, and so forth. Therefore, the priests of today are in an unbroken lineage to that momentous day of the Last Supper. This explains their unique role in the Church (see chapter 9). Catholics take 2 Timothy 2:2 as a reference to *four* generations in the "apostolic succession" where it says, "What *you* have heard from *me* before many witnesses entrust to *faithful men* who will be able to teach *others* also" (emphasis added). There is talk here of a clear succession running from *me* to *you* to *faithful men* to *others*.

Still, many wonder why confession should be made to a *priest*, and not to one another. In James 5:16, God commands us to confess our sins "to one another." Notice, first of all, Scripture does not say to confess your sins straight to God and only to God. Second, in Matthew 9:6, Jesus tells us that He was given authority on earth to forgive sins. Then Scripture proceeds to tell us, in verse 8, that God "had given such authority to men"—plural. But there is a next step. In John 20:21–23, Jesus tells the apostles to follow His example, "Jesus said to them again, 'Peace be with you. As the Father has sent me, even so I send you.' And when he had said this, he breathed on them, and said to them, 'Receive the Holy Spirit. If you forgive the sins of any, they are forgiven; if you retain the sins of any, they are retained.'" Thus, He delegated the power to forgive sins to the apostles. When Catholics confess their sins to a priest, they are simply following the plan laid down by Jesus Christ. He forgives sins through the priest—it is God's power, but Jesus exercises that power through the ministry of the priest.

Has it always been this way from the early Church on? There is historical evidence that committing very grave sins resulted in severe penance, sometimes even public penance—ten years' penance for abortion, for example, was common in the early Church. Early sources, such as the *Didache*, tell us that some sinners did publicly speak about their sins. Confession was not just something done in silence to God alone, but something done "in church," as the *Didache* indicates: "Confess your sins in church." Nevertheless, testimonies of the early Church show that in most cases offenses were known to the priest alone. Then, in the third century—a time of serious persecutions—multiple discussions ensued on how to exercise Church penance regarding grave sinners—lapsed Catholics, idolaters, adulterers, and murderers. In general, it may be said that if the sins to be forgiven were secret sins they could be confessed "in secret"; whereas if they were public sins (murder, adultery, rape, sorcery, perjury, and apostasy), then they had to be confessed "in public" before the whole community.

Early Christian writers, such as Origin (185–254), St. Cyprian (ca. 200–258), and St. Aphraates (or Aphrahat, ca. 280–345) state clearly that confession is to be made to a priest. Cyprian writes, "The forgiving of sins can take place only through the priests." St. Ambrose (339–397) says, "This right is given to priests only." Then a severe letter of Pope Leo I in 459 stated, "It is sufficient that the guilt which people have on their consciences be made known to the priests alone in secret confession." The connection between private confession and private penance was getting stronger and stronger. Gradually, it was the influence of Irish missionaries that contributed to a wider spread of the "private" and more frequent practice of penance, which does not require public and prolonged completion of penitential works before reconciliation with the Church. That's where we are now.

Currently, Catholics may use different terms in this context. Whereas "Confession" stresses the action of the believer in the sacrament, "Reconciliation" stresses the action of God, who uses the sacrament to reconcile us to Himself, and "Penance" expresses the proper attitude with which we should approach the sacrament—with sorrow for our sins, a desire to atone for them, and a firm resolve not to commit them again.

One more question might still be lingering: Doesn't the frequency of Confession in Catholicism make all of this a revolving-door event? It depends on how you look at it. Our sins keep piling up every day we live. Thanks to Confession, Catholics don't have to carry and heap up this increasing load of sins, for they can at any time unload their sins, and start with a "clean slate"—which does not mean the "slate" will stay clean, of course.

St. Augustine tells the famous story of how he stole pears from an orchard as a child. Then he astutely remarked about his stealing, "I had no wish to enjoy what I tried to get by theft; all my enjoyment was in the theft itself and in the sin." This is an example of the perverse will that chooses evil for its own sake—a consequence of Original Sin in which the will rebels against reason and becomes a slave at the command of passions. Just as the good can be loved for its own sake, as something intrinsically desired, so evil can be willed for its own sake. That's when someone's moral sense becomes desensitized, making evil appear to be good. A deep stain like that calls for Confession.

Thanks to Confession, no disruption of our relationship with God is forever. Confession is a sign of God's immense mercy and forgiveness. For Catholics, there is no "forever," as long as there is the sacrament of Confession. It brings reconciliation with God. But the Catholic practice is certainly not meant to encourage sin, for it requires quite some humility to confess one's sins.

Many people underestimate the power of Confession. Scientists and health-care providers may have tried to convince us that sinfulness is just a matter of sickness, genes, and chemicals—thus finding ways to get rid of its moral and religious dimension. But there is much reason to question this explanation.

Maybe addictions can be healed better by religious conversion than by medication. Perhaps child abuse can be better cured with self-discipline than with sedatives. Possibly, sexual abuse of children is not based on a pedophilia gene but on sinful behavior—another form of rape that requires self-discipline rather than genetic manipulation. It could very well be that a guilt complex—another name for a syndrome—doesn't require a shrink session but rather the therapy of the confessional.

When asked, "Why did you join the Church of Rome?" G. K. Chesterton answered in his autobiography as follows: " 'To get rid of my sins.' For there is no other religious system that does really profess to get rid of people's sins." How right Chesterton was—the Catholic Church is unquestionably a "hospital for sinners."

CONCLUSION

Catholics do *not* have an easy way out. Confession does not give Catholics a free pass to do the evilest things in life, but instead gives them the humble awareness that they are sinners. So this does not make for an easy way to Heaven, as some claim it does. On the other hand, Confession is more about Jesus than about us. The priest does not forgive sins, but Jesus does through the priest, who stands in for Jesus and thus shows God's enormous mercy and forgiveness, more so than our immense sinfulness. But the reality is that forgiveness can be given only to those who ask for it and repent. If the confessional seems like a revolving door, that is because of our habitual sinful nature. Whoever curtails the power of the confessional curtails the power of God's forgiveness. Besides, the confessional has actually an amazing therapeutic effect that can beat many a shrink session.

PART 3

CATHOLICISM AND ITS UNIQUENESS

12

CATHOLICS ARE NOT CHRISTIANS

THE LIE

The members of the early Church were not "Catholics" but "Christians." Catholics just introduced a new term for themselves—the Greek adjective *katholikos* is a contraction of *kata* and *holos*, which means "about the whole" or "universal"—and thus declared themselves as the only authentic members of the universal Church. But by doing so, they actually separated themselves from the core of Christianity.

Besides, these "Catholics" grew further and further away from their origin by incorporating foreign, pagan elements and new beliefs that were missing in the early Church.

THE TRUTH

"Catholic" or "Christian": What is the difference? Both terms have a very early origin. Paul started his missionary travels from the Church of Antioch in Syria, where the name "Christians"—believers in Christ—was coined. "In Antioch the disciples were for the first time called Christians" (Acts 11:26). But the term "Catholic" has also a very early origin. The term was used first, as far as we know, by Ignatius of Antioch before the turn of the first century: "Wherever the bishop shall appear, there let the multitude [of the people] also be; even as, wherever Jesus Christ is, there is the Catholic Church" (*Letter to the Smyrnaeans* 8). The casual way Ignatius uses the term "Catholic," without any further explanation, tells us he expects his readers to know it already as an accepted term. For Ignatius, "Catholic" means that the Church is more than a collection of isolated and disconnected congregations. It is not a regional cult but intended to include all people of the entire world—universal.

What does this mean for us? If you are a Catholic, should you call yourself "Christian," or "Catholic," or even "Roman Catholic"—or does it not matter which label you choose? There is some reason for choosing the term "Catholic," for in many people's minds nowadays, to be a Christian means to be a Protestant. One could even make the case that certain Protestant groups have hijacked the term "Christian." This is especially true in the Deep South of the USA, where you can hear people say, after they have left the Catholic Church, that they are no longer Catholic but Christian. But even on TV, when you see a "Christian" broadcast, it is usually on a Protestant channel. The pernicious idea behind this is that Catholics are not Christians but devotees of a cult similar to Jehovah's Witnesses or Mormons.

So should we call ourselves "Catholic"? Why not, for the term "catholic" simply means "universal"? When employing the term at the time of early Christianity, the early Church Fathers Ignatius of Antioch (35–108) and Polycarp of Smyrna (69–155) were referring to the Church that was already "everywhere," as distinguished from whatever sects, schisms, or splinter groups might have grown up here and there in opposition to the Catholic Church. So it is actually a very good term, as long as that doesn't mean that Catholics are not "Christian" in the sense of followers of Christ. In fact, they are both — both "Christian" and "Catholic."

So ultimately, both terms are almost equivalent. However, terms can change their meaning easily. Because there is nowadays a widespread confusion about what "Catholic" and "Christian" ultimately stand for, some have opted for the label "*Roman* Catholic," and in line with that, "the *Roman* Catholic Church." This does indeed make clear whom or what you are referring to, but it is very doubtful that it is a proper term for Catholics and their Church.

Here is why it's a questionable move. Kenneth D. Whitehead explains how the term "Roman Catholic" came in use. That term caught on mostly in English-speaking countries; it was promoted mostly by Anglicans, supporters of the "branch theory" of the Church — namely, that the one, holy, catholic, and apostolic Church of the Creed was supposed to consist of three major branches, the Anglican, the Orthodox, and the so-called Roman Catholic branch. Something similar happened in predominantly Calvinist countries such as the Netherlands.

Catholics should nevertheless beware of using the label "*Roman* Catholic," not only because of its dubious origins in Anglican and Calvinist circles suggesting that there just might be some other Catholic Church around somewhere besides the Roman one, but also because it often still is used today to suggest that the "Roman Catholic Church" is something other and lesser than the Catholic Church mentioned in the Nicene Creed.

Although the followers of Christ early became known as "Christians," according to St. Luke, the name "Christian" was never commonly applied to the Church herself. In the New Testament, the Church is simply called "the Church." There was only one. In that early time there were not yet any breakaway bodies substantial enough to be rival claimants of the name and from which the Church might ever have to distinguish herself. And the Church Fathers would also just speak of "the Church." But since the Reformation there have been serious breakaway groups, which forced some Christians to speak of "the Roman Catholic Church," to distinguish her from other Christian denominations.

Yet the Catholic Church never speaks of herself as "the Roman Catholic Church." First of all, there are more than twenty Churches in full communion with the pope of Rome that make up the Catholic Church, with the Latin (Roman) Church being only one of them; others include the Melkite Greek Catholic Church, the Armenian Catholic Church, and the Coptic Catholic Church. Nowhere in the sixteen documents of the Second Vatican Council, for instance, will you find the term "Roman Catholic." Pope Paul VI signed all the documents of the Second Vatican Council as "I, Paul. Bishop of the Catholic Church." Simply that—"Catholic Church." There are references to the Roman Curia, the Roman Missal, the Roman Rite, and so forth, but when the adjective "Roman" is applied to the Church herself, it refers to the local Diocese of Rome!

In general, though, speaking of "Christians" is fine as long as we don't use it to distinguish them from "Catholics." Especially in the works of the early Fathers, Catholics are Christians, and Christians are Catholics. In the fourth century, Bishop Pacian of Barcelona said, "Christian is my first name; Catholic is my surname. The former gives me an identity; the latter distinguishes me." How true that statement is. The name "Catholic" does not apply to heretics such as Montanus, Arius, Pelagius, or Donatus. Catholics distinguish themselves from all others—from all

Gnostics, Arians, Modalists, or Donatists. Catholics trace their identity back to the "one and only" Jesus Christ.

In other words, all Catholics live in "ecclesial communion" with each other. This communion, which we call "Church," not only extends to all Catholic believers in a specific historical period but also embraces all the epochs and all the generations. Pope Benedict XVI spoke of a "twofold universality": a *synchronic* one (uniting Catholics in every part of the world) as well as a *diachronic* one (uniting all Catholics of the past and of the future). It is the latter one that unites us today with the first Christians through the intermediaries of the Church Fathers. It is this historical link with the First Christians that makes and keeps us both Christian and Catholic. It is tradition that unites us with the First Christians. Tradition is the living river that links us to the origins—"back to the sources."

Did Catholics perhaps grow away from their Christian origin? Many Protestants still think that the history of the Church ended with the closure of the New Testament and picked up again with the sixteenth-century Protestant Reformation. In this view, all we need to know about the early Church can be found in the New Testament, in particular the Acts of the Apostles. But the apostles taught the early Christians much more than the Bible tells us; they told them also about the structure, the praxis, and the liturgy of the early Church. So this raises the question: Where else can we find what the first Christians believed? The answer is: in the early Church Fathers, who had known the apostles directly or indirectly, were taught by the apostles, and handed down what they learned from the apostles.

That is certainly surprising, for we tend to think that the further we get away from Jesus, the more tainted His original message becomes. When time progresses, the original enthusiasm of the first Christians seems to become diluted. We want to go back to the time when the Church was young—young, and not yet corrupted. One of the reasons we think that the early Church was purer and more genuine than today is that she had not been contaminated yet by heresies and other devious developments that pulled her away from her origin. It is rather common to think that the further away we get from Jesus—in time, that is—the more chance there is that the original purity gets tainted and corrupted by later developments, such as heresies and schisms.

The early Church Fathers were very aware of the problems that schisms and heresies can cause in the Church. A common goal of all Church Fathers was to preserve the unity of Christians—the unity around the Person of Jesus Christ and His message—in spite of the time that was separating them from Jesus. They justified their orthodox doctrine by showing a "chain" [*catena*] of unbroken teaching stretching from Father to Father, back to the apostles, and ultimately to Jesus. Heresies and schisms forced the Church and her teachers to be ever clearer in their expression of the Faith.

Even the Protestant Reformer John Calvin had to declare that for the first six centuries of her existence on earth the Church had remained "pure and undefiled." He wasn't very generous, but he at least acknowledged a kernel of the truth. Stephen Ray, a former Baptist Bible teacher, explained his conversion to Catholicism as follows: "The more I read, the more I realized that the early Church was Catholic and did not support my Evangelical conclusions." When we call the early Church young, that does not mean that now the Catholic Church is old. Perhaps she has grown more mature, but not really old.

The first Christians—whom we could as well call the first Catholics—are not much different from Catholics nowadays, at least not in their beliefs. They may not use the exact same words and wordings as Catholics do today, but their beliefs are basically the same, in spite of having gone through the stream of twenty centuries. We all go back to the "Word made Flesh," to the Jesus whom the apostles and their successors have handed down to us.

Cardinal John Henry Newman, a convert from Anglicanism, once wrote, "The principles and proceedings of the Church now, were those of the Church then; the principles and proceedings of heretics then, were those of Protestants now." And Steve Ray added, "The Reformation was not a recovery of what had been lost, but rather a radical departure from what had always been."

The Nicene Creed, for instance, was not imposed by the Roman Empire or Emperor Constantine, as some claim. What connects Nicaea with Jesus Christ is an impressive chain of Church Fathers who painstakingly followed Christ. And Constantine was not the beginning of corruption in the Church. Everything that happened before or after Constantine was kept in line by the Church Fathers, who were in constant battle with the Roman emperors and faithfully held on to what Jesus had taught them through the apostles. The Fathers are our testimony *against* the "puritanical" and anti-Catholic belief that the original and initial Christian Church has been covered over with creeds and doctrines of mere men.

CONCLUSION

Catholics are Christians to the core. The Catholic Church did not betray her Christian origins but vigorously protected what she had received from the Church Fathers and apostles, who had an unbroken link with Jesus Christ Himself. The Catholic

Church never broke with the early Church; instead it was the Protestant Church that broke away and separated itself from our common Christian roots. Catholics are Christians, and Christians should be Catholics.

13

CATHOLICS VENERATE MARY AS A GODDESS

THE LIE

Catholics pray to Mary, whom they call the "Queen of Heaven."
Praying to Mary means actually worshipping or venerating her
instead of God, or at least worshipping her next to God. This is
definitely in defiance of 1 Timothy 2:5: "There is one mediator
between God and men, the man Christ Jesus." As one Protestant
said, "When I go to a doctor, I don't want to talk to his mother."

Therefore, when Catholics pray the Rosary in honor of Mary,
they engage in blasphemy—it is antibiblical, it offends God, and
it venerates Mary instead of God.

THE TRUTH

It is hard for Protestants to deny that Mary plays an important
role in the Bible. Luke's Gospel mentions Mary most often,
identifying her by name twelve times, all of these in the infancy
narrative (1:27, 30, 34, 38, 39, 41, 46, 56; 2:5, 16, 19, 34). Matthew's Gospel mentions her by name five times, four of these in
the infancy narrative (1:16, 18, 20; 2:11) and once outside the

infancy narrative (13:55). Mark's Gospel names her once by name (6:3) and also mentions her as Jesus' mother without using her name (3:31). John's Gospel refers to her twice but never mentions her by name. In the Acts (1:14), Luke's second writing, Mary is mentioned in the company of the Eleven who are gathered in the upper room after the Ascension. The book of Revelation (12:1, 5–6) mentions the "woman clothed with the sun" but doesn't explicitly identify her as Mary of Nazareth, the mother of Jesus.

Unquestionably, Mary continues to play a pivotal role in the later life of the earliest Church. Acts 1:14 says, "These with one accord devoted themselves to prayer, together with the women and Mary the mother of Jesus, and with his brethren." Mary is also documented in Roman catacombs. Paintings from the second century show her holding the Christ Child. The earliest known Marian prayer is from around 270; it was discovered in 1917 on a papyrus in Egypt. The earliest church dedicated to the Virgin Mary dates to the late fourth century in Syria; among its ruins was found an inscription dedicating it to the *Theotokos* (the God-Bearer). St. Ambrose, the mentor of St. Augustine, venerated Mary as an example of Christian life and started a Marian cult of virginity as early as the fourth century.

Mother Teresa's words "No Mary, no Jesus" express a profound truth. God chose to bring His Son into the world through the cooperation of Mary. Without her cooperation, there would have been no Incarnation, and therefore no Redemption. As the Fall of man was a free act, so too the Redemption had to be free. Without the body of Mary, there would have been no body of Christ, for there is no child without the mother, and no mother without her child. It was her flesh that God took to make His own. Pope Paul VI made this very clear when he said, "If we want to be Christian, we must also be Marian ... which opens to us the way that leads us to him." The equations are obvious: Jesus = God; Mary = the Mother of Jesus; therefore, Mary = the Mother of God. Put differently, if Mary is not the Mother of God, then Jesus is not God.

Indeed, Mary is the Mother of God. Galatians 4:4 testifies to it: "When the time had fully come, God sent forth his Son, born of woman, born under the law." Elizabeth speaks of Mary as "mother of my Lord" (Luke 1:43). It was the Council of Ephesus in 431 that formally applied to her the description "Mother of God," in Greek *Theotokos*. Mary carried the Word of God in her body, kept it there, and bore it to the world. This was her essential role in the Incarnation. She bore in her womb "Emmanuel"—God with us, the Word made Flesh. For this reason, Catholics call Mary also "the Ark of the New Covenant." There is an obvious parallel between the Ark of the Old Covenant as the old dwelling place of God and Mary as the new dwelling place of God, between the Holy Spirit overshadowing the Ark and the Holy Spirit overshadowing Mary.

In addition, the Gospels of Matthew and Luke describe Mary as a virgin (παρθένος, parthénos). Matthew 1:23 quotes the prophecy of Isaiah 7:14: "Behold, a virgin [*alma* in Hebrew] shall conceive and bear a son." In the Septuagint—the Jewish translation into Greek of the Hebrew Bible (see chapter 2)—*alma* is translated into *parthenos* (virgin). No wonder then that the perpetual virginity of Mary was explicitly taught by the ecumenical Second Council of Constantinople in 553. It was St. Jerome who explained that Christ's "brothers," as mentioned in the Bible, were actually His cousins, since in Jewish idiom cousins were also referred to as "brothers." (We see something similar with "sisters": Mary stood at the foot of the Cross with her "sister" Mary, the wife of Clopas; the parents of the Blessed Virgin Mary were not so uncreative as to have given two daughters the same name.) So when Luke 2:7 says, "She gave birth to her first-born" we have to realize that "first-borns" were not given that title after there was a second-born. Even the Protestant Reformers—Luther, Calvin, and Zwingli—honored the perpetual virginity of Mary.

The book of Revelation (12:13) has a passage that many scholars consider to be a reference to Mary and her Son: "[T]he dragon ... pursued the woman who had borne the male child" (12:13). Therefore, Mary is often called "the new Eve." St. Bonaventure (thirteenth century) said about her, "That woman (namely Eve), drove us out of Paradise and sold us; but this one (Mary) brought us back again and bought us." So it is Mary's yes that reverses Eve's no. Cardinal Newman put it this way: "No one doubts that the 'man-child' spoken of is an allusion to our Lord; why then is not 'the woman,' an allusion to his mother?"

It is for all the above reasons that Mary has been given a special role in the salvation we received through her Son. Although not a formally defined dogma, the Second Vatican Council says:

> Therefore the Blessed Virgin is invoked by the Church under the titles of Advocate, Auxiliatrix, Adjutrix, and Mediatrix. Her role as Advocatrix is to immerse herself in Christ's role as our Advocate, to speak as our most powerful intercessor to her divine Son on behalf of the human race. For who is closer to the Son than his Mother?

From medieval times on, the Latin word *Advocata* signifies Mary's special power of intercession. It is first found in the writings of St. Irenaeus (120–203) "that the Virgin Mary should become the advocate of the virgin Eve." Much later, in 1894, Pope Leo XIII said in his encyclical on the Rosary, "The recourse we have to Mary in prayer follows upon the office she continuously fills by the side of the throne of God as Mediatrix of Divine grace." Then in 1935, during a radio broadcast, Pope Pius XI gave the title *co-redemptrix* to Mary. But keep in mind, the prefix "co-" in "co-redemptrix" doesn't mean she redeems "together with" Jesus; instead she is the woman "connected with" the redeemer.

In other words, *Co-Redemptrix* is not the same as Redeemer, *Mediatrix* is not the same as Mediator, and *Advocatrix* is not the same as Advocate. Never can Mary receive the worship due to God and Christ alone. Only Christ stands before God to redeem, mediate, and advocate. The Virgin Mary humbly kneels before Christ. She has no role of redemption, mediation, or advocacy of her own. She "mediates" between us, who are powerless, and her Son, who has all the power.

Yet we can still repeat what St. Teresa of Calcutta said about Mary: "Of course, Mary is the co-redemptrix. She gave Jesus his body, and the body of Jesus is what saved us." So we need to read properly, "There is one mediator between God and men, the man Christ Jesus." In the words of Pope John Paul II, "The text of St. Paul's Letter to Timothy excludes any other parallel mediation, but not subordinate mediation." The fact that Mary "mediates" salvation to us does not take away from the glory due to God alone for our salvation.

All of this may sound very Catholic, yet most Protestant Reformers would agree with the basics of it. The Protestant theologian Karl Barth is very definite about it: "This is the miracle of the Virgin Birth as it indicates the mystery of the incarnation" and "Born of the Virgin Mary means a human origin for God." It is interesting to hear how the first Protestant Reformer, Martin Luther, had very high words to say about Mary. In his sermon of August 15, 1522, he said, "There can be no doubt that the Virgin Mary is in heaven." In his sermon of September 1, 1522, he went even further: "The veneration of Mary is inscribed in the very depths of the human heart." In his sermon on the Feast of the Visitation, 1537, he actually spoke to her in the first person: "No woman is like you. You are more than Eve or Sarah, blessed above all nobility, wisdom, and sanctity." In line with this, Max Thurian (1921–1996), who was the subprior of the Taizé community, an ecumenical monastic community in France, wrote a book with the title *Mary, Mother of All Christians*. Not surprisingly, in 1988, Thurian converted to Roman Catholicism and was ordained a priest.

What we need to keep in mind, though, is that when Catholics ask Mary during each Hail Mary, "Pray for us sinners," they ask her to pray for sinners, not to redeem sinners. She brings them to her Son. This is the acid test of proper devotion to the Blessed Lady. Ultimately, Mary challenges us with the person and message of Jesus: "Do whatever he tells you" (John 2:5). Even in the great Marian churches of the world, such as Notre Dame de Paris, and Our Lady of Guadalupe in Mexico City, the central act of worship is the Mass—the Lord's Supper, the bloodless reenactment of his sacrifice on Calvary. The focus of worship is the altar, Cross, and tabernacle. Christ alone is the center of Catholic Faith. He is the one mediator between God and humanity. You won't find any Catholic priest offering a Mass to Mary; no, the sacrifice of the Mass is offered to God the Almighty Father, even on Marian feasts.

Being human, Mary was also redeemed herself, yet she is considered to have a special and unique relationship with God, as Christ shares DNA with her. Catholics believe that worship is due to God alone. Catholics do, however, venerate Mary. In other words, they honor the Blessed Mother with great reverence and devotion because she is the Mother of God. Mary is the model of perfect love and obedience to Christ. The former Protestant minister Scott Hahn, who eventually converted to Catholicism, says about prayers: "If there were 90 percent that goes to Christ and 10 percent that goes to Mary, 100 percent of it goes to God."

Can Catholics still call Mary the Queen of Heaven? In Jeremiah 7:18, God is indeed upset with the Israelites for worshipping a false goddess called the "queen of heaven." However, just because God rebuked them for worshipping the false queen of heaven, doesn't mean that we cannot pay honor to the true Queen of Heaven—the Blessed Mother. It is faulty logic leading one to believe that just because people worship a false god that they call "god," we, therefore, should not call the true God by that same name—God—because that's the same title the idolaters use for their god. In the same way, the fact that there is a false queen of heaven does not lead to the conclusion that we worship a false goddess when we call Mary the Queen of Heaven.

As a matter of fact, there is a true Queen of Heaven, which we see quite clearly in Revelation 12:1 where it says, "A great portent appeared in heaven, a woman clothed with the sun, with the moon under her feet, and on her head a crown of twelve stars." So in this passage, we read that there is indeed a woman, that she's indeed in Heaven, and that she has indeed a crown on her head. It is the true Queen of Heaven, Mary, the mother of the male child who is to rule the nations. We can pray to her, for she prays to God.

Even the most common and very Catholic prayer to her, the Rosary, is actually very biblical—each and every part of it! The prayer begins with "Hail Mary, full of grace, the Lord is with thee." This is nothing other than the greeting the angel Gabriel gave Mary in Luke 1:28. The next line says, "Blessed art thou among women, and blessed is the fruit of thy womb, Jesus." This comes from what Mary's cousin Elizabeth said to her in Luke 1:42. The final line says, "Holy Mary, Mother of God, pray for us sinners, now and at the hour of our death. Amen." Calling her holy is not an offense to God, for the Bible describes Christians in general as "holy" (Eph. 1:1; Phil. 1:1; Col. 1:2).

As Archbishop Salvatore J. Cordileone of San Francisco puts it, "To pray the Rosary is to look at Jesus through [Mary's] eyes." More in general, when Catholics pray, they always pray to God and Jesus alone, but frequently through and with Mary.

CONCLUSION

Catholics do *not* venerate Mary as a goddess. Mary is not a female deity in Catholicism. Catholics do not venerate her as a deity "next" to God, but they do honor her as the Mother of God, because she carried the Son of God in her womb and thus her yes helped God's Son to become man, as one of us. That's how she could play the role of the New Eve, who is now the Queen of Heaven.

14

CATHOLICS VENERATE STATUES

THE LIE

Not only do Catholics outfit their churches with an abundance of statues—practically in every corner, on every wall, in every painting or stained-glass window, they also often kneel in front of them and burn candles. They send their prayers up to a statue and expect answers from the statue or from whomever the statue represents, in spite of the fact that the Bible plainly rejects all of this.

Catholics who venerate a statue or kneel before a statue to pray are committing idolatry, for at least two reasons: (1) they are praying to a statue or worshipping a statue; (2) they are praying to a dead person, but you can't pray to dead people. Besides, Catholics make saints the mediators between God and man, in defiance of what St. Paul says in 1 Timothy 2:5, "There is one mediator between God and men, the man Christ Jesus."

The Catholic veneration of saints is a worship of false gods. It's as though the Roman Church has simply replaced the Greek and Roman pantheon with the pantheon of saints, so the old paganism of Rome is still alive and well in Catholicism.

THE TRUTH

The First Commandment seems very clear about this: You shall not bow before idols. How then could Catholics ever defend statues of saints in their churches? We have at least four avenues to approach this issue. To begin with, what does the First Commandment really forbid? Second, what are idols? Third, why are religious statues not idols? Fourth, why is bowing different from venerating?

Let's start with number one: What is at stake in the First Commandment? The First Commandment is not about using images of God. The Bible tells us that God did in fact reveal Himself under visible forms — for instance, in Daniel 7:9: "Thrones were placed and one that was the ancient of days took his seat; his raiment was white as snow, and the hair of his head like pure wool; his throne was fiery flames, its wheels were burning fire." Most of us make depictions of God the Father under forms like this. But, more importantly, in the Incarnation of Christ His Son, God showed mankind an "icon" of Himself. St. Paul said, "He is the image [*ikon* in Greek] of the invisible God, the first-born of all creation" (Col. 1:15). Christ is the tangible, divine "icon" of the unseen, infinite God. Genesis 1:26 tells us that all human beings are made in God's *image*; a coin may hold the emperor's image, but humans carry God's image. Yet, iconoclasts want to do away with any icon.

Apparently, the First Commandment does not say that we cannot use images of God. What the First Commandment does say is very different. This can perhaps be best explained by looking at the Exodus account about Moses and the golden calf. While Moses was in conversation with God at Mount Sinai, the people were wondering among themselves along these lines, "Why don't we make an image? A golden calf — a young bull, a symbol of power and fervid vitality, made of gold and silver, the most beautiful and profound things we have. Let this calf be the focus of our attention." They thought that nothing could represent the divine omnipotence more appropriately than this ancient symbol of power and fertility. Here was a material object worshipped as if it were God. However, all of this comes to an abrupt end when Moses suddenly reappears and takes dramatic action. Why?

What God forbids is not using images, but "worshipping them as gods," replacing the Unseen God with the images we carve, depending on them, and ascribing to them attributes which belong to God alone. However, in the light of God's countenance, every entity that calls itself a god, or deems itself to be a god, fades away and shrivels up. The mysterious power of nature turns out to be a tiny piece of God's creation for the mere use of human beings. The lights of the sun and moon and stars are merely lamps created to give people light and to show the time. Kings and governments are nothing but human institutions endowed with human limitations; their assignment is temporary and their power transitory. If you thought they were gods, the First Commandment clears the sky: God, and God alone! As Deuteronomy 6:4 puts it, "The LORD is our God, the LORD *alone*" (NABRE, emphasis added). This is about other gods, not icons of God.

Let's move on to the second question: What are idols? An idol is anything that replaces God but isn't God. It is something that is not God but that we venerate *instead of* God. The Bible wages a constant battle with "idols"—not to be confused with icons. An idol in itself can do nothing; left alone, it will deteriorate, rust, rot, or chip. Scripture calls idols literally "nothings" when it says, "For all the gods of the peoples are idols" (Ps. 96:5). The *Catechism of the Council of Trent* (in 1566) taught that idolatry is committed "by worshipping idols and images as God, or believing that they possess any divinity or virtue entitling them to our worship, by praying to, or reposing confidence in them." Think of the Rosary; the Rosary does not do anything on its own; it "works" when used in prayer, not when only left in the closet.

According to the *Catholic Bible Dictionary*, "Idols were more to ancient cultures than mere representations of their deities. The idol was the means by which the god could be appeased, worshipped, mollified, and communicated with. Thus the idol was treated with the same reverence and awe as the god itself. It was common for the idol to be given food offerings, to be washed and dressed, to be offered songs and sacrifices — in effect to receive all that might be given to the god." That's icons-turned-idols!

Do not think idols are something from the past, mere remnants of a pagan past. Idols may be nothings, but we still keep idolizing them. We idolize our movie stars, our sports heroes, our deities on TV, even our role models in *American Idol*. But we forget so easily that, in fact, they are idols — that is, nothings. So often, these idols tend to take over God's place in our minds. There is nothing wrong with using religious objects such as icons to enhance our faith, but the danger lies in losing focus — that is, when they pull our attention away from God. When Catholics "pray to statues," they pray actually to God, albeit through the intercession of the saint behind the statue. The only way to keep our faith from sliding into superstition and idolatry is to remember that spiritual blessings come not from created matter, such as statues and icons, but from the Creator of all matter.

The *Catechism* makes it very clear: "Man commits idolatry whenever he honors and reveres a creature in place of God, whether this be gods or demons (for example Satanism), power, pleasure, race, ancestors, the state, money, etc." (2113). The

Catechism (2116) also mentions various forms of divination: the use of horoscopes, astrology, palm reading, clairvoyance, mediums, and so forth. Those who think these are gods are committing idolatry.

Let's move on to the third question: Why are religious statues not idols? Even if we have an image of God—for instance, the image of God the Father, with white hair, sitting on His throne in Heaven—this image does not replace God, but only "pictures" God. Words are similar to pictures. When we speak about God in language, we describe what we imagine He is like; also when we visualize God in art or illustrations, we express how we picture what God is like. In either case, we try to make God more accessible to us. Even when we speak about God, we "imagine" something about God—not in pictures but in words. And the same holds for statues of saints. The Fourth General Council of Constantinople (869–870) makes the same comparison: "What speech conveys in words, pictures announce and bring out in colors." But, as we all know, a picture can be worth more than a thousand words. In this context it is worthwhile quoting St. Germanus (ca. 634–734), the patriarch of Constantinople, who battled the iconoclasts of his time with the words, "Pictures are history in figure.... We do not worship the colors laid on the wood."

Let's finally briefly address the last question: Why is bowing different from venerating? Even when Catholics bow before a picture or statue, they do not venerate that object. Though bowing can be used as a posture in worship, not all bowing is worship. Bowing is actually part of several cultures: Japanese bow to people; the Yoruba in Nigeria even prostrate themselves to the ground to greet an elder. These are acts of respect rather than adoration. Even the Bible acknowledges this. There are plenty of Old Testament references that distinguish veneration from worship—for instance, "Moses went out to meet his father-in-law, and did obeisance and kissed him" (Exod. 18:7, but also 1 Chron. 29:20 and 1 Sam. 24:8). Paying respect and venerating is not worshipping.

Although God forbids the worship of images as gods, He doesn't ban the making or using of images. We could actually say He commanded their use in religious contexts. The prophet Ezekiel (41:17–18) acknowledges this when he writes, "On the walls round about the inner room and [on] the nave were carved likenesses of cherubim." There is an important distinction between thinking a piece of stone or plaster is a god and merely desiring visually to remember God, Christ, angels, and saints by making "icons" in their honor. Icons help us to be Christian through all our senses.

Yet anti-Catholic rhetoric claims that statues are remnants of a pagan history. When in the year 609, Pope Boniface IV consecrated a famous Roman landmark, the Pantheon, as the Church of St. Mary and the Martyrs, the statues of the pagan gods were removed and replaced with the images of the saints. In this manner it became a church dedicated to all the saints instead of all the pagan gods. This is not paganism but a victory over paganism.

But what is the purpose of dedicating a church to dead people, let alone praying to them? The answer is simple. Catholics don't pray to dead people. They don't think Heaven is a "dead" place. Catholics believe people in Heaven are fully alive, even more so than we are. Their bodies may be dead, but their souls are not. Although the saints have physically died, they can still pray for us precisely because they are *not* dead.

Who are these saints? Aren't all Christians supposed to be saints? Indeed, in his Letter to the Colossians, St. Paul addresses them as "the saints and faithful brethren in Christ at Colossae" (1:2). Yes, all Christians are saints, for they have been "baptized into Christ Jesus" (Rom. 6:3), who is the source of all holiness. However, according to St. Paul in Col. 1:12, God "has qualified us to share in the inheritance of the saints in light." In other words, "the saints" on earth partake in part in what "the saints" in Heaven possess in fullness. Thus, it is fitting that the Catholic Church reserves the title of "Saint" for those she has declared to be in Heaven. They alone possess sainthood in its fullness, so to speak.

It is the "saints in Heaven" who are God's "masterpieces," if you will. They are examples for us to imitate. Therefore, St. Paul writes, "Be imitators of me, as I am of Christ" (1 Cor. 11:1). Likewise, chapter 11 of the Letter to the Hebrews lists many examples of faith that we should imitate. This listing could be called the Bible's "hall of fame." It presents numerous examples of the Old Testament saints for us to imitate. The author of the Letter to the Hebrews also stresses the importance of imitating true spiritual leaders: "Remember your leaders, those who spoke to you the word of God; consider the outcome of their life, and imitate their faith" (Heb. 13:7). The third pope, St. Clement I, said it right, "Follow the saints, for those who follow them will become saints."

So it is not detracting from God and Christ to recognize the holiness of the saints. They are saints precisely because they chose to cooperate with God's grace. When these saints died for their Faith, or when they lived a holy life, they were reflecting Christ, and it is this that we honor. It's not idolatry to hold up human examples of what it means to be like Christ. In the saints we see the extent of the transformative power of God's grace.

Can these saints in Heaven still pray for us? Does praying for others make any sense? The idea of praying for one another comes up in Scripture over and over again. Before St. Paul tells us in 1 Timothy 2:5, "There is only one mediator," he says emphatically in verse 1, "First of all, then, I ask that supplications, prayers, petitions, and thanksgivings be offered for everyone." Apparently, praying for others is very biblical. We know now that it is okay to ask others here on earth to pray and intercede for us. But if that is true, why can't saints in Heaven also pray for us and intercede for us with God?

In the Old Testament, we see that Moses, Abraham, and Job interceded on behalf of others — that is, they mediated between God and man. In 1 Timothy 2, Paul doesn't say that God wants us to communicate with Jesus alone. He says there is only one mediator between God and men, which is something else. In praying for one another, we are participating in the mediation, but we are not the mediators. Catholicss believe that saints in Heaven can pray for us just as well as — or even infinitely better than — our friends on earth. Catholics don't think that praying with the saints detracts from the worship of God any more than praying with friends detracts from worship of God. In other words, Catholics don't pray *to* the saints but *through* or *with* the saints. On All Saints' Day, they honor all who had a global impact on us, and, on All Souls' Day, those who had a personal impact.

Perhaps you accept that it's okay to have saints, and even to pray through and with them, but why would we need their statues? Think of this: just as it helps to remember your mother by looking at her photograph, so it helps to recall the example of the saints by looking at "pictures" of them. Statues can also be used for teaching purposes; in the early Church they were especially useful for the instruction of the illiterate. Even Protestants use pictures of Jesus and other Bible pictures in Sunday school for teaching children.

But what about kneeling before a statue? The fact that Catholics also kneel before a statue doesn't mean they are praying to the statue or venerating a statue, just as the fact that someone kneels to pray with a Bible in his hands does not mean this person is worshipping the Bible. Statues, paintings, and other artistic devices are used to call to mind the person or thing depicted.

It is hard to assume that this would amount to idolatry. True, sometimes Catholics use very imprecise terminology. When it comes to saints, they speak interchangeably of worship, adoration, veneration, and reverence — words most Protestants would use only for God. But it must be noted that in Scripture, the term "worship" is similarly broad in meaning. It was only later that theologians began to differentiate between different types of honor in order to make clearer which is due to God and which is not.

To make clear the difference between the honor due to God and that due to humans, we should use the words "adore" and "adoration" to describe the total, consuming reverence due to God, whereas the terms "venerate," "veneration," and "honor" are used to refer to the respect due to humans. Thus, Catholics sometimes say, "We adore God, but we honor His saints." But no matter what, when Catholics pray, they always pray to God alone, but frequently through and with the saints — either with or without a statue.

CONCLUSION

Catholics do *not* venerate statues. They pray not to statues but to the persons whom the statues represent; they pray through them, but ultimately to God. They do not venerate statues and icons. They do not expect answers from statues and icons. They are certainly not idolaters, for icons and statues are very different from idols. These are just "tools" to help their imagination — "salvation history in figure," so to speak. When Catholics pray, they always pray to God alone, but frequently through and with the saints — either with or without a statue. Saints have indeed physically died, but they can still pray for us precisely because they are *not* dead.

15

CATHOLICS LIVE BY RITUALS

THE LIE

Catholics are spellbound by repeating endless rituals and routines such as genuflecting, making the Sign of the Cross, bowing toward the crucifix—or, in a wider context, praying the Rosary, going to Mass every Sunday, going to Confession frequently, saying grace before each meal. They believe rituals or routines are supposed to work on their own and create an effect of their own—almost "auto-magically."

Catholics obscure the pure form of Christian worship with liturgical debris of a pagan past that accumulated over the centuries. They emphasize rituals and symbolism over "the Word of God," instead of a pure religion freed from rituals, ornaments, symbols, and other nonscriptural monstrosities.

THE TRUTH

Mention the word "ritual," and people's reactions are quite diverse. Some conjure up images of evil doings, magic practices, hexes, or spells. Others roll their eyes at religious rites that are performed over and over again, declaring them void of meaning.

But there are also others, Catholics, who honor religious rites and rituals.

It is hard to deny that rituals are marked by repetition. The Rosary is perhaps the most striking example of repetition: five times ten Hail Marys. The Mass is another example of repetition, because it has basically the same series of actions performed in the same order during each Mass. In rituals, each next step is generally predictable—with some, but not much variation. Since rituals seem monotonous, you might think a ritual is just a matter of routine.

Certainly, there is always some kind of *order* behind a ritual or routine. As Scott Hahn remarks, "Order makes life more peaceful, more efficient, and more effective.... Routines free us from the need to ponder small details over and over again; routines let good habits take over, freeing the mind and heart to move onward and upward.... The rites of the Christian liturgy are the set phrases that have proven themselves over time." That's why it makes no sense to complain during Mass that "I've heard most of this before."

Rituals are certainly not a later Catholic invention. The *Didache*—written as early as A.D. 70—contains already a rather fixed liturgical manual. Soon different regions developed their own styles of liturgical practice: Syrian, Coptic, Maronite, Roman, and so on. Yet, they share the same basic elements of the Eucharist in a fixed order: a rite of repentance, Scripture readings, a recitation of psalms, a homily, a Eucharistic Prayer, and Holy Communion. These elements are combined with certain gestures. At certain parts of the Mass, the congregation sits, stands, and kneels: they stand to pray, kneel to worship, sit to listen to teaching, and so forth.

A ritual is an action, or a series of actions, performed in a prescribed order and with partly identical texts. But, of course, not all rituals are created equal. Some simply add to the atmosphere of reverence, while others are a form of worship in and of themselves. Some rituals—kneeling at Communion rails, reverencing a bishop's ring, or wearing mantillas—have generally disappeared in most countries since Vatican II, while others—such as genuflecting, making the Sign of the Cross, and burning candles to remember the dead—have remained strong in today's Catholic culture.

Yet, there is always an immense power in religious rituals and ritual gestures. What all traditional gestures of Catholic ritual have in common is that they are physical actions to express the Catholic Faith. Ritual gestures are part of a wordless liturgical language. There is something inherently unifying in the fact that a Mass said in California is conducted through the same rituals as a Mass said in Italy or China. Similarly, there is something unquestionably comforting in knowing that the Rosary we pray today is practically identical to the Rosary prayed by our ancestors in faith around eight hundred years ago. Rituals form a common culture that connects Catholics from all parts of the world and gives identity to successive generations of Catholics throughout the history of the Church. This enables them to see, in spite of their diversity, that they are all members of the same Body.

It may look like rituals have taken a back seat since Vatican II, but the tide is turning, because Catholics have begun to realize what they had almost lost and forgotten—that rituals are an important part of the Catholic Faith. The Catholic Church is reviving the power of rituals among her faithful. As then-Cardinal Ratzinger said about kneeling, for instance, "Kneeling does not come from any culture—it comes from the Bible and its knowledge of God.... The man who learns to believe learns also to kneel, and a faith or a liturgy no longer familiar with kneeling would be sick at the core." The late French philosopher Jacques Maritain remarked that those who boast of no longer genuflecting before the tabernacle would happily bend their knee to the manifold spirits of this passing world. Kneeling is an expression of human nature.

Kneeling is definitely part of the ritual gestures Catholics make during worship. Gestures such as these are, as Fr. Romano Guardini observed, "a form of speech by which the plain realities of the body say to God what its soul means and intends." By the "body language" of our ritual gestures we unite the physical with the mental and spiritual aspects of our worship of the Lord and express our unity with Him through our entire being.

Undoubtedly, the most important ritual for Catholics is the Sacrifice of the Mass, which could be called the "ultimate ritual" (see chapter 17). So it is not surprising that, in *Sacramentum Caritatis*, Pope Benedict XVI stressed the need for formation and instruction about the Sacred Mysteries of the Eucharist, which he called "mystagogical catechesis." He was very emphatic about this: "A mystagogical catechesis must also be concerned with presenting the meaning of the signs contained in the rites.... More than simply conveying information, a mystagogical catechesis should be capable of making the faithful more sensitive to the language of signs and gestures which, together with the word, make up the rite." Even the power of silence is part of the rite.

Very recently, this issue became even more prevalent when new attention was drawn to the way the Mass used to be celebrated. Since Vatican II — but not because of Vatican II — the priest who celebrates a Mass has often been considered a mere "presider," facing the people through the entire Mass, typically standing behind a four-legged table. This position is called *versus populum*. The celebration of Mass *versus populum* places the priest front and center, with all of his eccentricities on display. We would never ask cardiologists why they don't smile while performing heart surgery, or scientists why they don't crack a joke while taking measurements. This is because the dignity and gravity of their work demands concentration, precision, and reflection. The same demands are made of the priest when he celebrates Mass.

That's why there used to be another way of saying Mass: *ad orientem* — "facing the East." This posture of the priest is still practiced in the Eastern rites but has become exceptional in Roman Catholic churches. It is often misinterpreted as the priest "turning his back" to the people. Not so. Rather, the priest faces east — not always in a literal way, though — to direct the faithful's attention away from himself and toward the horizon symbolizing the Resurrection. As then-Cardinal Ratzinger put it, "Looking at the priest has no importance. What matters is looking together at the Lord." This is surely not just a matter of mere rituals or routines.

Most recently, Cardinal Robert Sarah, prefect of the Congregation for Divine Worship, said during the keynote opening address of the Sacra Liturgia conference that took place in London in 2016, "The liturgy is not about you and me.... The liturgy is first and foremost about God and what he has done for us.... It is very important that we return as soon as possible to a common orientation, of priests and the faithful turned together in the same direction — eastwards or at least towards the apse — to the Lord who comes." It is obvious that this whole discussion is about the role of rituals and gestures in the liturgy. Ritual requires one to prepare and focus on the event or activity and to be fully aware. While ritual is often solemn, sacred, and rhythmic in nature, it is always thought-provoking at the same time.

Unfortunately, however, there is also a darker side to rituals: a ritual can be habit-forming and can easily turn into a mere routine. The congregation often reacts to certain expressions of a priest—such as "The Lord be with you"—with an automatic response, or they routinely respond with "Amen," even when it is not called for. I even know of a woman who had made the ritual of genuflecting before entering the church pew such an automatism that she once did it routinely before entering her row in a movie theater. Rituals are not a goal in themselves but a tool to a much higher goal: divine adoration. When they become a goal of their own, they turn into some kind of superstition—the mistaken belief that rituals can achieve something all by themselves.

God is not against the use of rituals per se; He is only against empty rituals that are performed with no heart behind them. Rituals can be a very meaningful part of adoration, but as Matthew 6:7 says, "In praying, do not babble like the pagans." Yet rituals are universal, even among Evangelicals who lift their hands when they sing praise music, or interject sermons with Hallelujahs.

CONCLUSION

Catholics do *not* live by rituals. Rituals, rites, and routines do not work on their own in the Catholic Church. They are not remnants of a pagan past. They are sets of phrases and actions that have proven themselves over time—over a long time of Christian history from the earliest stages of the Church on. Ritual gestures are part of a wordless liturgical language that unites believers from all over the globe. They also unite body and soul, as long as they don't become mere routines. They are bodily expressions of what the soul intends.

16

CATHOLICS WALLOW IN CHRIST'S PASSION

THE LIE

Catholics have an obsession with Christ's Passion. That's why they crucify Christ over and over again in every Mass. That's why they love crucifixes more than crosses. Instead, they should replace their Catholic crucifix and its naked corpse with the Protestant cross, with its vacant wood, or the Orthodox icon, with its gold, because Christ is no longer on the Cross but has ascended into Heaven. Catholics should focus on the Resurrection, not on the Crucifixion. Besides, the Resurrection shows God's triumph, the Crucifixion His defeat.

THE TRUTH

Indeed, a Catholic crucifix is very different from a Protestant cross, but its use has nothing to do with masochism. The crucifix is a cross with the figure of Christ crucified upon it. The word "crucifix" comes from the Latin words *cruci* and *fixus*, meaning "one fixed to a cross." To show Jesus on the Cross is not incompatible with His Resurrection. Just as Jesus is "still" in the manger, during and after Christmas, so is Jesus "still" on the Cross. Both events are "timeless"; they were, and still are, key events in our salvation history. They had to happen before the Resurrection could occur. Their impact is beyond space and time. An old, sixth-century hymn expresses it well: "O hail the cross, our only hope" (*O Crux ave, spes unica*).

Before the crucifix emerged in Catholic history, the cross was a very common symbol among the first Christians. We find St. Ignatius of Antioch (ca. 35–108) stating at the end of the first century, "My spirit bows in adoration to the cross, which is a stumbling-block to those who do not believe, but is to you for salvation and eternal life." And Tertullian (ca. 150–225) comments in several places that the Christians of the second century routinely and universally "crossed themselves" with the "sign of the cross" on their foreheads.

Roman pagans called the Christians "cross worshippers" and ironically added, "They worship that which they deserve." Perhaps it is this sarcasm of the heathens that prevented Christians from openly displaying this sign of salvation. They were somewhat reluctant to show the means of the Lord's execution since it was a grisly and cruel Roman institution. Had Christ died in our generation, one would not expect Christians to portray the electric chair as a sign of victory shortly after such an execution.

Whereas, in early Christian art, the Crucifixion was represented by the bare Latin cross, by the fifth century the body of Christ was painted on the Cross, and later became sculpture attached by four nails, one in each hand and foot. One of the earliest-known representations of Christ being crucified is a fifth-century panel on the brass door of Santa Sabina in Rome. The Church added the figure of Christ to remind the faithful of the great suffering that had brought about their redemption.

Very soon in the history of the Church crucifixes began to outnumber crosses. But that changed suddenly when the Protestant Reformers entered the scene. Whereas Martin Luther was rather tolerant, John Calvin was very radical in his opposition to what he called the "pagan" images and statues of the Roman Catholic Church. The Calvinist theologian Beza (1519–1605) wrote vehemently against the Lutheran tolerance of images, including crosses and crucifixes, with the words, "Our hope reposes in the true cross of our Lord Jesus Christ, not in that image." Most Protestant churches removed all statues and paintings from their interior—which included also crucifixes and even crosses. Many Reformed churches still have the rooster on their steeples instead of the Cross, although the Cross is coming back in many Protestant churches. The issue of cross versus crucifix now is mostly a matter of distinguishing between Catholic and Protestant.

Why is the crucifix so important to Catholics—and why should it be to all Christians? The main reason is given by St. Paul: "We preach Christ crucified, a stumbling block to Jews and folly to Gentiles, but to those who are called, both Jews and Greeks, Christ the power of God and the wisdom of God" (1 Cor. 1:23–24). So one might even say that some folks did away with the crucifix because it is a stumbling block and foolishness.

Of course, Catholics believe in the Resurrection, but they also know that there is no crown without a Cross. Without the Crucifixion, there would be no Resurrection; without the Crucifixion, there would be no salvation. If the Cross is a hoax, then the whole economy of salvation is up for grabs, for there is no light of Easter morning without the dark of Good Friday afternoon. And this is why Catholics want to keep their crucifixes, because they are wary of Christianity without a Cross. The crucifix tells us at what price our salvation had to be bought: Jesus had to *die* for us. It is precisely the crucifix that shows us the cruel suffering of Jesus' death and the depth of Christ's passion and love. The Passion of Christ—from the Latin word *passio*, which means "suffering"—refers to those sufferings our Lord endured for our redemption, from the agony in the Garden until His death on Calvary. Jesus suffered and died for us: that's what the crucifix reminds us of.

What can express all of this better than the crucifix? A simple cross may be fine, but it hides an important part of the story. St. Cyril of Jerusalem (313–386) could not express this more clearly: "We proclaim the Crucified, and the devils quake. So don't be ashamed of the Cross of Christ."

Another early Church Father, St. Alexander of Alexandria (ca. 250–327) put it this way: "Oh, the new and ineffable mystery! The Judge was judged. He who absolves from sin was bound; He was mocked who once framed the world; He was stretched upon the cross who stretched out the heavens; He was fed with gall who gave the manna to be bread; He died who gives life. He was given up to the tomb who raises the dead."

CONCLUSION

Catholics do *not* wallow in Christ's Passion. They are not masochists when they venerate the Cross with their Savior stretched out upon it. Instead they are very aware of the "scandal of the Cross," which is actually the "mystery of the Cross." They do not deny the Resurrection, but they venerate the crucifix because they realize at what cost the Resurrection and our salvation were bought. They do not crucify Christ over and over again in every Mass. The "sign of the cross" is not a later development in the

Church but runs like a vital thread through Church history. The crucifix did certainly not emerge as a pagan icon but instead was vehemently rejected by pagans as being a symbol of execution, not victory.

17

CATHOLICS CONSUME JESUS' BODY AND BLOOD

THE LIE

Catholics do not merely commemorate Jesus' death during the session of a communion meal, but they actually pretend to consume Jesus' Flesh and Blood. Even the pagan Romans knew that this is a disgusting abomination—they called Christians "cannibals." Catholics base their practice on the outdated belief of transubstantiation—a weird form of metamorphosis once implemented by the Catholic Church.

"Hocus pocus" is a generic term for a magic trick. The term originated from a mockery of the Catholic liturgy of the Eucharist, which contains the phrase *Hoc est enim corpus meum*, meaning "For this is my body." The Anglican prelate John Tillotson was right when he wrote in 1694: "In all probability those common juggling words of hocus pocus are nothing else but a corruption of *hoc est corpus*, by way of ridiculous imitation of the priests of the Church of Rome in their trick of Transubstantiation."

THE TRUTH

What we have here is a myth, and yet it isn't. What the pagan Romans then, and the Protestant Calvinists nowadays, say about Catholics eating Jesus' Flesh and drinking His Blood is the truth. For the early Christians, as well as for modern Catholics, the Eucharist is not just a memorial meal but a sacramental meal, where the ones present literally consume Jesus' Body and Blood, sacrificed for us. John 6:53 could not put it more clearly, "Unless you eat the flesh of the Son of man and drink his blood, you do not have life within you."

It was the distortion of this fact that made pagan Romans accuse Christians of "cannibalism" and "human sacrifice." Although early Christian apologists took this up in order to dismiss it as a myth, we can see through the distorted lens of pagan gossip what the most identifiable element was, and still is, of Christian life and worship: to be a *Christian* is to go to Mass to eat Jesus' Body and drink His Blood.

The last sentence should probably be reworded nowadays: to be a *Catholic* is to go to Mass. Why? Because many Christians, as a consequence of the Protestant Reformation, will no longer identify themselves by going to Mass; they go to a "service" that consists mainly of a long sermon, sometimes combined with a communion service. The late Fr. Benedict Groeschel makes no bones about it: "I've been a priest for forty years, and I never conducted a 'service' called a Mass. I was a 'stand-in' for the High Priest ... functioning *in persona Christi* — in the person of Christ, the High Priest of the Epistle to the Hebrews. People do not come to Mass to receive my body and blood, and I could not have given it to them if they did. They come for communion with Christ."

This is certainly a mystery. Religious faith necessarily deals with mysteries that cannot be understood completely. But although the mysteries of the Catholic Faith may be beyond reason, they are not against reason—they are not even unreasonable. They can be defended, though not proven, by arguments based on reason (see chapter 27). A mystery is not something about which we can't know anything, but something about which we can't know everything. The reason that there are mysteries is that God is infinite but our intellects are finite.

To make this mystery of the Eucharist a bit more accessible and understandable, St. Thomas Aquinas used the concept of *transubstantiation* centuries ago. It was a sophisticated effort to explain philosophically how elements used in the Eucharist, bread and wine, can change into the Body and Blood of Jesus Christ without changing their appearances.

The concept of transubstantiation hinges on the distinction between two sorts of change: accidental and substantial. Accidental change occurs when nonessential appearances change without a change in substance. Water, for instance, can take on the appearance of ice, while remaining the same substance (H_2O) all the way through. Substantial change, on the other hand, occurs when the substance changes, but the appearances may or may not change. In most cases, both substance and appearance change—the food we're eating, for instance, changes in both substance and appearance when it is digested; the change from sodium and chlorine to salt is another example of a substantial change.

But it is hard to find cases in which the substance changes while the appearances remain the same, for in our everyday experience, a change of substance is always accompanied by a corresponding transition of accidents, appearances, or properties. Yet that is exactly what happens in the Eucharist: the substance changes from bread and wine into the substance of body and blood, without any change in appearance. This is what is called *transubstantiation*. Thus, the substance, wine, can change into the Blood of Christ even though the smell and taste of wine do not change — what you see is not what you get.

Is this hard to believe?

As Cardinal John Henry Newman put it, "What do I know of substance or matter? Just as much as the greatest philosophers, and that is nothing at all." As the late physicist Sir James Jeans said, "There is in principle no permanence in substance; it is mere bottled energy." Besides, we could point out that if a cow can change grass into milk, then God can certainly change wine into Jesus' Blood. St. Ambrose used a simple comparison: "If the word of the Lord Jesus is so powerful as to bring into existence things which were not, then *a fortiori* those things which already exist can be changed into something else."

The Catholic Church at the Council of Trent (1545–1563) accepted Aquinas's concept of transubstantiation as the best explanation of the changing of the bread and wine into the Body and Blood of Jesus Christ. When at His Last Supper, Jesus said: "This is my body," what He held in His hands still had all the appearances of bread. But it all depends on what "is" is, to use a popular phrase. When Jesus made that declaration, the underlying reality (the "substance") of the bread was converted to that of His Body. Hence, the essential reason Catholics are not guilty of cannibalism is the fact that they do not receive the Lord Jesus Christ in a cannibalistic form. They receive Him, His Body and Blood, in the form of bread and wine, yet qualitatively the bread and the wine are entirely different. In the words of the hymn "Tantum Ergo," "Faith will tell us Christ is present, when our human senses fail."

The Catholic Church considers the doctrine of transubstantiation — which is about *what* is changed, not about *how* the change occurs—the best defense against what it sees as two mutually opposed interpretations: on the one hand, a merely figurative understanding of Christ in the Eucharist—teaching that the substance remains the same—and on the other hand, an interpretation that would amount to cannibalistic eating of the Flesh and corporal drinking of the Blood of Christ. This way the Catholic Church teaches that the accidents that remain are real, not an illusion, and that Christ is "really, truly, and substantially present" in the Eucharist. Thus, in the Eucharist, the bread ceases to be bread in substance, and becomes the Body of Christ. As St. Thomas Aquinas observed, Christ is not quoted as saying, "*This bread* is my body," but "*This* is my body." When Tertullian (ca. 150–225) says that the bread "represents" the Lord's Body, he means "re-presents," that is, makes it present again.

In his book *The Lamb's Supper*, Scott Hahn, a former Presbyterian minister and now a Catholic theologian, tells us how he learned to understand the mysterious book of Revelation by attending a Catholic Mass for the first time. He quotes Revelation 4:1, "After this I looked, and lo, in heaven an open door" and then he says, "And the door opened onto ... Sunday Mass in your parish church." He realizes, though, that our weekly experience of Mass is anything but heavenly. In his own words:

> In fact, it's an uncomfortable hour, punctuated by babies screaming, bland hymns sung off-key, meandering, pointless homilies, and neighbors dressed as if they were going to a ball game, the beach, or a picnic. Yet, I insist that we do go to heaven when we go to Mass, and this is true of every Mass we attend, regardless of the quality of the music or the fervor of the preaching.

Discussions about the Real Presence of Christ in the Eucharist tend to hinge, often fruitlessly, on the word "is" in "This is my body." But instead we should draw attention to the tense of this verb, and to the tenses of the surrounding statements: Jesus declares that the bread which He presents *is* His Body (present tense), which *is* given for us (present tense). His words indicate that what He was giving was being given in that very instant—so surely He did not mean, "My Body, which I will give for you when I suffer." For Jesus, speaking at the Last Supper, the moment of His suffering had already come and will always remain present when we celebrate the Eucharist: Jesus is literally and wholly present—Body and Blood, Soul and Divinity—under the appearances of bread and wine.

CONCLUSION

Catholics do *not* consume Jesus' body and blood as cannibals do. Yet, their Catholic understanding of the Eucharist goes back to the way the first Christians understood what they were celebrating every Sunday, on the Lord's Day. The doctrine of transubstantiation is the best defense of what is actually taking place during the Eucharist. It also explains why Catholics are not cannibals, because they do not receive the Lord Jesus Christ in a cannibalistic form.

18

CATHOLICS ARE REQUIRED TO
BELIEVE IN APPARITIONS

THE LIE

What God has revealed to us through the Bible and through Jesus Christ is apparently not enough for Catholics. They want more, they need more, and thus they create more. They find their "spiritual needs" fulfilled in what they call "apparitions" — especially Marian apparitions.

Catholics deny that God's revelation has found its final fulfilment in Jesus Christ, so they are required to believe in new revelations, especially apparitions. They don't realize apparitions may be the devil posing as an angel of light. Since the devil's purpose is to deceive us, he would cleverly word his message in such a way that it would appear to be from Heaven.

THE TRUTH

Catholic apparitions of Mary as well as belief in miracles have always been part of the rich tapestry of Catholic history. While skeptics are quick to dismiss miracles and visions as either madness or coincidence, there is a long record of documentation proving the authenticity of such events. Apparitions such as Our Lady of Guadalupe and Our Lady of Fatima are well documented, where there is either physical evidence, as in the case of Our Lady of Guadalupe, or thousands of witnesses, as in the case of Our Lady of Fatima. Even antireligious newspapers reported the event.

Apparitions are often called "private revelations." But it must be stated first that apparitions are not *new* revelations. They are about what has already been revealed to us in the Bible and in Jesus Christ. Apparitions do not reveal anything new, let alone anything that is contrary to God's revelation in the Old Testament and in Jesus Christ. The *Catechism* says, "No new public revelation is to be expected before the glorious manifestation of our Lord Jesus Christ. Yet even if Revelation is already complete, it has not been made completely explicit; it remains for the Christian faithful gradually to grasp its full significance over the course of the centuries" (66). This leaves some room for apparitions. Nevertheless, it must also be stated that while the Catholic Church may declare particular visions to be truly "Heaven sent," she doesn't oblige Catholics to believe that whatever is contained in these visions is required as a matter of faith to get into Heaven.

In "private revelations," according to St. Thomas Aquinas, God continues to reveal Himself to individuals, "not indeed for the declaration of any new doctrine of faith, but for the direction of human acts." Since they occur after the close of public revelation, the Church separates the content of such revelations to individuals from the public deposit of the Faith by calling them "private revelations." The *Catechism* adds, "Christian faith cannot accept 'revelations' that claim to surpass or correct the Revelation of which Christ is the fulfilment, as is the case in certain non-Christian religions and also in certain recent sects which base themselves on such 'revelations'" (67).

So the test of the authenticity of *private* revelations is always its consistency with *public* revelation as guarded faithfully by the Catholic Church. For example, alleged revelations that propose to improve upon, correct, or entirely replace public revelation are rejected by the Church as inauthentic, regardless of the claims made for them. Just as some Scripture books claimed to be apostolic but were not, so did some private revelations claim to be authentic but were not. Such revelations include those of Muhammad in the Qur'an, Joseph Smith in the Book of Mormon, the writings of new-age mystics, psychics, and the like. Religious beliefs cannot authenticate themselves: claiming, for instance, that the Qur'an must be true because the Qur'an says so does not automatically make it true (see chapter 20). More is needed.

Again, private revelations cannot correct or add anything essentially new to public revelation. However, private revelations may contribute to a deeper understanding of the Faith, or provide new lines of theological investigation (such as was suggested by the revelations to St. Margaret Mary about the Sacred Heart), or make a prophetical call to mankind as to how to live the Gospel (as at Fatima). In so doing, a private revelation may recall defiant individuals to the Faith, stir the devotion of those who are already faithful, or encourage prayer and penance on behalf of others, but it cannot substitute for the Catholic Faith, the sacraments, and hierarchical communion with the pope and bishops.

Therefore, apparitions are private revelations that do not require acceptance by Catholics. As Pope Benedict XIV stated, "It is possible to refuse to accept such revelations and to turn from them, as long as one does so with proper modesty, for good reasons, and without the intention of setting himself up as a superior."

Although belief in private revelations is never required by the Church, some of them are approved by the Church, whereas some are not. What about private revelations *without* Roman approval? Catholics must often judge for themselves whether they are credible. If the person (whether living or dead) has a reputation for sanctity (for instance, Padre Pio at one point), then clearly any mystical revelations have considerable credibility prior to any formal evaluation by the Church. The witness of prudent priests, especially the person's spiritual director, is a key element in determining credibility. However, even then care must be taken, for false mystics have been known to "shop" for gullible, extremely aged, or incompetent spiritual directors—and then the devil may indeed be posing as an angel of light.

Today there are a myriad of alleged private revelations and apparitions vying for the attention of the faithful and the approval of the Church. None have been definitively judged by the Holy See, some have been approved by local authority (e.g., Akita, Cuapa, Betania), others have been found lacking in authenticity (e.g., Medjugorje, Garabandal), a few have been condemned (e.g., Necedah, Bayside) and finally, the vast majority have received no attention from Church authorities whatsoever.

Currently, there are at least nine major officially approved Marian apparitions: Our Lady of Guadalupe, Mexico; Rue du Bac, Paris, France; La Salette, France; Lourdes, France; Pontmain, France; Knock, Ireland; Fatima, Portugal; Beauraing, Belgium; Banneux, Belgium; and recently, Champion, Wisconsin.

Apparently, the Church must walk a fine line here between belief in the supernatural and an errant belief in the occult. Therefore, apparitions in particular must be subjected to all relevant theological and human tests of credibility. Bishops evaluate evidence of an apparition according to the following guidelines: (1) the facts in the case are free of error; (2) the persons receiving the messages are psychologically balanced, honest, moral, sincere, and respectful of Church authority; (3) no doctrinal errors are attributed to God, our Lady, or to a saint; (4) theological and spiritual doctrines presented are free of error; (5) moneymaking is not a motive involved in the events; (6) healthy religious devotion and spiritual fruits result, with no evidence of collective hysteria.

All of this testifies that the Catholic Church does not easily give in to what some consider a spiritual need of Catholics for "special" visions, revelations, and apparitions. She puts everything carefully to the test, following St. Paul's advice in 1 Thessalonians 5:21, "Test everything; retain what is good." The most positive verdict the Church gives to an apparition is: "worthy of belief." The *Catechism* gives this verdict: "Throughout the ages, there have been so-called 'private' revelations, some of which have been recognized by the authority of the Church. They do not belong, however, to the deposit of faith. It is not their role to improve or complete Christ's definitive Revelation, but to help live more fully by it in a certain period of history" (67).

CONCLUSION

Catholics are *not* required to believe in apparitions. Although not required, belief in approved apparitions is recommended to Catholics to enrich, deepen, or strengthen their faith. Apparitions that are approved by the Church have a long record of documentation proving the authenticity of such events. They do not create new revelations or new doctrines, but they help direct the way Catholics live their religious lives.

PART 4

CATHOLICISM AND OTHER RELIGIONS

19

CATHOLICS THINK HEAVEN IS ONLY FOR THEM

THE LIE

The centuries-old claim of the Catholic Church is that outside the Church there is no salvation. Thus, Catholics reserve Heaven for themselves and send non-Catholics directly to Hell, thinking that what a person believes in terms of religion determines whether God sends him to Heaven or Hell.

Catholics ignore what Jesus said: "There are many mansions in heaven" (see John 14:2). They deny that there must be many roads leading to Heaven—for everyone, even non-Catholics, perhaps even the road atheists follow.

THE TRUTH

"Outside the Church there is no salvation" (*extra ecclesiam nulla salus*) is one of the most misunderstood teachings of the Catholic Church. We need to find out first how the teaching office of the Church, the Magisterium, understands its own teaching.

First of all, we need to acknowledge that St. Cyprian was the first to coin this expression, but in a very different context. It was his opinion that baptism performed by heretics, enemies of the Church, could not be valid. In his own words, "If they are not in the Church … how can they baptize with the Church's baptism?" Cyprian was later condemned for this error. However, his statement remained popular and soon acquired an entirely different meaning.

Catholic apologist Jim Blackburn points out that in recent times, the Church did realize that her teaching about the necessity of the Catholic Church for salvation has been widely misunderstood, so she has "reformulated" this teaching in a more positive way. Here is how the *Catechism* begins to address this topic: "How are we to understand this affirmation, often repeated by the Church Fathers? Reformulated positively, it means that all salvation comes from Christ the Head through the Church which is his Body" (846). In other words, there is no salvation *without* Christ, but because this salvation has come to us through the Church, salvation cannot be found anywhere else—only *inside* the Church.

Even before it was fully revealed that He was the Messiah, Jesus Himself taught that "salvation is from the Jews" (John 4:22). In a similar fashion, now that the Messiah has established His Church, Jesus might say, "Salvation is from the Catholics"! Without the Jews, we would have had no Savior, and without the Church, we would not know about His salvation. This teaching is consistent with Jesus' teaching about those who reject Him: "If I had not come and spoken to them, they would not have sin" (John 15:22). But once people come to know the truth, they must embrace it, or they will be culpable of rejecting the truth. We hear this in Jesus' words to the Pharisees: "If you were blind, you would have no guilt; but now that you say, 'We see,' your guilt remains" (John 9:41). They rejected the truth they could have known!

Does salvation really have anything to do with us? It is God who decides ultimately who goes to Heaven and who does not. But He does not make His decisions randomly or arbitrarily. What we do and what we believe is also taken into account. Because we are free human beings, we will be held accountable for our choices in life. Depending on *our* choices, God makes *His* choices (see chapter 8).

Does this mean that Hell is as real as Heaven? God's love calls us to Heaven, but God's justice may also have to send some into Hell. However, God does not cast persons into Hell against their will. As said earlier, if there is evil and if there is eternity, then there can be Hell — it is a consequence of our own free choice. C. S. Lewis says, "There are only two kinds of people — those who say to God, 'Thy will be done' and those to whom God says in the end, 'Thy will be done.'" Although redemption is for everyone, salvation is not. For some there is salvation, for some damnation.

So when we say there is no salvation outside the Catholic Church, does this mean non-Catholics are bound for Hell? Not necessarily so. Let's face it: some (or perhaps many) *non-*Catholics may make it to Heaven, whereas some (or perhaps many) Catholics may *not* make it to Heaven. Only God knows why some people do not believe in Him, in Jesus, or His Church. Perhaps other Catholics did not teach them properly, or did not give them proper examples of living a Catholic life, or exposed them to anti-Catholic experiences. Only God knows what is in our hearts, which is often not visible or accessible from the outside. So we do not really know who have intentionally and consciously positioned themselves "outside the Church." Some have rejected the Catholic Church because they have been bombarded with the anti-Catholic myths that are the very targets of this book.

So we need to acknowledge that not everyone may have had a "fair" chance to become acquainted with the Gospel, the Church, and her teachings. Although the document *Lumen Gentium* (*LG*) from Vatican II still confirms that those who have been given knowledge of Christ, but fail to act, "could not be saved," the Council also added a caveat:

> Those who, through no fault of their own, do not know the Gospel of Christ or his Church, but who nevertheless seek God with a sincere heart, and, moved by grace, try in their actions to do his will as they know it through the dictates of their conscience — those too may achieve eternal salvation. (16)

The late theologian Karl Rahner introduced the term "anonymous Christian" — similar to the much older notion of a "virtuous pagan" or a "righteous Gentile." Although some took the phrase "anonymous Christian" as derogatory for non-Christians and even paternalistic toward those who have not expressed any desire for it, it does convey an important message by declaring that people who have never heard the Christian Gospel, including the ones who lived before Jesus was born, might still be saved through Christ. It accepts that, without Christ, it is impossible to achieve salvation, but it does not accept that people who have never heard of Jesus Christ would *not* be saved. This is like repeating Jesus' words, "Forgive them, for they do not know what they are doing" (see Luke 23:34).

This view seems to give us the impression that salvation is for everyone — whether inside or outside the Catholic Church — regardless of their religion. Not too long ago, Pope Francis may have enforced that same impression when he said, "The Lord has redeemed all of us … not just Catholics … even the atheists."

Was that the end of "Outside the Church there is no salvation"? Not so, if one reads these statements carefully and focuses on their exact wording. Vatican II and all the popes since (and before) speak of "*redemption* for all," not of "*salvation* for all." Let us not confuse these two notions: Redemption is universal, but salvation is not. Redemption is indeed for all, because Christ "died for all," in the words of St. Paul (2 Cor. 5:15). The *Catechism* puts it very emphatically, "There is not, never has been, and never will be a single human being for whom Christ did not suffer" (605).

But again, redemption is not the same as salvation. Salvation results from accepting Jesus' redemption and living one's life accordingly. But those who do not accept this gift of universal redemption — unless it is "through no fault of their own" — may still miss out on salvation. The *Catechism* makes it very clear that God gave us "the hope of salvation, by promising redemption" (55). Redemption has opened Heaven for all, but that does not mean that everyone will be led to Heaven and to salvation. Although redemption is for everyone, salvation is not; for some there is salvation, for some there is damnation. Heaven is for those "on his right," while Hell is for those "on his left" (see Matt. 25:34, 41). Catholics may end up on either side — and so may non-Catholics.

In light of the above, we can now say that Pope Francis only confirmed that redemption in Christ is for all, not just Catholics — even for atheists. However, it does not follow from this that people from other religions, not to mention those without a religion, have accepted this gift of redemption and therefore will "automatically" receive salvation. Again, redemption is universal, but salvation is not. Redemption has opened Heaven for all, but that does not mean that all will end up in Heaven.

Forty Anti-Catholic Lies

So it could be said that Pope Francis used St. Peter's Square as a present-day Areopagus: he was evangelizing—trying to bring salvation within the reach of as many people as possible, for there are many roads leading to Rome. His message was not a declaration of universal salvation but a universal invitation to salvation—in an effort to make salvation as universal as possible.

It is only thanks to the Church that we know about salvation and realize that salvation is possible for each one of us. In other words, salvation cannot be found anywhere else—not in any other religion, not in communism, not in any other kind of ideology, not in any other religion. That's why the Catholic Church can say that salvation cannot be found "outside" or "without" the Church.

CONCLUSION

Catholics do *not* think Heaven is only for them. The famous, or infamous, quote "Outside the Church there is no salvation" can easily be misunderstood. Because salvation has come to us through the Church, salvation cannot be found anywhere else—only *inside* the Church. Without the Church there would be no salvation—or at least we would not know about it. But Catholics also realize that we do not know why some people are *outside* the Church. There can be many reasons for this, very often beyond their own faults. Only God decides.

20

CATHOLICS CLAIM TO OWN THE TRUTH

THE LIE

Catholics ignore the fact that all religions claim they own the truth. So this claim by itself cannot authenticate their claim as true, not even for Catholics.

Catholics also forget that all monotheistic religions worship the same God—no matter whether they call God by the name of Lord, Yahweh, Allah, or Krishna. So it must be that each religion captures part of the truth—and together perhaps the whole truth. We are presumably all united in "faith," although our beliefs may differ.

The Catholic Church claims a monopoly position in defiance of the fact that the commonalities between religions trump their differences by a wide margin. Religions have so much "common ground" that there is no longer reason for a Catholic monopoly.

THE TRUTH

The fact that there are so many religions and that most of them claim to own the truth has led to various positions.

Position 1: Since there are so many religions with different truth claims, *none* of them can be true. This position is hard to defend, though. It is like saying that if many people have a different answer to a specific complex mathematical calculation, there must be no correct answer at all.

You cannot consistently claim that there is no truth. If there is no truth beyond your belief that something is true or false, then you cannot hold your own beliefs to be true. Or if you believe that all truth is relative to one's frame of reference, you cannot at the same time claim that this belief itself is absolutely true, an exception to its own rule.

Instead, the truth is that truth is truth, even if you do not accept it; and untruth is untruth, even if you claim it. Truth is truth for everyone, anywhere, at any time. The existence of God, for instance, is a factual issue of yes or no: God either exists or He doesn't — that's not a matter of opinion, but of truth or untruth. You can have your own opinions, but you can't have your own facts.

This means that the idea of truth is essential, even in religion. The late British philosopher Gilbert Ryle used to say that there can be no counterfeit coins without genuine currency — in translation, if there were no truth, there could not be any untruths. Even those who swear by "trial and error" must admit that errors exist only by the grace of truth. That's why Karl Popper, the champion of falsification and falsifiability, had to admit that the very idea of error is inconceivable without the idea of truth.

Not surprisingly, G. K. Chesterton was eager to debunk the argument that the diversity of religions hampers any truth claims:

> It is perpetually said that because there are a hundred religions claiming to be true, it is therefore impossible

that one of them should really be true.... It would be as
reasonable to say that because some people thought the
earth was flat, and others (rather less incorrectly) imag-
ined it was round, and because anybody is free to say that
it is triangular or hexagonal, or a rhomboid, therefore it
has no shape at all; or its shape can never be discovered.

Position 2: All religions have only *part* of the truth, but together they may have the whole truth. To illustrate this position,
some use the ancient fable of six blind men who visit the palace
of a king and encounter an elephant for the first time. As each
one touches the animal with his hands, he feels a different part
of the elephant, announcing an elephant to be all trunk, all tail,
and so forth. An argument ensues, each blind man thinking his
own perception of the elephant is the correct one. Awakened
by the commotion, the king calls out from the balcony, "The
elephant is a big animal. Each man touched only one part. You
must put all the parts together to find out what an elephant is
like."

The message is clear: each one had found only part of the
truth. In an analogous way, the different truth claims of all religions must be equivalent to each other, for no one has the
entire picture, just pieces of it. Ultimately, all religions are supposedly equal in being inadequate. Had these people searched
more completely, they would have discovered their half-truths.
In this view, Catholics must be misinformed too, or at least only
partially informed.

However, there is a real problem with the assumptions behind
this position. To come to a conclusion like this, we must have
a full and accurate view of the entire picture — just as the king
had of the blind men and the elephant from his balcony. The

king was in a position of privileged acccss to the truth. Because he could see clearly, he was able to correct those who were blind. If everyone truly is blind, then no one can know if he or anyone else is mistaken. Only someone who knows the whole truth can. In this story, only the king can know the truth—no one else.

The Christian apologist Greg Koukl words the issue correctly: "If the story-teller is like one of the six who can't see … how does he know everyone else is blind and has only a portion of the truth? On the other hand, if he fancies himself in the position of the king, how is it that he alone escapes the illusion that blinds the rest of us?" So we must come to the conclusion that position 2 is indefensible. It's like saying, "Each of us is blind," and then adding, "but I'll tell you what the world really looks like." That's a clear contradiction.

Position 3: All religions are based on a set of *beliefs*—that's why we call them "faiths." Seen this way, an interfaith dialogue is merely an exchange of different beliefs. Just as we invented different languages, so we invented different religions.

Each one of them claims to be true. Does that make them true? When defendants in court plead innocent, does that mean they *are* innocent? Similarly, when religions claim to be true, does that *make* them true? Not so!

Therefore, we need at least another important deciding factor to determine which beliefs are true and which are not. Well, this deciding factor is *reason* (see chapter 27). Religious beliefs that are against reason cannot be true; religious faith that is not open to reason cannot be true; religions that are irrational and incoherent cannot be true. In fact, reason is the interreligious criterion to judge a religion's truth. Not all religions are created equal. Pope Benedict XVI even spoke of "sick and distorted forms of religion." Religions based on extraterrestrial sources or

on books that only some people are supposed to have access to
or on books that no longer exist have a hard time passing the
test of reason.

In other words, not everything that calls itself religion may be
regarded as a legitimate religion. The canons of reason are needed
to weed out what is plausible or implausible in what a certain
religion tells us about God. Not all religious beliefs are of the
same quality—some can be very weird. What about the Church
of the Flying Spaghetti Monster, to name just one extreme case?
In 2016, even a federal judge in the USA ruled that this church
is not a real religion—let alone a *true* religion. Not all "religious
beliefs" have a claim to our respect—we must respect their members, and perhaps even their beliefs, but not necessarily their truth
claims. This might eliminate quite a few of them. Questionable
candidates would be, for instance, the Branch Davidians, Nu-
waubianism, the Scientology Church, the Nation of Yahweh, the
Unification Church, and the list is growing. Recently "freedom of
religion" has been used to allow afterschool programs for Satanism, which is not even a religion but an antireligion.

So we must conclude that position 3 is indefensible too. Not
all "religious beliefs" qualify as a legitimate form of religion, unless they pass at least the test of reason. The fact that someone
believes in UFO religions, also referred to as "UFO cults" or
"flying saucer cults," does not authenticate them as true.

Position 4: All religions share the *same* truth: God. If so,
then there is more that unites them than what separates them.
This is often called the idea of "common ground." It is indeed
a frequently heard argument that all religions worship the same
God—no matter whether they call God by the name of Yahweh, Allah, Brahman, Krishna, or you name it. It is based on
the notion that if we abstract enough from particular beliefs

about God, we will eventually arrive at some "god" on whom we can all agree.

This seems to be especially true of the so-called monotheistic religions, such as Judaism, Christianity, and Islam. The argument used here is based on the distinction between *reference* and *description*. Yahweh and Allah, for instance, have the same reference — referring to the same God in Heaven — although their descriptions are rather different. There are similar cases. Aristotle's "sun" refers to the same sun as Galileo's "sun," but their descriptions are very different. The same can be said about the Morning Star, the Evening Star, and Venus: they come with different descriptions but refer to the same thing in the sky. Based on this distinction, the argument goes as follows: if, according to monotheism, there can in principle be only one God, then Christians, Jews, and Muslims must be worshipping the same God.

The "common ground" approach has been very popular and has been used to promote "ecumenism" between Christian denominations, or even "interfaith dialogue" across an increasingly wide board, from Catholics to Protestants, from Christians to Jews and Muslims, from revealed religions to Buddhism and Hinduism, from monotheism to polytheism.

Is the "common ground" approach a viable option? It is hard to see how it could be. Declaring all religions equal is as dubious as the statement that all dogs are equal. Equal in what sense? It is very obvious that there are many differences between dogs, although they all eat dog food. Religions are definitely not equal in the sense of all being true, as there are obvious contradictions between them. If the descriptions of God in different religions are in contradiction with each other, then they cannot all be true at the same time. So we have to decide which description is true. There must be more to it than having the same reference.

This does not mean "interfaith" dialogue is out of the question, but we have to put it in the right perspective. Any kind of dialogue between religions must be honest about the differences that separate them — sparing us a false impression of common ground, for God is also "in the details." Pope Benedict's encyclical *Charity in Truth* articulates very well that the aim of any religious dialogue is ultimately truth. All dialogue should come to the truth, but with respect and love. Respect for other religions does not mean we have to let go of any truth claims — we don't have to go along to get along. Those who think differently confuse respect for people with respect for beliefs. Pope Benedict XVI was right when he expressed a deep respect for Muslims, but that is not the same as having respect for Islam as true. We can and should agree respectfully to disagree.

So we need to keep in mind that these different religions entertain very different descriptions of God. Judaism, for instance, teaches that Jesus is not the Son of God, whereas Christianity teaches that He is. Well, Jesus either is the Son of God or He's not. These two claims can't both be right. The notion that Christianity and Judaism are equally true is contradictory, just as a "square circle" is. Contradictory claims can't be simultaneously true.

Something similar can also be said about the differences between Christianity and Islam. They may both refer to the same God in Heaven, but the way they talk about this common reference is very different. Yes, they both talk about "love of God and neighbor," but for Muslims this extends only to other Muslims. The Muslim God commands Muslims to kill or subjugate Jews and Christians, unless they accept the God of Islam. But most of all, the Christian God is a "triune" God — not three Gods, but one God in three persons: Father, Son, and Holy Spirit. That's certainly not so in Islam. So we should ask the question, as is done in the title of a recent book: Is the Father of Jesus the God of Muhammad? Or are they essentially different instead? Even the Qur'an itself suggests that the God of the Qur'an is radically different from the God Christians worship. The Qur'an specifically tells us that Christ was not divine, was not crucified, and that believing in the Trinity is polytheism. To affirm these teachings constitutes blasphemy for Muslims. Their religion, in short, cannot be "just like ours."

If indeed monotheism maintains that there is only one God, this can mean at least two very different things—either all religions venerate the same God, or all religions have their own gods, but only one of them is the real God. The latter view can be found all over the Bible, especially in the Old Testament. This has made some believe that Yahweh and Allah not only carry different descriptions but also different references.

To use our example of Venus again: talking about "Venus" may refer for some to a planet, for some to a goddess, for others to a horoscope—which are not only different descriptions but also very different references. In this view, the difference between Yahweh and Allah is more like the difference between Yahweh and Baal. Baal is *a* god, but not *the* God. The Old Testament very often makes a distinction between God, on the one hand, and gods, idols, or demons, on the other hand. Only Yahweh is God, but all the other gods are not God but God's creations which rebelled against Him and became fallen spirits.

In this context, Roy Schoeman, who converted from Judaism to Catholicism, makes an interesting observation in his book *Salvation Is from the Jews*:

> Of all the major religions of the world, only Islam arose after God's full revelation of Himself to man in His

incarnation in the person of Jesus Christ. Thus all of the other major religions are either fully true (Christianity); fully true up to the time of their origin, but lacking the later revelation (Judaism); or based on the incomplete revelations available to mankind before God chose to make Himself truly known. Only Islam's revelation came after Christ, aware of Christianity yet contradicting it.... If of supernatural origin, did it come from God or from fallen spirits? It is difficult for a Christian to consider the source of the revelation to be of God, given its contradictions with Christian revelation.

No matter how far we want to go in this discussion, the idea of "common ground" is very questionable, or there is so little in common between religions that the idea is not very useful. The only "common ground" we have is the world we live in. So we may conclude for now that the positions 1, 2, 3, and 4 do not prevent us from taking on a fifth position.

Position 5: Only *one* religion has the truth: Catholicism. How do we know this? The briefest answer is: because the King has spoken—not the king of the elephant fable, but the King of Heaven. God has revealed Himself in the history of Judaism and in the life of Jesus Christ. Because of this, one religion may have the whole truth—the "elephant," so to speak. That's what the Catholic Church claims. But she adds to this that other religions "often reflect a ray of that truth which enlightens all men" (Vatican II, *Nostra aetate*, no. 2). They possess some aspect of the truth, with varying degrees of clarity. But only the Church possesses the fullness of the truth, of God's revelation. That's why many people have converted to Catholicism, for there they found the full truth.

Truth is the keyword here, together with another related keyword, *reason*. Truth can't be against reason. If a certain belief is irrational or unreasonable, then it can't be true, for truth is more than what we believe to be true. A belief in square circles can't be true. A counterfactual belief can't be true: if the earth is round, my belief cannot make it flat. You can't have your own facts.

But how can Catholics know their religion is true? If it is hard to claim that the Bible is true because the Bible says so, then it is equally hard to claim that a certain religion is true because that religion says so, which is something almost all religions do. So there must be external reasons or arguments or evidence for making such a claim.

We could go into a long list of reasons here, but let's narrow them down to the following basic facts. If Jesus never existed, the Word did not become flesh. If Jesus did exist but was never crucified, we were not redeemed. And as the apostle Paul wrote, "If there is no resurrection of the dead, then Christ has not been raised; if Christ has not been raised, then our preaching is in vain and your faith is in vain" (1 Cor. 15:13–14).

Rabbi Israel Zolli, the chief rabbi of Rome during the Nazi occupation, who converted to Catholicism after World War II, gave another reason when he explained why he chose the Catholic, rather than the Protestant, Church: "The Catholic Church was recognized by the whole Christian world as the true Church of God for fifteen consecutive centuries. No one can halt at the end of those 1,500 years and say that the Catholic Church is not the Church of Christ without embarrassing himself seriously."

The fact remains that the Catholic Church is the world's largest, and Christianity's oldest, religious body. Her one billion members inhabit the width and breadth of the earth, comprising almost one-fifth of the total human population. How could she remain such a large body? One of the prime reasons is her central authority rooted in Jesus Christ, St. Peter, and his uninterrupted line of successors. Joel Peters asks the right questions: "Who says which verses in the Bible you take literally and which ones you don't? For that matter, who says which beliefs in the Bible you need to follow and which you can explain away? Who says which moral teachings are in the Bible and which are not? How do they decide? Are they following a particular religious teacher? Isn't that what Jesus warned against?"

Catholics do have the answer to such questions because the Church—not one individual—is the right and proper interpreter of Sacred Scripture. The whole Church alive in the world today and down through the ages offers the interpretative authority by which we decide which parts of the Bible we take literally and which we do not. That's how Catholics can claim to own the truth, for the truth is something beyond the reach of individual interpretations and opinions. Jesus Christ, and the long line of apostolic succession, is the foundation of Catholicism. Without these historical facts, the Catholic Faith would be "built on sand" (see Matt. 7:26). Our Faith is not based on fairy tales, but on very specific events and names: Isaiah and Moses, Peter and Paul, Mary and Joseph, Pontius Pilate, and countless others. The culmination of all of this is the Incarnation around the year 4 B.C. Chesterton speaks of "ten thousand reasons all amounting to one reason: that Catholicism is true."

CONCLUSION

The fact that all religions claim their own truth does not mean that all these truth claims are worth the same. We need some "external" standard to judge their claims, which is *reason*. This explains why not everything that calls itself religion may be regarded as a legitimate religion. The idea that all religions share a "common ground" obliterates the fact that there are essential, often contradictory, differences between them. This leads to at least three positions: they are all false, they are all partially true, or only one of them is fully true. The Catholic Church has many reasons to claim she has the full truth, but other religions may have "rays" of this full truth.

21

CATHOLICS TAKE ORDERS FROM THE POPE

THE LIE

The Catholic Church appears to be one big monolithic, well-oiled organization of believers, headquartered in Rome, from which all orders come and flow downward. But where does her authority come from? If Scripture alone determines what is true in Christianity, then no authority from outside Scripture can decide what is true or false in Christianity—certainly not a pope.

The Catholic doctrine of "infallibility" for popes is a monstrous idea. The Catholic Church does not have the authority to tell Christians what to believe, nor does her leader, because "the church" is an invisible entity, which refers collectively to all Christian believers—not to one well-defined organization or to a particular person.

THE TRUTH

Since early Christian history, someone or something has had to make doctrinal decisions. We discussed earlier that Scripture itself does not and cannot decide what belongs in Scripture (see chapter 3). So how could one know which books were "apostolic" or "biblical"? That's where the Church comes in. Without the Church, there would, in fact, not be a New Testament. Even if we did not have Scripture, we would still have the Church. Members of this Church were the ones who wrote Scripture, preserved its many texts, and eventually canonized it. The Gospel was passed on by spoken tradition before it was written down.

Of course, this does not necessarily mean that the Church is a hierarchical organization. Yet, that is what Catholics claim, because the Church has one head, Jesus Christ. So, in their view, the Church is not a human institution, not a debating society, not a democracy, not a collection of individual and independent congregations—it is "one Body under Christ," the Body of Christ. Therefore, it is not an organization but an *organism*—and organisms usually have a hierarchical structure. For Catholics, that means: a hierarchy of pope, archbishops, bishops, priests, and laypersons—all under the head of Jesus Christ. So the Church's teachings do not come "from below," as in a democracy, but "from above." In order to know what the apostles commanded and taught in the name of God and Jesus Christ, there has to be a "mechanism" by which we can recognize the apostles' teachings.

In 1 Timothy 3:15 we read, "You may know how one ought to behave in the household of God, which is the church of the living God, the pillar and bulwark of the truth." It is not the Bible, but the Church—the living community of believers founded upon St. Peter and the apostles and headed by their successors—that is "the pillar and bulwark of truth." The immediate, or direct, rule of faith is the teaching of the Church today; the Church takes her teaching from both the written Word, called Sacred Scripture, and the oral or unwritten Word, known as Sacred Tradition. The teaching authority, or Magisterium, of the Catholic Church (headed by the pope), has a God-given mission to interpret and teach both Scripture and Tradition. Scripture and Tradition are the sources of Christian doctrine, the Christian's remote, or indirect, rule of faith (see chapter 3).

The Church has used the authority bestowed on her by Christ for centuries. Take, for instance, the question of whether Arius was correct in his belief that the Son was created. All modern-day Christians agree that, although Arius presumably "compared Scripture with Scripture," he nonetheless arrived at an erroneous interpretation and conclusion. The very fact that Christians agree now that Arius's interpretations were heretical implies that an objectively true, or "right," interpretation does, in fact, exist for the biblical passages he used. How do we know? There must be, out of necessity, an infallible authority to tell us so. It was that infallible authority, the Catholic Church, that declared Arius heretical. Had the Catholic Church not been both infallible and authoritative in its declaration, believers would have had no reason whatsoever to reject Arius's teachings, and the whole of Christianity today might have comprised modern-day Arians.

Something similar happened when, in the second and third centuries, the writings of the Gnostics — teaching that Jesus was not God and that the God of the Old Testament was not the God of Jesus Christ — were rejected on the basis of not matching up to the apostolic tradition. Private, personal interpretations of Scripture do not matter. As 2 Peter 1:20 puts it, "No prophecy of scripture is a matter of one's own interpretation." St. Peter is obviously contrasting genuine, apostolic teaching with false prophets and false teachers, and he makes reference to private interpretation as the pivotal point between the two. Based on private interpretations, Protestants have become divided into thousands of denominations; they have churches, but no Church, or at best a very fragmented church. The clear implication is that private interpretation can easily become a pathway whereby an individual turns away from authentic teaching and begins to follow erroneous teaching. Without the Catholic Church, we could very well all have been Gnostics.

Protestants should at least concede a point, which Martin Luther also admitted, namely, that the Catholic Church safeguarded and identified the Bible. In his own words, "We are obliged to yield many things to the Catholics—(for example), that they possess the Word of God, which we received from them; otherwise, we should have known nothing at all about it." G. K. Chesterton said it right: "It was only the Roman Catholic Church that saved the Protestant truths.... Even the very selection of dogmas which the reformers decided to preserve had only been preserved for them by the authority which they denied."

Ultimately, the problem of private interpretations can be resolved only through the intervention of an infallible teaching authority that speaks on behalf of Christ. Catholics know that this authority is the Catholic Church and its Magisterium, or teaching authority.

But be aware that Catholics do not claim that the Church is infallible because Scripture says so. The Church is infallible because Jesus said so! Because Scripture itself is open to various interpretations, Scripture is subject to fallible interpretation. The only source of infallible teaching is an infallible interpreter—that is, the Church in the person of Peter's successor. Without that infallibility, the certainty of Christian belief is not possible.

Although Revelation came to its fullest manifestation in Jesus, the Son of God, its understanding would still need further completion. Jesus told His disciples, "I have yet many things to say to you, but you cannot bear them now. When the Spirit of truth comes, he will guide you into all the truth" (John 16:12–13). What we see here is that divine revelation is progressive in nature—that is, over time, we are granted a fuller and fuller knowledge of God in general, including a fuller understanding of the meaning of prior revelation, including Scripture. It is for this reason that the doctrine of the Faith undergoes a process of development through time, guided by Scripture, Tradition, and the authority of the Church. The formulation of revealed truth develops through the discernment of new truths that are formally implicit in what the apostles handed on to us. This process of growth resembles the way a river grows—it gets wider and deeper, while remaining the same river.

So we could conclude from this that both Scripture and Tradition are the inspired sources of Christian doctrine, while the Church—a historical and visible entity dating back to St. Peter and the apostles in an uninterrupted succession—is the infallible teacher and interpreter of Christian doctrine. Catholics do not follow papal *orders*, but they do follow papal *teachings* that flow directly and indirectly from Jesus through the "bed" of Tradition.

When the First Vatican Council declared the pope *infallible*, this was certainly not done in an unlimited manner. The history of popes clearly shows there is no unlimited infallibility in being pope. Popes are not saints by definition. It is the Church that is called "holy," not her members, not even her popes. Only a few popes have made it to sainthood, and certainly not because they were pope.

Yes, the pope is infallible, but only when he speaks *ex cathedra*. That situation does not happen often, nor does it come easily. Besides, it is wrong to assume that whenever the pope says something in an infallible way, Catholics will then automatically fall in line to carry out the pope's "orders." Some, or perhaps many, are "cafeteria" Catholics who take "orders" of their own liking. Just think, for a comparison, of the effect of the many strong and repeated statements that the last three pontiffs have regularly made against legalized abortion.

Obviously, St. Augustine's famous saying "Rome has spoken; the cause is finished" (*Roma locuta; causa finita est*) often does not lead Catholics to abide by what Rome has decided. Nonetheless, the pope does carry a heavy authority and responsibility. Encyclicals, for instance, are papal letters containing the pope's views on Church teaching and doctrine in particular areas. Although encyclicals do not set down new Church doctrine, they are still, in essence, official statements and are considered authoritative teaching, since popes speak for the Church. Officially, they are "authoritative" but not infallible.

However, there are papal statements that are indeed infallible. Since infallibility is such a controversial issue among non-Catholics, it needs a bit more attention. It requires several caveats. First of all, we should not confuse the charism of papal infallibility with impeccability. Catholics know very well that popes, beginning with the first pope, St. Peter, are far from perfect, let alone sinless, but they are infallible in a very specific and restricted way.

Second, infallibility is a protection, a safeguard, from *error*, which is clearly something different from inspiration. According to Vatican I, the pope is preserved from the possibility of error "when, in the exercise of his office as shepherd and teacher of all Christians, in virtue of his supreme apostolic authority, he defines a doctrine concerning faith or morals to be held by the whole Church."

Third, infallibility belongs not only to the pope but also to the body of bishops as a whole, when, in doctrinal unity with the pope, they solemnly teach a doctrine as true. Yet infallibility also belongs in a special way to the pope as head of the bishops when he speaks ex cathedra, with the power of the keys that Jesus promised to Peter alone in Matthew 16:19. He does so by using ex cathedra introductions such as "We declare," "We define," or "We pronounce." Interestingly enough, the decrees of Vatican II were never stamped with the note of infallibility, Pope Paul VI having personally requested that this Council not be considered doctrinal, but only pastoral.

The legendary American writer and essayist Flannery O'Connor, who died in 1964, said about infallibility: "Christ never said that the Church would be operated in a sinless or intelligent way, but that it would not teach error. This does not mean that each and every priest won't teach error, but that the whole Church speaking through the pope will not teach errors in matters of faith."

CONCLUSION

The authority of the Catholic Church, and in particular of her pope, goes back to what Jesus had instituted himself. It is thanks to the authority of the Church that we have been saved from numerous heresies in Church history. Non-Catholic Christians who refuse to submit themselves to the secure teaching authority of the one man designated as supreme shepherd by Christ Himself have actually conferred that same awesome authority upon people such as Luther and Calvin, or upon themselves—individually!

PART 5

CATHOLICISM AND ITS HISTORY

22

CATHOLICS CELEBRATE
PAGAN HOLY DAYS

THE LIE

The Catholic Church happily adopted pagan holidays and feasts. She introduced Christmas, which coincides with the date of the Roman celebration of "the day of the unconquered sun" (*Dies Natalis Invicti Solis*). She also took on Easter, which is connected to the ancient Babylonian goddess Ishtar and her Aramean counterpart, Astarte.

These Catholic inventions should be rejected because of their pagan origins. Not only did the English Puritans and Scottish Presbyterians reject them, but so have new sects such as Seventh-Day Adventists, Mormons, and Jehovah's Witnesses. They agree that Catholicism has been polluted by paganism.

THE TRUTH

Undoubtedly, Christmas and Easter are key events in the Catholic calendar. Some Catholics go to church only on Christmas and Easter. They hear the beginning of the Gospel on Christmas and the end of the Gospel on Easter but miss out on what happened in between. They have in fact become "CEO" Catholics—Catholics with "Christmas and Easter Obligations." Are they just celebrating pagan feasts?

It's a popular belief. The Catholic convert and apologist James Akin notes that the pagan claim of Easter is made "by some Christian Fundamentalists (who want to do away with or re-brand Easter), by some atheists (who want to undermine Christianity), and by some neo-pagans (who want to undermine Christianity and claim Easter for their own)." The fact that pagan feasts and Catholic feasts sometimes coincide with each other does not mean there is a causal connection. Every day is a pagan holiday somewhere on earth or in history. Christmas is no more "pagan" or less "pagan" than the Jewish celebration of the feast of Tabernacles, which happened to coincide with a Canaanite festival celebrating the grape harvest. Similarly, the fact that Hindus purify themselves by being submerged in the Ganges River does not make Baptism by immersion pagan. Besides, one could make the opposite claim, that the adoption of certain pagan customs may rather have been viewed by early Christians as a victory for Christ over paganism.

So let us find out what the real connections are, beginning with Easter. Whatever it meant for ancient pagans, for Christians Easter is the celebration of Christ's Resurrection. Again, the fact that the feast of the Resurrection seemed to coincide with pagan celebrations doesn't mean it was derived from them. The Jewish Passover (on which Christ was crucified) also coincided with pagan celebrations, yet this didn't mean it was pagan. Actually, the date for Easter is determined on a lunisolar calendar similar, but not identical, to the Hebrew calendar.

There is nothing pagan about basing a calendar system on the annual cycle of the seasons or on the phases of the moon.

God specifically made the sun and the moon to be timekeepers. As Genesis 1:14 says, "Then God said: Let there be lights in the firmament of the heavens to separate the day from the night; and let them be for signs and for seasons and for days and years." In a time before modern clocks and calendars, there was simply no other way to maintain any sort of calendar other than using the seasonal signposts of the sun and the moon.

In the Church's Western tradition, Easter is celebrated on the first Sunday following the new full moon that occurs on or immediately after the vernal, or spring, equinox. Because it is not connected to a pagan calendar but to the Hebrew calendar, Hebrew Christians, the first to celebrate the Resurrection of Jesus, timed the observance in relation to Passover. The full moon referred to is called the Paschal full moon, which is not an astronomical full moon, but the fourteenth day of a lunar month. Nisan 14 of the Hebrew calendar is "the Lord's Passover," according to Leviticus 23:5. It is not known how long the Nisan 14 practice continued. But both those who followed the Nisan 14 custom and those who set Easter on the following Sunday had in common the custom of consulting their Jewish neighbors.

But the chief complaint against this custom was that the Jewish communities sometimes erred in setting Passover to fall before the northern hemisphere spring equinox. This problem was formally resolved by the First Council of Nicaea in 325. Sunday Easter service was already the norm throughout Christianity by this time. The issue at the council was what the best way would be to calculate when Easter should occur. The desire was to have all the congregations celebrating on the same date, which was not possible by depending on the rabbis' determining the month by physical observation; dependency on such physical calculations might even allow Passover to be celebrated twice in one solar year. So the Council sought to keep the Passover of Christ from being arbitrarily decided and to have the date uniformly kept throughout the Church at large. Nothing in their discussions or in any of the surviving evidence suggests that these dates were chosen or influenced by any pagan practice or teaching.

Since then, using the Gregorian calendar, Western Christianity has Easter always fall on a Sunday between March 22 and April 25, within about seven days after the astronomical full moon. (The Orthodox Churches follow a different dating system and will thereby celebrate Easter one, four, or five weeks later.)

So this makes us wonder how the myth of a "pagan connection" could ever arise. Surprisingly, it began with the Venerable Bede (672–735), a Catholic monk and scholar, who asserted in his book *De Ratione Temporum* that Easter was named after the goddess Eostre, also known as Eastre. Bede spoke also about Eostur-monath, the month of the goddess Eostre. Then the name Eostre disappeared for more than a thousand years, until 1835, when Jacob Grimm published his work on *Teutonic Mythology* and mentioned the name of the goddess Eostre again. He says that it "must in heathen religion have denoted a higher being, whose worship was so firmly rooted, that the Christian teachers tolerated the name, and applied it to one of their own grandest anniversaries." Since then the name "Easter" has been connected with the Babylonian goddess Ishtar, also known as Astarte or Ashtoreth in other pagan cultures that the Israelites encountered in biblical times.

This claim is basically based on the fact that "Ishtar" *sounds* like "Easter." But it is hard to see how Babylonian influence could jump all the way across the Mediterranean to the European continent after so many centuries and then turn up in Germany and

England among the early Anglo-Saxons. As a matter of fact, there is no historical evidence to prove any Babylonian connection between these deceivingly similar names. The best explanation is mere coincidence!

Besides, a look at non-English speaking Christians shows there is actually a disconnect between Easter and pagan deities. As a matter of fact, there are only two languages in which the name seems to have any pagan associations at all: the name "Easter" in English and the name "Oster" in German. But in virtually every other European language, "Easter" is derived from the Jewish word *Pesach*, or "Passover." Thus, in Greek and in Latin the term for Easter is *Pascha*. From there the term passed into the Romance languages. So in Spanish it is *Pascua*, in Italian it is *Pasqua*, in French it is *Paques*, and in Portuguese it is *Pascoa*. It also passed into some non–Romance languages: in Dutch it is *Pasen*, and in Danish it is *Paaske*.

Thus, only in the highly Protestant countries of Germany and England, where the Reformation developed deep roots, could the term "Easter" have any plausible pagan associations at all. In early English translations of the Bible made by Tyndale and Coverdale in 1569, the word "Easter" was substituted for the word "Passover," but only in some verses. Exactly why the English language did not consistently utilize the Hebrew-Greek-Latin root is a riddle.

A similar account can be given regarding the origin of Christmas. While Easter is a movable feast that follows the cycles of the moon, Christmas is a fixed feast. It is about the birth of Christ. The Bible does not tell us when Jesus was born. Some early Christians, most notably Origen of Alexandria (185–254), strongly opposed the celebration of Christ's birth. Pointing out that only Pharaoh and Herod celebrate their birthdays in the

Bible, Origen argued that birthdays were for pagans, not Christians. Yet there is some evidence that Christmas may have been celebrated in Rome on December 25 as early as the year 205. This was certainly true by the year 336, when we have the first clear record of the Nativity being celebrated in Rome.

So where did December 25 come from? It is very tempting to connect that date with another pagan celebration. One of the candidates is an ancient Roman festival called Saturnalia in honor of the deity Saturn, held from December 17 through 23. The holiday was celebrated with a sacrifice at the Temple of Saturn. Another candidate is a pagan feast that Emperor Aurelian officially established as the principal cult of the empire on December 25, in 274: worship of a Roman version of a sun god, under the name of Sol Invictus. But there are many reasons to reject such claims.

First of all, the Saturnalia festival always ended on December 23 at the latest. Why would the Catholic Church, eager to divert the attention of her faithful from a pagan celebration, choose a date two days after that party had already ended? It makes no sense. No serious scholar believes this claim.

Second, the Catholic Church had been celebrating Christmas long before Emperor Aurelian decided to establish his solar feast. So it is much more likely that the action of Aurelian was a deliberate attempt at trying to undercut the Christian celebration. It seemed to be a response, rather than the other way around, to the growing popularity and strength of the Catholic religion, which was celebrating Christ's birth on December 25.

So what then is the real origin of the Christmas date? The earliest known accounts about Jesus' birth date came from the early Church Father Irenaeus (130–202), who connected Mary's conception of Jesus with the Passion Week (starting with Palm

Sunday). Using March 25 as his Passion Week date, Irenaeus calculated forward nine months to December 25 as a birth date. Another Church Father, Hippolytus of Rome (170–236), specifically related December 25 to the birth of Jesus, though he may have made this decision based on the earlier tradition of Irenaeus. And then there is Sextus Julius Africanus (160–240), who in the year 221 also noted December 25 as the date of Jesus' birth—which is long before 274, when Emperor Aurelian officially established Sol Invictus as the principal cult of the empire on December 25.

Once the date of the Annunciation and Incarnation was established, it was a simple matter of adding nine months to arrive at the date of our Lord's birth—December 25. This date would not be made official immediately, but was established long before Aurelian and Constantine. It had nothing to do with pagan festivals. In the year 350, Pope Julius I officially declared that Christ's birth would be celebrated on December 25, despite the day's possibly pagan significance and association.

So, Christmas and its date are not pagan inventions but are Catholic to the core. No wonder then that we cannot derive the English word "Christmas" from any pagan root. The old English term for it, *Christes maesse*, means "Christ's Mass." So when you wish people a merry Christmas, you are wishing them a good "Mass of Christ" for December 25. What's in a word? Sometimes a lot!

CONCLUSION

Catholics do *not* celebrate pagan holidays. There are no indications that the Catholic Church celebrates feasts that have a pagan origin. All arguments to the contrary are based on misinformation, flawed reasoning, highly unreliable sources, and very unlikely hypotheses. Christmas and Easter were already celebrated in the early history of the Church as deeply Christian events. Even the names of these feasts are Christian, not pagan.

23

CATHOLICS ARE CRUSADERS AGAINST ISLAM

THE LIE

The Catholic Crusades were a series of holy wars against Islam led by power-mad popes and fought by religious fanatics against innocent, tolerant, and peaceful Muslims. There is no way Catholics can defend these wars. The Crusaders were the real aggressors who waged a holy war against Muslims; the Muslims were merely victims who had to defend themselves. That's why Mehmet Ali Ağca, the man who attempted to assassinate Pope John Paul II, explained what he did: "I have decided to kill Pope John Paul II, supreme commander of the Crusades."

THE TRUTH

The anti-Catholic myth of the Crusades has been growing stronger and stronger over a long period. One of the first milestones was the rhetoric of the Protestant Reformer Martin Luther, the first within Christianity who argued in a very forcible way that to fight in the Crusades as a Christian would be the same as fighting

181

Christ Himself. He believed that Christ had sent the Turks to punish the Catholic Church for its infidelity to God.

A second milestone was the rise of the Enlightenment. It was its anti-Catholic propaganda that invented the name "crusade," just as it invented the term "Dark Ages" to describe a period of darkness and fanaticism in between the splendors of Antiquity and the Renaissance (see chapter 28). The word "crusade" first appears in *L'Histoire des Croisades* written by the Franciscan friar Archange de Clermont and published in 1638—nearly six centuries after the First Crusade took place in 1095.

The third milestone was the spread of European colonialism after the breakup of the Ottoman Turkish Empire in the early twentieth century. It was not until then that the Crusades came to be used in anti-imperialist propaganda. Interestingly enough, the first Arabic history of the Crusades was not written until 1899.

There are usually at least two sides to a story. So it is time to find out the other side of the story—arguably the true story behind the Crusades.

The first question is: What were the real motives behind the Crusades? The world had dramatically changed before the First Crusade began. During the first century of the second millennium things had come to a head. In 1010, the Muslim caliph al-Hakim had already ordered the destruction of all Christian shrines and churches in the Holy Land. The arrival of the Seljuk Turks (non-Arab Muslims), who conquered Jerusalem from the Egyptian Muslims in the late eleventh century, critically altered the landscape for the Christians. In 1065, the Seljuks began a campaign of persecution against Christian pilgrims in the Holy Land. During this campaign, the bishop of Bamberg, for instance, and twelve thousand pilgrims were massacred by the Muslims only two miles from Jerusalem. In 1071, the Muslim Seljuk Turks defeated the Christian Byzantine forces and cut off the pilgrimage routes from the west.

In 1095, an assembly of churchmen called by Pope Urban II met at Clermont, France. Messengers from the Byzantine emperor Alexius I had urged the pope to send help against the armies of Muslim Turks, for by the end of the twelfth century, the Muslim Turks had turned their attention to the Near East. The conquering Muslim hordes swept through the Christian East and finally turned toward Constantinople. The new emperor, Alexius, realized his weakened state and appealed to Western Christendom for help to protect his crumbling empire. This required action.

So Pope Urban II called for the First Crusade, stressing three important reasons for his plea: the molestation of pilgrims in the Holy Land, the desecration of holy Christian places, and the plight of Eastern Christians in distress. In 1095, when the pontiff proclaimed the First Crusade, his main goal was to restore Christian access to the holy places in and near Jerusalem. Because pilgrimages to the Holy Land were very popular at the time, it was no surprise that the disruption of pilgrimages by conquering Seljuk Turks prompted strong support for the Crusades in Western Europe.

A second question is: Who were the real crusaders? Those who joined the Crusades had no idea they were in a "crusade" — that term is a much later invention, as we saw. They were known by various terms, including "the Franks," "the faithful of St. Peter" (*fideles Sancti Petri*), or "knights of Christ" (*milites Christi*) — but never "crusaders." The origin of the word "crusader" may be traced to the cross (*crux*) made of cloth and worn as a badge on the outer garment of those who took part in these enterprises.

This "taking of the cross" meant taking a vow, which was made in public, before witnesses, and was binding in the eyes of God and the Church. Only eventually did the word become associated with the entire journey. In other words, the crusaders saw themselves as undertaking a journey, or a peregrination. It is essential to understand that the crusades were actually penitential pilgrimages: "taking the cross" meant taking a vow. But, of course, high ideals may not always guarantee a good outcome.

One of the contributions Crusaders made to history was the formation of knightly orders such as the Knights Templar, the Teutonic Knights, and the Hospitallers. These were orders of religious knights, working from a monastic rule to defend the Holy Land and to protect pilgrims on their way to Jerusalem. The members of these orders were monks and knights at the same time; that is, to the monastic vows of poverty, chastity, and obedience, they added a fourth vow, which bound them to protect pilgrims. In other words, these orders were both a response to the desperate need for manpower in the East and an example of the way the Church was attempting to tame and even monasticize the warrior class. In Jerusalem, for instance, they managed a massive hospice that started as an aid station for pilgrims, but would soon look more like a modern hospital specifically caring for the sick and doing simple operations, while serving Muslims and Jews as well.

A third question is: Were the Muslims really the target of the Crusades? No, the real target was Jerusalem and free access for Christian pilgrims to the Holy City — but certainly not the Muslims themselves. It is revealing to note that at no point did the Crusaders attack the Muslim homeland, Arabia, but only those originally Christian territories that the Muslims had conquered and blocked for access by Christian pilgrims.

Catholics are crusaders against Islam

As a matter of fact, Muslims who lived in Crusader-won territories were generally allowed to retain their property and livelihood, and always their religion. Throughout the history of the short-lived Crusader Kingdom of Jerusalem, Muslim inhabitants far outnumbered the Catholics. This is probably also the reason Muslims did not pay much attention to the Crusades until very recently. Besides, the crusades were never successful in establishing the permanent liberation of the Holy Land. Crusaders were not out to kill infidels, as some Muslims are.

A fourth question is: Who were the real aggressors? To answer this question, we need to realize that Christianity at the time was suffering a long, protracted history of Muslim invasions and occupation. Imperialism is certainly not a Western invention; Muslims see it as the normal exercise of power. Here are some milestones of Muslim invasion: Syria, and the surrounding lands, all Christian, including Palestine (636), Iraq (637), Jerusalem (638), Iran (638–650), Egypt (639–642), North Africa (643–707), Cyprus and Tripoli (644–650), followed by Spain (711–718). This changed the Mediterranean into a "Muslim Lake."

It is only against this background that the Crusades can receive a fair assessment. The situation had come to a head when the Holy Land, and especially Jerusalem, was desecrated and destroyed and was no longer accessible to pilgrims.

So the idea that the Crusaders were the aggressors, and that the Muslims were merely victims who had to defend themselves cannot be accurate. If you want to use war terminology, the Crusades to the East were in every way *defensive* wars, and certainly not aimed at Muslims as such. They were a direct response to Muslim acts—an attempt to reverse Muslim conquests of Christian lands or defend Christian lands against further Muslim conquests.

It is often said that the word "Islam" means "peace," but a more accurate translation is "submission" ("salam" means peace). When Christians use violence in wars and the like, they are not following the gospel or the example of Christ; but when Muslims use violence, they are following the Qur'an and Muhammad's example. Given this distinction, the Crusaders did not wage a "holy war" but a "just war"—to keep Jerusalem accessible to Christian pilgrims.

In recent years, a powerful social movement has demanded that the West, and specifically the Catholic Church, apologize for the entire medieval crusading movement. Underlying the request for an apology, though, is the assumption that religious frontiers are somehow carved in stone, and that Muslim states of the Near East must always and infallibly have been destined to be part of the world of Islam. In contrast, an equally good case can be made that the medieval Middle East was no more inevitably Muslim than other regions conquered by Islam and subsequently liberated, such as Spain and Hungary. Nor, curiously, do Westerners suggest that Muslims apologize for the aggressive acts that gave them power over those various, originally Christian lands in the first place.

A fifth question is: Which ties do Muslims have with Jerusalem? There is no doubt that Jerusalem and the Holy Land serve as the home not only of the Jewish faith but also of the Christian faith. With Emperor Constantine's conversion, Jerusalem became a Christian city and was thereupon adorned with great shrines and churches commemorating all aspects of Christ's final days—with the most glorious edifice being the great Church of the Holy Sepulchre. It commemorated the hill of Crucifixion and the tomb of Christ's burial. No wonder Jerusalem was a favorite destination for many a pilgrimage. In short, the city of Jerusalem bore, and still bears, a holy significance for the Christian religion.

But isn't this also true for Muslims? you might ask. Not really. The Qur'an recounts that, in a dream or vision, Muhammad was taken by night "to the farthest mosque"—wherever that might be. Nowadays, the Arab world considers that "farthest mosque" to be the Mosque of Omar on the Temple Mount in Jerusalem. However, as Roy Schoeman remarks:

> When Muhammad died in A.D. 632, Jerusalem was still a Christian city and had no mosques at all; in fact, up until A.D. 638, when Jerusalem was captured by Khalif Omar, a Christian church known as Saint Mary of Justinian stood on the site. It was converted into a mosque only around A.D. 711 by Abd El-Wahd, who ruled Jerusalem from 705–715.

Thus, not only is it certain that Muhammad was never physically present in Jerusalem, but the mosque on the Temple Mount to which he supposedly went in his dream was not built until three generations after his death. Ironically, during the several centuries that the Temple Mount was held by the Muslim Turks, no repairs were done on the Dome of the Rock and the El-Aksa mosque. Photographs taken of them at the time show them in a state of disrepair, with missing roof tiles and high grass growing through the paving stones. But the real kicker is this: Jerusalem is not mentioned a single time in the Qur'an. So what "link" is there?

A sixth question is: Why did the Crusades not work out according to plan? There were at least eight Crusades against the Muslim caliphates of the Near East, but ultimately they were not successful and were often marred by scandals and internal conflicts. The main problem during each Crusade was that there was no unified command. True, it was always popes who proclaimed or approved the Crusades, but they had great difficulty controlling the Crusaders, and besides, they were not "in the field." Those who were in the field were not under a unified command, and those whom we consider "leaders" of each Crusade often acted independently of each other, or even against each other.

So what should our final assessment of the crusades be? Viewed in the light of their original purpose, the Crusades were failures. They made no permanent conquests of the Holy Land or Jerusalem. They did not retard the advance of Islam. Far from aiding the Eastern Empire, they hastened its disintegration.

As with all great human endeavors, the crusades had their high points and their low points. As the poet T.S. Eliot once wrote,

> Among [them] were a few good men,
> Many who were evil,
> And most who were neither,
> Like all men in all places.

CONCLUSION

Catholics are *not* crusaders against Islam. Those who would blindly defend the Crusades and the Crusaders, and those who would seek to apologize for them without any question, are probably equally misguided. But the fact remains that Catholics were not crusaders against Islam, but against the occupation and desecration of holy Catholic places. As Muslims speak out clearly when they perceive an attack on Islam, so can Catholics speak out clearly when they perceive an attack on Christianity. However, myths and lies and fabrications have obscured the real history behind the Crusades.

24

CATHOLICS KILLED THOUSANDS DURING THE INQUISITION

THE LIE

The Catholic Church masterminded a vast, papal-controlled Inquisition that targeted non-Catholics and Jews but also rounded up Catholic dissidents, tortured them, and executed them. It killed tens of thousands of innocent people, Christian and non-Christian alike, and was eager to burn witches.

THE TRUTH

In the eyes of many, one of the greatest villains in Catholicism is the Inquisition. The anti-Catholic myth of the Inquisition developed over a rather short period. Needless to say, people or groups of people targeted by inquisitors tried very hard to spread a negative image of the Inquisition as an institution. But the real explosion in anti-Inquisition rhetoric came during the rise of Protestantism.

Probably the main reason the Inquisition myth could spread so quickly was the invention of the printing press. The Protestants were happy to use this potent new weapon against their

Catholic enemies and their inquisitors. For instance, in Germany in 1567, two Spanish Protestants under the pseudonym Montanus published a one-sided, extremely biased book that would be reprinted and advertised throughout Europe. It was considered the definitive source on the Inquisition for more than two hundred years. Most Inquisition "histories" written thereafter would rely on Montanus's dubious work. That's how the legend of the Inquisition could grow larger and larger than its history. So it is time to find out the true story behind the Inquisition.

The first question is: Of which Inquisition are we speaking? It is tempting to talk about *the* Inquisition, but there is no such thing. Most people do not realize that the term "the Inquisition" refers to a group of rather diverse institutions. First, there was the Medieval Inquisition, from 1184 to the 1230s, established by Pope Lucius II, and later formalized by Pope Gregory IX, as a special court to curb the spread of heresy—in particular the heresy of the Albigensians (or Cathars) in southern France and the Waldensians in France and Italy. Then there were the Spanish Inquisition (late fifteenth century), the Portuguese Inquisition (sixteenth century), and the Roman Inquisition of the sixteenth century onward. In more recent history, the Roman Inquisition would survive as part of the Roman Curia. In 1908 the name of the Congregation became "The Sacred Congregation of the Holy Office." After the Second Vatican Council, it was replaced in 1965 by the "Congregation for the Doctrine of the Faith," which maintains vigilance in matters of faith.

One could even say that almost all Inquisitions were predominantly local phenomena. A vast, papal-controlled, grand and singular Inquisition never existed in Europe—it is a fabrication. Local bishops, or members of the Mendicant orders (Dominicans and Franciscans), established local ecclesial courts for the investigation of heresy. They used procedures rather common to secular legal procedures. What had begun in the thirteenth century as a papal-designated juridical system to remove "heresy-hunting" from control of the mob and from secular authorities evolved rather quickly into a means for local churches and secular authorities to address local, and later national or dynastic goals. As a result, it is impossible to speak of "the Inquisition" in the singular.

A second question is: Who were the targets and victims of the Inquisitors? The answer can be very brief: never any particular group outside Christianity, neither Jews nor Muslims, but only Christians, and in particular, heretics. The primary task of the Inquisition was to keep the Catholic Church free of heresy. As its name indicates, the Inquisition *inquires*. The job of the Inquisition, then, is twofold: put in negative terms, its task is to detect heretics, but also, in positive terms, to clear those who were falsely accused of being heretics (e.g., Ignatius of Loyola).

This raises the question why heresies and heretics are such an important issue for the Church. Especially nowadays, many tend to see the condemnation of heresy as a violation of "freedom of expression" (see chapter 36). In this assessment, there are no heretical views—they are merely harmless, perhaps dissident, alternative views. Well, in science, no one would defend such a position. Saying, for instance, that disinfection before surgery makes no sense is not just an alternative view but is definitely "anathema" in science. Something similar holds for heresy in religion—it is *anathema*.

Heresy is a perpetual threat to Christianity. In his farewell to the Ephesian church (Acts 20:30), St. Paul says, "From among your own selves will arise men speaking perverse things, to draw away the disciples after them." So something like an inquisition is basically a necessary tool to protect Jesus' Church from errors and false truths (see chapter 20). Let us state clearly again, the target of Inquisitors is Christians only—who were exclusively Catholics until the sixteenth century.

A third question is: What methods did the Inquisitors use? They basically used methods that civil courts would also use at the time. Before the existence of the Inquisition, people accused of heresy in the early Middle Ages were brought to the local lord for judgment, just as if they had committed theft or vandalism. Yet in contrast to those crimes, it was not so easy to discern whether the accused person was really a *heretic*. So there was a growing need for some kind of clerical Inquisition, done by clerical experts.

Therefore, in 1184, the Medieval Inquisition started when Pope Lucius III sent a list of heresies to Europe's bishops and directed them to take an active role in determining whether those accused of heresy were, in fact, heretics. Rather than relying on secular courts, local lords, or unruly mobs, bishops were to see to it that accused heretics in their dioceses were examined fairly by churchmen of expert knowledge and blameless reputation, in whose hands the Church could trust the decision as to the orthodoxy or heterodoxy of a given teaching.

In general, the ecclesiastical courts functioned the way civil courts had operated in the more recent past. Codes and manuals were developed that detailed how an Inquisition court was to function. It began with the arrival in an area of the inquisitors, usually members of the Dominican order. They would preach a sermon to the clergy and the laity of that area on the dangers of heresy. A "period of grace" would then be extended to allow for confessions of dissenting practices without subsequent trial. Trials were held only for those who refused to confess under the period of grace. For those who returned to the Church, forgiveness was granted and some form of penance imposed.

Although, for the most part, these courts did function similarly to their secular counterparts at that time, their sentences and penances were generally far less harsh. Many people preferred to have their cases tried by ecclesiastical courts because the secular courts had fewer safeguards. In fact, historians have found records of people intentionally blaspheming in secular courts so they could have their case transferred to an ecclesiastical court, where they would get a better hearing. The simple fact is that the Inquisition saved uncounted thousands of innocent (and even not-so-innocent) people who would otherwise have been roasted by secular lords or mob rule.

A fourth question is: Did Inquisitors use torture and execution? Yes, they did use torture, but never execution. Torture was used, but not as punishment, as in the secular courts. Modern researchers have discovered that the Spanish Inquisition applied torture in 2 percent of its cases. Each instance of torture was limited to a maximum of fifteen minutes. In only 1 percent of the cases was torture applied twice, and never for a third time. If you have ever heard of gruesome lists of instruments of torture, be aware they were an invention of the post-Reformation propaganda machine rather than the reality of the Catholic inquisitions.

Whereas torture was possible in ecclesiastical courts, execution was not. The reason for this is quite obvious. From the perspective of secular authorities, heretics were traitors to God and king, and therefore deserved death. From the perspective of the Church, on the other hand, heretics were lost sheep who had strayed from the flock. Being shepherds, all popes and bishops had a duty to bring those sheep back into the fold, just as the

Good Shepherd had commanded them. While medieval secular leaders were trying to safeguard their kingdoms, the Church was trying to save souls. If that did not work, there was one option left: handing the heretics over to civil authorities. Only the civil authorities had the power to execute people, often by burning them at the stake.

So execution was not part of the ecclesiastical court. The final step of execution—but only for unrepentant, obstinate, or relapsed heretics—was put in the hands of civil courts. The regular expression for such heretics was this: "Since the Church can no further punish their misdeeds, she leaves them to the civil authority."

A fifth question is: Were the Catholic Inquisitions unique? When most people speak about "the Inquisition," they usually have the Catholic Inquisition in mind. But that is basically another part of the myth. Protestants had their own state-run kind of inquisitions. One of their regular inquisitions was set up in Saxony, for instance, with Luther's associate Melanchthon on the bench; under it many persons were punished, some with death, some with life imprisonment, and some with exile.

It is well known that belief in the justice of punishing heresy with death was so common among the sixteenth-century Reformers—Luther, Zwingli, Calvin, and their adherents—that we may say their open-mindedness began where their power ended. To the great humiliation of the Protestant churches, religious intolerance and even persecution unto death were continued long after the breach with Rome. In Geneva, severe persecution was put into practice by state and church, including the use of torture and even the admission of the testimony of children against their parents. All of this was done with the sanction of John Calvin. Also, conservative estimates indicate that thousands of English and Irish Catholics were put to death—many by being hanged, drawn, and quartered—for refusing to become Protestant. An even greater number were forced to flee to the Continent for their safety.

There is strong evidence that the Protestant "witch" burnings in Germany alone killed more people than all the various actions of the Inquisition in Catholic Europe combined. Soon America would have its own "witch trials" performed by Protestant Puritans. In general, one could say that all countries that had dissolved their ties with the Catholic Church had witch trials conducted by secular courts under the control of Protestant leaders.

A sixth question is: What about the Spanish Inquisition, arguably the worst of all Inquisitions? The Spanish Inquisition began with the reign of King Ferdinand II of Aragon and Queen Isabella I of Castile. At the time in Spain, the Catholic Faith was endangered by what some considered pseudo-converts from Judaism (*marranos*) and Islam (*moriscos*). This danger was not based on their being Jews or Muslims, but on their being false Catholics. Over the years, the "Old Christians" began to see the new converts as opportunists who secretly maintained the faith of their non-Catholic forefathers. The task of the Spanish Inquisition was to determine whether they were real converts or pseudo-converts.

However, rather soon Fray Tomás Torquemada would become the true organizer—and for many the true villain—of the Spanish Inquisition. On November 1, 1478, at the solicitation of Their Spanish Majesties, Pope Sixtus IV empowered the Catholic sovereigns to set up their own Inquisition. Soon Their Majesties bestowed on Torquemada the office of Grand Inquisitor, the institution of which indicates a decisive new step in the development of the Spanish Inquisition.

Especially when Torquemada came to be the Grand Inquisitor, the Spanish Inquisition became infected with inhuman cruelty. Because the Spanish Inquisition had no jurisdiction over the Jews in Spain, Torquemada urged the sovereigns to compel all the Jews either to become Christians or to leave Spain. To frustrate his designs, the Jews agreed to pay the Spanish government thirty thousand ducats if left unmolested. But Torquemada expressed his objection to such a deal. Mainly through his intervention, the Jews were officially expelled from Spain in 1492.

Pope Sixtus IV was alarmed about these developments in Spain. On April 18, 1482, he wrote a letter to the bishops of Spain. King Ferdinand was outraged when he heard of the letter. He wrote back to Pope Sixtus, openly suggesting that the pope had been bribed with gold from pseudo-converts. That was the end of the papacy's role in the Spanish Inquisition. From then on, it would be an arm of the Spanish monarchy alone, detached from any papal authority.

Soon, Torquemada was replaced by the cardinal archbishop of Toledo, Francisco Jimenez de Cisneros, who worked hard to reform the Spanish Inquisition, removing bad apples and reforming procedures. Once these reforms had been implemented, the Spanish Inquisition had very few critics left. Staffed by well-educated legal professionals, it was one of the most efficient and compassionate judicial bodies in Europe. As historian Thomas Madden has written: "The Spanish Inquisition was widely hailed as the best run, most humane court in Europe."

Nevertheless, the Spanish may have defeated Protestants on the battlefield, but they lost the propaganda war. These were the years when the famous "Black Legend" of Spain was forged. Innumerable books and pamphlets poured from northern presses, accusing the Spanish Empire of horrible atrocities, thus putting all other Catholic Inquisitions in a bad light. They erroneously created an image of the Spanish Inquisition as the epitome of Catholic terror and barbarity.

CONCLUSION

Catholics did *not* kill thousands during the inquisition. The Inquisition was not one monolithic and papal-controlled enterprise. It did not target non-Catholics and Jews, but only Catholics or make-believe Catholics. It did not execute them, and torture was rarely used. It was an ecclesiastical court system that followed strict legal rules, often much better than those of civil courts. But it did have extremely partisan enemies in the Protestant camp, which controlled powerful printing presses, while having at the same time its own kind of inquisition.

25

CATHOLICS HELPED ESTABLISH HITLER

THE LIE

Nazism was an offshoot of Catholic anti-Semitism. Many in the Nazi leadership were Catholics. Adolf Hitler was born Catholic, Joseph Goebbels went to a Franciscan boarding school, Reinhard Heydrich was Catholic, as was Heinrich Müller.

Following the Nazi takeover, the Catholic Church sought an accord with Hitler's government. She closed a pact with Hitler, called a Concordat, which Pius XI officially signed in 1933.

THE TRUTH

The myths that surround the relationship between Nazism and Catholicism form such an intricate web that we need to address some questions separately and in more detail in order to uncover the truth. Here are a few of those questions:

Question 1: Did Nazism itself have Catholic roots? Indeed, Hitler was born Catholic (although he had not practiced the Catholic Faith since childhood), as were Goebbels, Heydrich, and Müller. Hermann Goering, on the other hand, had a mixed

Catholic-Protestant parentage, while Rudolf Hess, Martin Bormann, Albert Speer, and Adolf Eichmann were from Protestant backgrounds. But even if some in the Nazi leadership were Catholics, the most we can say is that they were *former* Catholics who had renounced their religion.

A special case was Heinrich Himmler, a devoted Catholic as a student. He made it his business to assemble an extensive library about the Jesuit Order. He even dreamed at one stage of training his elite Waffen SS combat troops along Jesuit lines and went so far as to propose that the principal officers undergo a form of Ignatian Spiritual Exercises—adapted, however, to a mad blend of the new Nordic cult of Wodin, Siegfried, the Holy Grail, and the Teutonic Knights of old. The plan never succeeded, but even Hitler knew of it and joked about Himmler as "our very own Ignatius Loyola." So there may be some tiny Catholic roots here, but they were largely overgrown by weeds from very different origins.

The long-term aim of the Nazis was to de-Christianize Germany. Hitler believed that in the long run National Socialism and religion would not be able to coexist, and he stressed repeatedly that Nazism was a secular ideology, founded on modern "science"—the pseudo-science of racial superiority, that is. Joseph Goebbels, who led the Nazi persecution of the Catholic clergy, wrote that there was, as he said, "an irreconcilable opposition between the Christian and the heroic-German world view." Hitler's chosen deputy, Martin Bormann, saw Christianity and Nazism as "incompatible," as did the official Nazi philosopher, Alfred Rosenberg, who wrote as early as 1930 that Catholics were among the chief enemies of the Germans.

As to the question "Did Nazism have Catholic roots?" we must come to the conclusion that there were no such roots. Quite the opposite: Nazism wanted to root out all Catholic roots. The Dachau concentration camp, for instance, was used by the Nazis to kill many of its most hated enemies—among them Catholic priests. Indeed, of the 2,720 clergy sent to Dachau, 2,579 were Catholic priests, 411 of them were German priests; most of them were Polish priests—1,748 in all. Of the 1,034 priests who died in the camp, 868 were also Polish. The priests were housed in a special "priest block" and were targeted for particularly brutal treatment by the SS guards.

Question 2: Did Catholics bolster Nazism? Initially, Hitler and the Nazis tried to present a moderate and reassuring face to Catholics. But the instinctive reaction of many Catholics to the Nazis was a negative one, and only small numbers of Catholics voted for the National Socialists in the elections prior to 1933. Sure enough, it was soon after the elections that the Nazi Party began to show its true face. Thugs from the Sturmabteilung (SA) stormed a gathering of the Christian trade unions and the Catholic Centre Party and brutalized many of those in attendance.

After that, Catholics witnessed attacks on the Catholic press. A special Editors' Law was decreed in December 1933. Catholic newspapers and publications soon closed their doors, as they were unable to comply with government limitations on freedom and were unwilling to print Nazi propaganda on such horrendous issues as enforced sterilization and euthanasia. At the start of 1933, there were more than four hundred daily Catholic newspapers in Germany. By 1935, there were none.

The next step was that German Catholics were discouraged from sending their children to Catholic schools. Nazi propaganda called those schools disloyal and havens of corruption, and families were eventually required to appear before authorities to declare officially why they had decided to betray the regime. By 1939, all Catholic denominational schools had been disbanded or converted to public facilities.

What was the reaction of Catholics to all of this?

On the one hand, many average Catholics, like most other Germans, were not yet fully aware of the dangers of National Socialism. Some saw the Nazis as a potential ally against the spread of communism. On the other hand, when they realized they were deceived, they had already been surrounded by a very oppressive regime that would mute any dissident voices. But it must also be emphasized that the Catholic press and the Catholic German Centre Party were distinctly hostile to the Nazis.

In general, Catholic Bishops were more suspicious of National Socialism than all other established forces in Germany — media, academia, business, and the arts — even more so than their Protestant counterparts. In early 1931, the bishops' conference of Cologne, followed by the bishops of the regions of Paderborn and Freiburg, condemned National Socialism. Powerful names that come to mind are Cardinal Faulhaber of Munich, Bishop Preysing of Berlin, and Bishop Galen of Munich. In their sermons and speeches they expressed strong words against Hitler, Nazism, and anti-Semitism. This does not mean, of course, that all Catholics in Germany immediately followed suit.

Question 3: Did the Church make a pact with Hitler? It is true that, following the Nazi takeover, the Catholic Church sought an accord with the new government in the form of a concordat, an agreement between the Holy See and a sovereign state that defines the relationship between the Catholic Church and the state in matters that concern both. On July 20, 1933, Pius XI signed a concordat with Hitler. While attacked today as a Catholic capitulation to the Nazis, the concordat was viewed in its time in terms similar to those of the concordat of 1800 with Napoleon Bonaparte.

Before his election to the papacy as Pope Pius XII, Eugenio Pacelli was papal nuncio to Germany (1917–1929). While in Germany as nuncio, Pacelli had some experience with negotiating concordats: a favorable concordat between the Holy See and Bavaria in 1924, and a less favorable one with Prussia in 1929.

Concordats were quite common. In general, they allowed the Church to organize youth groups, make ecclesiastical appointments, run schools, hospitals, and charities, or even conduct religious services.

This specific concordat with Hitler's Germany did something similar. It specified that certain activities—education, youth associations, Church rallies—were legally guaranteed by the Reich. In return, the Church's support for the Centre Party would be withdrawn. Actually, the Centre Party, under relentless pressure from the Nazis, had already voted itself out of existence even before the final signing of the concordat, a fact that distressed Pacelli, as it frustrated his negotiating stance. Besides, Nazi violations of the concordat commenced almost immediately after it was signed.

Interestingly enough, the initiative for the treaty did not come from the Vatican this time, but from Hitler, who wanted to remove Catholic clergymen from party politics. Franz von Papen, a Nazi in Catholic garb, was sent to Rome to conclude such a pact, but received a cool reception from the now secretary of state Pacelli, who was fully aware of how little faith could be placed in Hitler's promises.

When a new negotiator was sent to Rome, Cardinal Pacelli continued to refuse agreement to the withdrawal of clergy from political activity, until it became clear that the Catholic Centre

Party in Germany was about to dissolve itself as the last German party to hold out against Hitler. Then things moved quickly. The concordat was initialed in Rome on July 8, 1933. The concordat was meant to protect Catholics in Germany, but certainly not Hitler. Let's also make utterly clear that this concordat with Hitler had nothing to do with anti-Semitism; in 1938, Pope Pius XI memorably declared that, in his own words, "anti-Semitism is a movement in which we Christians can have no part whatsoever.... Spiritually we are Semites."

Question 4: Did the Church ever condemn Nazism? As early as March 1937—Hitler had been in power only for four years—Pope Pius XI issued the encyclical *Mit Brennender Sorge* (With Burning Concern). It was co-drafted by Cardinal Faulhaber of Munich, Bishop Preysing of Berlin, Bishop Galen of Munich, and the Vatican secretary of state, Cardinal Pacelli, the future Pope Pius XII. All of these had been very vocal voices denouncing Nazism and its anti-Semitism. Cardinal Faulhaber, for instance, had been a member of a group called "Friends of Israel" and had a menorah emblazoned on his bishop's coat of arms. In this encyclical, Pope Pius XI noted on the horizon the "threatening storm clouds" of religious wars of extermination over Germany. The encyclical used very clear language:

> Whoever exalts race, or the people, or the State, or a particular form of State, or the depositories of power, or any other fundamental value of the human community—however necessary and honorable be their function in worldly things—whoever raises these notions above their standard value and divinizes them to an idolatrous level, distorts and perverts an order of the world planned and created by God; he is far from the true faith in God

and from the concept of life which that faith upholds.
(no. 8)

It certainly was a more-than-daring encyclical—written in
German for a change, not Latin, to make sure it would "reach"
Germany. And it certainly did! Priests, nuns, and laypeople en-
sured that *Mit Brennender Sorge* was read everywhere. Despite
the concerted efforts of the Gestapo, thousands upon thousands
of copies were printed through a vast underground network and
then distributed through parishes across Nazi Germany. As was
to be expected, the Nazis responded with an intensification of
Church suppression. The Gestapo arrested hundreds of Catholics, including children who were caught handing out copies of
the encyclical. The security services watched Catholic clergy
very closely—instructing agents to monitor every diocese, to
obtain the bishops' reports to the Vatican, and to report the
bishops' activities. Priests were frequently denounced, arrested,
or sent to concentration camps—many of them to the dedicated
clergy barracks at Dachau.

Question 5: What were the real roots of Nazism? On a closer
look, Nazism turns out to be a fervently anti-Catholic ideology
occasionally concealed behind a Catholic face. When studying
what lies behind Nazism and the Holocaust, we come across
an intricate network of ideological and spiritual forces. Perhaps
surprising to some, those forces were not of Christian or Catholic
origin. Roy Schoeman's book has an excellent overview of this
issue, from which I heavily borrowed for this discussion.

First of all, there was a quasi-scientific preparation for the
Holocaust. The anti-Semitism of the Nazi regime did not stem
from anything Catholic; instead it was based on the ideology of
eugenics—a version of Darwinism, advocating the improvement

of human genetic traits through the promotion of more frequent reproduction of people with desired traits (positive eugenics) and less frequent reproduction of people with less-desired or undesired traits (negative eugenics).

Second, there was an intellectual preparation for the Holocaust. The beliefs of intrinsic superiority of the "Aryan race" and the inferiority of the Jews can be traced back to the Second Reich. Bismarck's "blood and iron" policies had created a powerful, even dominant nation, ready for a strident economic and political nationalism. Many Germans had come to believe the myth of a "master race" destined to conquer the world and subdue "lesser races." None of this had any Catholic origins.

Third, there was a "spiritual" preparation for the Holocaust. From the outset, the pseudoscience of racial superiority was deeply intertwined with occultism. There were many links in this chain. One of them was Madame Blavatsky with her version of occultism known as Theosophy. She claimed to have learned her occult doctrines during seven years she spent in Tibet studying under Hindu masters. Her contempt for Jews and Judaism was undisguised. Another important link was Dietrich Eckart from the Thule Society. He predicted the imminent coming of a German messiah who would free Germany from the chains of Christianity. He also claimed to have "initiated" Hitler into occultism—a rite by which "higher centers" are opened, enabling extrasensory powers. In reality, it entails the introduction of demonic entities into a person. Finally, there is Heinrich Himmler, who was never without his copy of the Hindu scriptures. He established an institute in Berlin to study the potential of harnessing for the war effort occult forces of power, including black magic, spiritualist mediums, pendulum practitioners, and astrologers.

Question 6: What was the real force behind Nazism? The crux of the answer is that Hitler—and those with him—had made a pact with the devil. There are many indications that Hitler's relationship to the satanic was intentional, explicit, and extensive. We should not forget that Eckart had "initiated" Hitler into occultism. On at least one occasion, Hitler referred to Eckart as his "John the Baptizer."

In retrospect, all that Nazism stood for looks like a master plan. Who or what could have orchestrated such a master plan that appears to be beyond mere human power? There seems to be only one explanation: what we have here is a cosmic warfare between good and evil, between God and Satan. The contrast between these two could not be more decisive: God's goal is salvation for all, Satan's goal is perdition of all; Catholicism follows God's goal, Nazism favors Satan's goal. Pope Benedict XVI, who lived under Hitler's regime as a youth, would later write in his *Memoirs*, "Hitler was a demonic figure."

Only religious persons see all of history as a cosmic and constant warfare between God and Satan, waged daily and everywhere on a global scale. They grasp how the power of evil and the darkness of Satan can enable a man like Hitler—or Stalin and Mao, for that matter—to spellbind and enslave the minds and spirits of millions, creating hell right here on earth. This explains how such evil tyrants, who have sold their souls, can follow "orders" that stem from sources far beyond their own resources. Only religious people recognize this dimension of history that historians usually miss. After all, could Hitler have ever done what he did by relying on human power alone? Satan was and is happy to lend such people "spiritual" help from "beyond," giving them more than mere human power—extraordinary, superhuman power. Without that power, Hitler could have never done what he did.

CONCLUSION

Catholics did *not* help establish Hitler. Nazism was certainly not an offshoot of Catholic anti-Semitism. Although some in the Nazi leadership were Catholics, they were at best *former* Catholics. The roots of Nazism were not in Catholicism, but in anti-Catholic ideologies. The Catholic Church did not close a pact with Hitler through a concordat, but instead actively opposed and condemned Hitler through her encyclicals, through anti-Nazi members of the Catholic hierarchy, and initially through the Catholic Centre Party and the Catholic Press in Germany, but all of these were silenced by the Nazis.

26

CATHOLICS WERE TOLD TO IGNORE THE HOLOCAUST

THE LIE

The Catholic Church was actively involved in ignoring the Holocaust, especially through Pope Pius XII, who always remained silent and was just hiding in the Vatican. Pope Pius XII was more interested in the Vatican's investment portfolio than in the Holocaust. He can be best described as "Hitler's pope," who supported Hitler's evil plans.

THE TRUTH

The facts contradict the myths that have been spun around the image of Pope Pius XII. Here are the main facts.

Fact 1: Pope Pius XII was not silent about what was going on in Germany. Having lived thirteen years there as apostolic nuncio, he knew Germany from the inside. So when Pacelli became Pius XII—following the death in early 1939 of Pius XI, who had been very vocal against Hitler—he became the main Catholic figure of World War II. His first encyclical, *Summi Pontificatus*—subtitled "On the Unity of Human Society"—was issued in 1939, on October 20, within two months after Hitler's invasion of Poland. In this encyclical, the pope expressed dismay at the invasion of Poland, reiterating Church teaching against racial persecution and calling for love, compassion, and charity to prevail over war.

Fact 2: Pope Pius XII had no other power than his spiritual authority. What was his real secular power? The pope's worldly power—as ruler of fewer than a thousand inhabitants of Vatican City—is negligible, but depends "upon the spiritual sovereignty of the Holy See" which is indeed *sui generis* and wields an enormous, though imponderable, spiritual authority. The matter is succinctly summed up in Stalin's remark, "How many divisions has the pope?" and in Churchill's answer, "A number of legions not always visible on parade."

Although he did have spiritual authority, it is exceedingly naïve to imagine that Catholic Church leaders can simply issue "orders" to their flocks with the expectation that what they say will be carried out (see chapter 21); yet this seems to be a common assumption among many who fault Pius XI and Pius XII for not having issued the proper "orders." On several occasions, Pius XII explained that he was not speaking out because he did not want to make the situation worse. In view of the conditions found in Nazi-occupied Europe for those who lived there, perhaps the pontiff understood better than his critics what the consequences might have been of public challenges by him to the Nazis. Several sources have alleged that Hitler was plotting to kidnap Pope Pius XII and bring him to Liechtenstein.

Numerous people urged the pontiff to flee—and a lesser man would have done so—but instead Pius XII remained solidly at his post in Rome, leading the Church and also the anti-Nazi resistance. Between 2003 and 2006, the archives of the pontificate of Pius XII's predecessor, Pius XI, were released, demonstrating that as secretary of state, Pacelli fiercely opposed Nazi doctrine and practices and supported the Third Reich's many victims.

Fact 3: Pope Pius XII was never Hitler's pope. How, then, could he be called "Hitler's pope"? It was a fabrication promoted by John Cornwell. In his 1999 book, *Hitler's Pope*, Cornwell suggests that Pacelli, the pope-to-be, had visited Hitler, when in fact, Pacelli never set foot on Nazi soil after he left Germany for good in 1929—which is four years before Hitler obtained power. As a matter of fact, Pius XII never even met Hitler, much less collaborated with him. The two were relentless opponents.

The photograph on the front cover of the American edition of Cornwell's book was manipulated to give the impression Pius was leaving from a visit to Hitler in March 1939, the month that Pacelli was made pope, when, in fact, the photo had been taken in 1927, before Hitler had taken over, as Pius was leaving a reception held for German president von Hindenburg.

Not only did Pius XII speak out against the Holocaust; he was also one of the first ones to do so, authorizing Vatican Radio explicitly to condemn Nazi atrocities against Jews and Catholics in Poland, and personally confronting German Foreign Minister Joachim Ribbentrop over them. Robert Kempner, a prosecutor at the postwar Nuremberg Tribunal, publicly praised Pius XII for issuing countless protests against German war crimes.

Fact 4: Pope Pius XII was in fact heavily and personally involved with the protection of Jews. An event that has been overshadowed the most by the pope's distorted image took place on October 16, 1943—famously called "Black Saturday." In the early hours of that day, occupying Nazi troops descended upon Rome's Jews, estimated to be at least eight thousand. Although the ruthless Nazis were able to round up more than twelve hundred Jews during Black Saturday, and would deport more than a thousand of these to the Auschwitz-Birkenau extermination camp in Poland, the vast majority of them—some 85 percent—survived. They were hidden and protected in Church-run institutions with Pius XII's knowledge and support. The pope even opened his own summer residence at Castel Gandolfo to take in Jews targeted for death. As the U.S. Holocaust Memorial Museum notes: "For every Jew caught by the Germans in Rome, at least ten escaped and hid, many in the Vatican."

The event has been immortalized in the well-known movie *The Scarlet and the Black*. Regrettably, the movie creates the impression that Monsignor Hugh O'Flaherty, the main player in the movie, acted on his own, without any guidance from Pope Pius XII. However, writings of and memories about the Monsignor have revealed that he was acting on the orders of Pius XII, whom O'Flaherty loyally, wholeheartedly, and enthusiastically served.

The same can be said about another underground network, portrayed in the movie *The Assisi Underground*. In September 1943, Fra Ruffino Niccacci was the guardian of the Franciscan Monastery of San Damiano in Assisi. At the direction of Bishop Placido Nicolini and Aldo Brunacci, secretary to the bishop and chairman of the Committee to Aid Refugees, Padre Ruffino provided Jews with false identity cards and gave them sanctuary in local monasteries and convents. Again, the orders to do so came ultimately from the Vatican.

Fact 5: Pope Pius XII was widely praised for what he did during World War II. There was almost unanimous praise for Pius XII during and immediately after the war. Commenting on the pope's 1942 Christmas address, the *New York Times* called the pope "a lonely voice crying out of the silence of a continent." Chaim Weizmann, who would become Israel's first president, wrote in 1943 a letter in which he offered thanks for "the support the Holy See was giving to lend its powerful help whenever it can to mitigate the fate of my coreligionists." Winston Churchill called the pope "the greatest man of our time."

The same happened at Pius XII's death on October 9, 1958. It took the *New York Times* days to print the tributes from New York City rabbis alone. Israel's foreign minister Golda Meir said, "In a generation afflicted by wars and discords, he upheld the highest ideals of peace and compassion." Similar sentiments were expressed by Rome's Chief Rabbi, Israel Zolli. One of Zolli's successors, the chief rabbi of Rome, Elio Toaff, said the same. But matters would change soon, which brings us to the next fact.

Fact 6: Pope Pius XII was vilified by Moscow. In the midst of all endorsements for the pope, there was one important exception. As early as the winter of 1944–1945, the Soviet newspaper *Pravda* called the pope a fascist and an ally of Hitler. At the end of World War II, the Soviet Union continued an aggressive campaign to defame Pius XII. The framing of Pope Pius XII began on June 3, 1945, when Radio Moscow mendaciously alleged that he was "Hitler's pope." This set a whole train of events into action, eventually culminating in the production of the stage play *The Deputy* ("Der Stellvertreter" in German) by the then thirty-two-year old German Rolf Hochhuth. The author—who had been a junior member of the Hitler Youth!—portrayed Pope Pius XII as a coldhearted cynic, not interested in Hitler's slaughter of the Jews.

There was a clear connection between this play and the Soviet campaign of defaming Pius XII. A first indication of a wider plot was the fact that the play was translated into more than twenty languages by translators who all "happened" to be Western communists or sympathizers. Interestingly enough, the first producer of the play, Erwin Piscator, had joined the German Communist Party in 1919 and had worked for Soviet intelligence in Moscow during World War II. Without Piscator, the play that framed Pius XII would most likely never have seen the light of day.

Most recently, General Ion Pacepa, a former high-level official in Romania's Communist dictatorship of Ceausescu and the highest-ranking official ever to defect from the Soviet Union, has given us details about the Soviet plot to defame Pius XII. Pacepa revealed that he himself had played an important role in this "disinformation" machinery, and that he had sent Romanian agents to the Vatican disguised as priests. They gained access to the archives, then copied and falsified documents which were made available to Hochhuth, who was then doing "research" in Rome.

CONCLUSION

Catholics were *never* told to ignore the Holocaust—certainly not by Pope Pius XII. He was the one constantly condemning the Holocaust. His first encyclical was aimed at Hitler. When times got worse, he remained solidly at his post in Rome, leading the Church and also the anti-Nazi resistance. He was not "Hitler's pope": he never even met him, much less collaborated with him. He was personally involved with the protection of Jews and even opened his own summer residence at Castel Gandolfo to take in Jews targeted for death. Just after the war, he was widely praised for all his efforts during WW II, until anti-Catholic Soviet propaganda began to smear his name with numerous fabrications.

PART 6

CATHOLICISM AND SCIENCE

27

CATHOLICS DON'T USE THEIR HEADS

THE LIE

Catholics accept their beliefs on the authority of their Church, without asking for any explanation or evidence. They swallow whatever their Church tells them to swallow. When it comes to faith, they just don't use their heads.

They speak about faith mainly in terms of a "leap of faith"—a leap into the irrational. When questioned about their faith, they answer, "You just have to have faith." Their slogan is "Don't think, just believe."

In Catholic eyes, "religious faith" is synonymous with "blind faith," immune to any rational argumentation. Mark Twain put this view in a nutshell: "A man is accepted into a church for what he believes, and he is turned out for what he knows."

THE TRUTH

It might be true that some, perhaps even many, Catholics don't "use their head" in matters of faith. But their Church certainly does "use her head," and so should her members if they want to call themselves Catholic. The Catholic Church is known for her motto "Faith *and* Reason" (*Fides et Ratio*). She is arguably unique in Christianity, and even among other religions, for so strongly advancing the role of reason in religion. She does not accept beliefs that go against reason or are otherwise unreasonable (see chapter 20).

It is her deepest belief that reason comes from God as much as faith does. St. Augustine could not have said it more clearly, "Believers are also thinkers: in believing, they think, and in thinking, they believe." In his 1998 encyclical *Fides et Ratio*, John Paul II warned of "a resurgence of fideism, which fails to recognize the importance of rational knowledge and philosophical discourse for the understanding of faith, indeed for the very possibility of belief in God."

Apologetics is actually an important activity in the history of the Church. Its goal is to show how reasonable faith is, or at least to demonstrate that faith is not against reason. Apologetics has come up with "proofs of God's existence," and with empirical evidence based on the fact that there is design, fine-tuning, intelligibility, rationality, and morality in this universe. Individually, these arguments may not provide conclusive evidence, but combined they make a strong case for the Catholic Faith. How could nature be intelligible if it were not created by an intelligent Creator? How could there be order in this world if there were no orderly Creator? How could there be scientific laws in nature if there were no rational Lawgiver? How could there be design in nature if there were no intelligent Designer? How could there be human minds if the universe itself were mindless?

The only *rational* answer to all of these "rhetorical" questions seems to be that there is indeed an intelligent, rational, orderly, lawgiving Creator God who made this universe the way it is. In this case, belief in a Creator God is more or less like "connecting the dots"—although some may connect the dots differently, and others may connect different dots. But the fact remains that belief in God makes the world much more understandable. C. S. Lewis beautifully summarized this: "I believe in Christianity as I believe that the sun has risen: not only because I see it, but because by it I see everything else."

So what then is the role of *reason* when it comes to faith? Thomas Aquinas summarizes what reason does for faith as follows: (1) reason prepares the mind for faith; (2) reason explains the truths of faith; (3) reason defends the truths of faith. This perspective on reason has a long history in the Catholic Church. It can be traced back to St. Anselm's two famous phrases (eleventh century), "Faith seeking understanding" and "I believe in order that I might understand." But it goes even further back to St. Augustine's two famous formulas (ca. 400), which express the coherent synthesis between faith and reason: "Believe in order to understand" (*Crede ut Intelligas*), but also, and inseparably, "Understand in order to believe" (*intellige ut credas*). In other words, in order to find God and believe, you must scrutinize truth *and* reason.

Some find this hard to accept. When the father of a college student heard his daughter was learning that theology was "Faith seeking understanding," he exclaimed: "But faith doesn't have to seek understanding—that's why they call it faith!" People like him seem to think that if God's existence were a matter of reason, then it would no longer be a matter of faith—therefore, it cannot be a matter of reason. Some Christians trace this erroneous idea back to the German Reformer Martin Luther. Although Luther did not place "faith" explicitly counter to reason, he did put it in opposition to any human efforts—with reasoning being one of them. Interestingly enough, entirely on his own, Luther added an extra word, "alone" (*allein* in German), to Romans 3:28 in his Bible translation: "For we hold that a man is justified by faith [alone] apart from works of the law." When challenged about this, Luther responded: "If your papist is annoyed with the word 'alone,' tell him straightway, Dr. Martin Luther will have it so."

Indeed, the Catholic conception of "faith and reason" is quite radical. What we know through reason can never be in conflict with what we know through faith, and what we know through faith can never be in violation of what we know through reasoning. Nevertheless, some people think that when we begin to use reason, we have no choice but to abandon faith; conversely, they think that if we have faith, we must leave reason behind. Aquinas argues the opposite. We should be faithful in our reasoning and reasonable in our faith—even when, or specifically when, it comes to God. We cannot live by faith alone or by reason alone, but only by a harmonious combination of faith *and* reason. Sometimes we need understanding before we can believe; at other times we need faith before we can understand. Faith tells us more than we could know by reason alone, so we need to become "faithful" in our reasoning. On the other hand, reason tells us more than we could know by faith alone, so we need to become "reasonable" in our faith.

It should not surprise us then that the Catholic Church follows St. Thomas Aquinas, a Doctor of the Church, in defending the principle that faith cannot be against reason. When something is against reason, God cannot create it. Aquinas is adamant on this issue because God is reason: He cannot act against His own nature by doing what is contradictory. God is absolutely free, but His freedom is not arbitrary, so He cannot go against what is true and right. We know this because our own power of reason is rooted in creation and thus participates in God's power of reason.

As a consequence, God's being all powerful does not mean that God is able to do what is logically contradictory. Aquinas gives many examples: God cannot create square circles; He cannot make someone blind and not blind at the same time; He cannot declare true what is false; He cannot undo something that happened in the past, and the list goes on. To use a silly example: God does not have the power to make a stone so heavy that He Himself cannot lift it—that would be contradictory, and therefore against reason. God cannot act against His own nature—and reason is part of His nature.

The *Catechism* summarizes all of this very nicely: "Though faith is above reason, there can never be any real discrepancy between faith and reason. Since the same God who reveals mysteries and infuses faith has bestowed the light of reason on the human mind, God cannot deny himself, nor can truth ever contradict truth" (159). In the words of Pope John Paul II, "Faith and reason are like two wings on which the human spirit rises to the contemplation of truth; and God has placed in the human heart a desire to know the truth—in a word, to know himself—so that, by knowing and loving God, men and women may also come to the fullness of truth about themselves." Combined, faith and reason form the cradle of truth. Therefore, we need to reject both a faith-alone approach and a reason-alone approach.

Let us come to a conclusion. Why should we believe something? Because others believe it? Not so! Because it feels good? Not so! The only reason is: because it is *true*. How do we know what is true? Faith can tell us so "from above," but faith can never rightly tell us what is against reason; and reason can tell us so "from below," but reason can never rightly tell us what is

Forty Anti-Catholic Lies

against faith. Reason tells us more than we could know by faith alone, and faith tells us more than we could know by reason alone. Reason needs to purify faith, and faith needs to purify reason. Discovering the truth through reason can never destroy faith, and discovering the truth through faith can never destroy reason. Therefore, we should always be "faithful" in our reasoning, and "reasonable" in our faith.

CONCLUSION

The answer to the question "Do Catholics use their heads?" is "Yes, they do and should." According to some Protestants, the answer is "Yes, even too much." Yet the Catholic Church holds on to her motto of faith and reason. Catholicism is arguably the most rational and coherent of all religions. When it comes to faith, Catholics are encouraged to use their heads. They don't believe that religious faith is immune to rational argumentation and scrutiny by reason. Catholics are thinkers: in believing they think, and in thinking they believe.

28

CATHOLICS STILL LIVE
IN THE DARK AGES

THE LIE

Catholics have never been able to pull themselves out of the grip
of the Dark Ages, when the Catholic Church was in charge, because they rejected the Enlightenment—an eighteenth-century
movement in Europe that challenged Catholic doctrines and
dogmas and could have opened their eyes for a new world.

They completely missed out on what people such as Voltaire,
Denis Diderot, Jean-Jacques Rousseau, David Hume, and Adam
Smith had tried to teach them: the overthrow of religion and
the rejection of traditional authority in favor of the development of free speech and thought. Because Catholics rejected
these ideas, they have never been able to pull themselves out
of the Dark Ages.

THE TRUTH

The terminology "Dark Ages" and "Middle Ages" is a little confusing and has changed over time. The idea of a "Dark Age" originated with Francesco Petrarch in the 1330s. Later, the Protestant

Reformers called all of the Middle Ages "dark," because they saw it as a time of corruption by the Catholic Church. Then followed the Enlightenment thinkers, who considered all that happened between the fall of Rome and the Enlightenment period an era of darkness. Nowadays, most historians make a distinction between the "Dark Ages" (ca. 500–ca. 1000) and the "Middle Ages" (ca. 1000–ca. 1500). Some rather speak of "Early Middle Ages" and "Late Middle Ages." What's in a name? Sometimes a lot.

If the "Dark Ages" were indeed "dark," that was not so because of the Catholic Church, but rather because of the massive and disruptive influx of invaders into Europe. The civilized world of the Roman Empire was overrun by uncivilized barbarians from outside the empire. As a matter of fact, the only reason any achievements, scientific and other, made it through these "dark" ages was because of the Catholic Church's hiding all her books from the rampaging and pillaging Huns, Vandals, Visigoths, and Vikings. Had it not been for the Catholic Church, all schools of learning and their libraries would have been lost during these "Dark Ages."

Some consider even the Middle Ages as a "dark" period. They usually do so because everything is considered dark that happened before the Enlightenment, when the reign of faith was finally ended and gave way to the so-called Age of Reason. They consider all that had happened between the fall of Rome and the Enlightenment period as an era of darkness under the control of the Catholic Church. This myth has even been perpetuated into the twenty-first century. Rather recently, the astronomer Carl Sagan, in one of his many books, makes it look as if nothing happened in the natural sciences between 415 and 1543.

However, when "enlightened" thinkers claim that there was no science at all during the "Dark Ages" and not even during the Middle Ages, they need to think twice (see chapter 30). It is becoming more and more evident, and has been accepted by a growing contingent of historians, that science was born in the Catholic cradle of the Middle Ages. The following list of some of its pioneer crafters testifies to this. As early as the seventh century, the English Benedictine monk Bede studied the sea's tidal currents. At the end of the first millennium, Pope Sylvester II had already used advanced instruments of astronomical observation, driven by a passion for understanding the order of the universe. He also endorsed and promoted study of arithmetic, mathematics, and astronomy, reintroducing to Europe the abacus and armillary sphere, which had been lost to Europe since the end of the Greco-Roman era. He is also said to be the first to introduce in Europe the decimal numeral system using Arabic numerals. All of these would be important tools for science. The currently rather popular idea that classic Greek texts had been lost in Europe during the Middle Ages and then were given back to Europe by Muslims ignores the fact that they had been preserved and transmitted by Catholic scholars such as Boethius, the monks of Mont Saint-Michel, William of Moerbeke, and Catholic Greeks in the Eastern part of the empire.

In fact, it is hard to ignore the role of the Catholic Church in preserving her intellectual heritage and promoting science during the Middle Ages. Even during the "Dark Ages," monasteries of that era were diligent in the study of medicine. As early as 633, the Council of Toledo required the establishment of a school in every diocese, teaching every branch of knowledge, including medicine. Then, around 800, King Charlemagne decreed that each monastery and cathedral chapter establish a school, and in these schools, medicine was commonly taught. It was at one of these schools that the later Pope Sylvester II taught medicine.

Clergy were active at the School of Salerno, the oldest medical school in Western Europe. Famous physicians and medical researchers included the abbot of Monte Cassino (Bertharius), the abbot of Reichenau (Walafrid Strabo), and the bishop of Rennes (Marbodius of Angers)—and last but not least, Hildegard of Bingen (1098–1179). Hildegard, a Doctor of the Church and one of the most distinguished of medieval Catholic women scientists, wrote a text on the natural sciences (*Physica*) and a text on "Causes and Cures" (*Causae et Curae*).

Science prospered even more during the next period, the so-called Middle Ages (ca. 1000–ca. 1500). During this era, Bishop Robert Grosseteste introduced the scientific method, including the concept of falsification, while the Franciscan friar Roger Bacon established concepts such as hypothesis, experimentation, and verification. In other words, the scientific project—even the scientific method itself—was an invention of these Catholic pioneers.

Had it not been for the Catholic Church, the scientific revolution would most likely never have happened. After all, science did not take root in South America, Africa, the Middle East, or Asia—it took place in Christian Europe. It was during the Middle Ages that the first universities arose. The Middle Ages were, of course, Catholic, so these first universities of the world were Catholic universities. They were the hotbed for a period of great technological and scientific advancements, as well as achievements in nearly all other fields of knowledge.

When the French physicist Pierre Duhem (1861–1916) studied the works of Catholic medieval mathematicians and philosophers, such as John Buridan, Nicholas of Oresme, and Roger Bacon, their sophistication surprised him. He consequently came to regard them as the founders of modern science, since they had, in his view, anticipated many of the discoveries of Galileo and later scientists (see chapter 31). Thus, he came to regard the medieval scholastic tradition of the Catholic Church as the origin of modern science. Duhem had to come to the conclusion that "the mechanics and physics of which modern times are justifiably proud [came] from doctrines professed in the heart of the medieval schools." Needless to say, those schools were undeniably Catholic.

Pierre Duhem did pathfinding work in the history of science when he showed that the doctrines of the Church have been a permanent ally of, rather than an obstacle to, the success of the scientific enterprise in the West. He opened the eyes of many to the fact that it was actually the often-despised metaphysical framework of medieval Catholicism that made modern science possible.

Many historians of science and other scholars would later follow his lead. The sociologist Rodney Stark, for instance, argues that the reason science arose in Europe, and nowhere else, is because of Catholicism: "It is instructive that China, Islam, India, ancient Greece, and Rome all had a highly developed alchemy. But only in Europe did alchemy develop into chemistry. By the same token, many societies developed elaborate systems of astrology, but only in Europe did astrology lead to astronomy." So Stark was forced to come to the conclusion that "science was not the work of Western secularists or even deists; it was entirely the work of persons who were devout believers in an active, conscious, creator God."

In other words, the claim that Catholics still live in the "Dark Ages" has no leg to stand on. History shows us that medieval Catholics created a hotbed for science, personally contributed to scientific achievements, and honored and spread scientific advances through their schools and colleges. Another name that should be mentioned in this context is that of St. Albert the Great (*Albertus Magnus*), the teacher of St. Thomas Aquinas. Albert (1193–1280) had quite a scientific track record for his time: he discovered the element arsenic; he experimented with photosensitive chemicals, including silver nitrate; and he made disciplined observations in plant anatomy and animal embryology.

Although Thomas Aquinas (1225–1274) himself was more directly focused on philosophy and theology than on science, he was certainly indirectly involved with science. He addressed many problems we would now assign to astronomy, physics, chemistry, and the life sciences. For instance, he regarded gravitation as the natural motion of a heavy object to its natural place but denied that it was caused by some absolute principle. In this he implicitly rejected the absolute space and attractive forces later proposed by Newton's followers, and opted instead for relational concepts that have more affinity with those of modern relativity theory.

Aquinas also took up the problems of magnets as well as tidal variations and was intent on reducing them to natural, instead of occult, causes. In astronomy, this man who has been vilified as a "geocentrist" voiced his expectation that Ptolemy's theory would one day be superseded by a simpler explanation, since all such theories are based on hypothetical reasoning. In Aquinas's own words, "Maybe the phenomena of the stars can be explained by some other schema not yet discovered by men" (see chapter 31). In the life sciences, St. Thomas wrote a treatise on the heart in an attempt to trace lines of causality of blood in motion.

One could even make the case that Aquinas touched on chemical issues and thus prepared the ground for chemistry. Based on the doctrine of so-called *minima naturalia* (the smallest parts into which a homogeneous natural substance could be divided while still retaining its essential character), he indirectly contributed to the development of atomistic, corpuscular theories in science. He taught how elements are present in compounds, holding that they are not present there actually or potentially, but only "virtually." So, while there is only one substance that results from the composition of various elements, the new substance has the combined powers of the elements that came together in its composition—which makes for a new compound, instead of a mixture of the original elements.

To explain this with a modern example: when the substances hydrogen and oxygen change into a new substance, water (H_2O), the change cannot be attributed merely to the rearrangement of the elements involved. The two elements are present in themselves as gases before change takes place. Since change does occur, some different substance comes to be. If it were the elements that caused the change, two gases in themselves would be substantially the same as water, which they are not. Besides, hydrogen and oxygen can be rearranged to make things other than water, such as hydrogen peroxide (H_2O_2). These elements in themselves are not the reason hydrogen and oxygen, when combined, produce water. The essence of water is different from the essence of either hydrogen or oxygen, and each of these essences is different from the other. In other words, although Aquinas did not work with chemicals, he did prepare a significant analysis of such work. And the list could go on and on.

But there is another reason Aquinas was crucial for the upcoming rise of science. He saw very clearly the possibility of a science that does not depend on divine revelation but is based merely on sensory experience and the intellectual processing of that experience. This opened the way for an autonomous, rational enterprise called science. He also anticipated its future diversity. The different scientific disciplines we know today are generated by the fact that we can consider the things of nature from different perspectives. Aquinas holds that the division of sciences can be accounted for by the power of *abstraction*, which allows the intellect to leave out of consideration certain characteristics. Social scientists, for instance, can study behavioral processes of human beings, while abstracting from their physiological processes, such as heartbeat. It is also through abstraction that the knowledge of a single individual human being, based on concrete sensorial experience, can become usable for *all* human beings. Even the technique of representative sampling, for instance, is based on this idea. All of this makes science a universal enterprise. It is at the heart of science to use generalizations in relation to individuals.

It is thanks to Catholic thinkers such as Albert the Great and Thomas Aquinas, and many others, that the basis for the later scientific revolution was laid. So it is hard to believe that Catholic thinkers like them were still living in the "Dark Ages." They turned the light on for us. They made many other Catholics see the light and follow them to play a pivotal role in the further advancement of science. To name just a few: Canon Nicolaus Copernicus (heliocentric solar system), Abbot Gregor Mendel (quantitative genetics), Bishop Nicolas Steno (stratigraphy and modern geology), and Monsignor Georges Lemaître (the big bang theory).

Yet, most of this has been kept secret from people living in the third millennium. The nuclear physicist Stephen Barr testifies to this: "Ask a Catholic audience whose name they associate with the Catholic Church and science. 'Galileo!' they shout. Ask them about Lemaître, Grimaldi, Stensen, Secchi—or Piazzi—and you get blank stares. Is it any wonder the science-religion warfare myth persists?" Indeed, this myth keeps repeating that the Catholic Church is still living in the "Dark Ages." They are "dark" only for those who have not seen the light yet and are still living in "darkness" themselves.

CONCLUSION

Catholics do *not* live in the "Dark Ages." The so-called Dark Ages were not so dark as many try to make us believe. The term is actually a creation of the Enlightenment, which sought to make all that happened between the fall of Rome and the Enlightenment look like an era of darkness. Nothing is further from the truth. It was actually the Catholic Church that protected and maintained culture, literature, and knowledge against the invading Huns, Vandals, Visigoths, and Vikings during this time. It has actually been shown that science was born in the Catholic cradle of the Middle Ages. Had it not been for the Catholic Church, the scientific revolution would most likely never have happened. So it does not make sense to say that Catholics were never able to pull themselves out of the grip of the "Dark Ages."

29

CATHOLICS BELIEVE IN DOUBLE TRUTH

THE LIE

Catholics who believe in science as well as in religion are "schizophrenics" who celebrate religion on Sundays and science on weekdays. When they are occupied with science, they are critical, look for proofs, and believe something only if it has been proven. Then on Sundays, while on their way to church, they turn a mental switch. In the pews, they set their understanding to zero and their gaze on infinity. They swallow everything without any proof.

THE TRUTH

There are not different truths for Sunday and for weekdays. There is only one truth, but there are two ways of getting to the truth: by *reason* and by *faith*. This does not mean, though, that one set is for Sundays in church and the other set is for weekdays while on the job. And certainly they are not the Sunday truths versus weekday truths that anti-Catholics talk about.

No matter how we distinguish them, what they all have in common is this: truth is truth, even if you do not accept it; and untruth is untruth, even if you claim it. Truth is truth—for everyone, anywhere, at any time. It is a matter of fact that the earth is round; believing that it is flat does not make it flat. Likewise, it is a fact that God exists; believing that He does not exist does not make Him disappear. Indeed, Catholicism is not just a personal, private feeling but rather a conviction about facts and truths, as, for instance, stated in a Creed: "I believe in ..." To put it more directly, God's existence is not dependent on our experience of Him. God either exists or He doesn't—that's not a matter of opinion or feeling. You can have your own opinions and feelings, but you can't have your own facts. Frank Cronin of Aquinas College expresses this as follows: "If it turns out God doesn't exist, it isn't that our faith was wrong—our facts were wrong.... Our faith is wrong because we got the facts wrong."

The distinction between natural truths that we gain through *reason* and supernatural truths that we gain through *faith* has quite some consequences. When we speak of faith and reason (see chapter 27)—or theology and philosophy, or religion and science—we are making a distinction, not a separation. We can distinguish them without putting them in conflict with each other. Human truth comes from so-called natural revelation based on reason, whereas divine truth comes from so-called special revelation based on faith. Something similar can be said about science and religion: science masquerading as religion is as unseemly as religion masquerading as science. Instead, they convey two very different kinds of truth. Science has *theories* to help us understand, but they are subject to change—so let us not make science more than what it is. Religion, on the other hand, has *dogmas* we try to understand, but they never change—so let us not make religion less than what it is. Truth is truth, but we may not fully understand the truth yet.

The moment we try to mix up or merge science and religion, religion usually ends up being at the mercy of science. All attempts of merging science and religion into one concoction can easily be seen as trying to create a mixture of "oil and water"—two components that just do not mix well. Yet some people like this mix. They tend to speak in terms of "reconciliation," as if science and religion were just two different ways of expressing the same truth. Such people basically want to "reconcile" the data of religion with the data of science—which usually means that science annexes religion by "interpreting" the data of religion so as to leave the data of science intact. That puts religion at the losing end.

The reason some promote this move is that scientific facts are considered to be "safe" and "proven." Hence, the latest scientific developments are supposed to lead to a revamping of religious doctrine. However, there is no reason religion should necessarily bend to the criteria of science. Science cannot claim such authority (see chapter 35). First of all, science is not omnicompetent—it's not a know-all or cure-all. Science has a rather narrow scope restricted to what can be measured, dissected, counted, and quantified. But there is so much more that cannot be measured, dissected, counted, or quantified. That's why the late University of California at Berkeley philosopher of science Paul Feyerabend, for instance, could say that "science should be taught as one view among many and not as the one and only road to truth and reality." Even the "positivistic" philosopher Gilbert Ryle expressed a similar view: "The nuclear physicist, the theologian, the historian, the lyric poet and the man in the street produce very different, yet compatible and even complementary pictures of one and the same 'world.'" Science provides only one of these views. The astonishing successes of science have not been gained by answering every kind of question, but precisely by refusing to do so.

There is another reason science cannot claim absolute authority. What we call "proven" scientific knowledge is proven only until a new set of empirical data disproves what was previously considered proven. Francis Crick, one of the two scientists who discovered DNA, couldn't have said it better: "A theory that fits all the facts is bound to be wrong, as some of the facts will be wrong." In science, whatever is thought to be true today may no longer be thought to be true tomorrow.

Here is just a small selection of scientific theories that were believed to be true but sooner or later turned out to be false. (1) The expanding-earth hypothesis stated that continental drift could be explained by the fact that the planet was gradually growing larger. (2) Prior to the notion that the universe was created as the result of the big bang, it was commonly believed that the size of the universe was an unchanging constant. (3) For some thirty years, the number of human chromosomes was supposed to be forty-eight, until it was found to be forty-six in 1955. (4) Until the mid-twentieth century, most paleoanthropologists preferred Asia over Africa as the continent where the first hominids evolved.

Science is always a work in progress. Religion, on the other hand, is very different from science. What is true of Catholic doctrine today will also be true tomorrow. But not so in science: science is always an ongoing process, perhaps even never-ending; what is true today may have to be revised tomorrow based on new or better tests and experiments. Scientists must submit their minds to the data of experiment; religious believers must submit theirs to the data of revelation.

The contrast we painted here may raise some questions. It is easy to see that what is true today in science may have to be revised tomorrow. But would this not also be true of Catholic doctrine? Didn't the Church have to revise her interpretations of the Bible regarding the place of the earth and of human life in the universe? The answer depends on what we mean when we speak about revelation. That's because, over time, we are granted a fuller and fuller knowledge of God in general by coming better to understand the meaning of prior revelation. For instance, the New Testament did not abolish the truth of the Old Testament but extends and deepens it. Although revelation came to its fullest manifestation in Jesus Christ, its understanding would still need further completion. Many of the central doctrines of Christianity, including the Trinitarian nature of God, the divinity of Jesus, the Incarnation of Jesus, and the perpetual virginity of Mary, only gradually became clear in the centuries following Jesus' death (see chapter 3). As we said earlier, this process of growth resembles the way a river grows—it gets wider and deeper, while remaining the same river.

During this continuing process, some truths were proclaimed by the Church as divinely revealed, so they became dogmas. Dogmas must be held by all as essential for Catholic faith. Hence, the Church cannot deny in one age what she has affirmed in a previous age as essential dogma. But this does not hold for scientific theories. Heliocentrism, for instance, has never been declared a dogma, and evolution will never be declared a dogma. Our salvation does not depend on whether we believe in heliocentrism, evolution, or any other scientific theory; instead it depends on what God has revealed to us in Scripture and Tradition.

One more question should be addressed in this context: If there are indeed two kinds of truths—natural versus supernatural—can they be in conflict with each other? At the time of Thomas Aquinas, Islamic philosophers had introduced the idea that there can be "double truth." The concept of double truth meant that religious knowledge and philosophical knowledge may arrive at different, contradictory truths, but without detriment to either. By placing the "truths" of philosophy and science in one category and the "truths" of faith and religion in another, one could hold mutually exclusive positions as long as one believes that the opposing views are in separate departments of the mind—one for Sundays and one for weekdays, if you will.

In Islam, Allah could will one thing today and its opposite tomorrow. His latest affirmation is always the binding one, but it can change the following day. According to this view, since truth is not grounded in reasoning, but in "willing," the only way we could know that the sun will rise in the morning is if Allah wills it and we believe it. This means that we cannot really rely on "nature" for anything.

Aquinas considered this view unsustainable. He saw with utter clarity that all truth comes from God, and therefore there can never be, ultimately, any conflict between the outcome of reason and the beliefs of faith, or between the data of the sciences and the facts of revelation, or between philosophical truths and theological truths. He claimed that faith and reason, or theology and philosophy, play, in his own words, "complementary roles in the quest for truth. Grace does not destroy nature but fulfills it."

We have the Catholic Church and St. Thomas to thank for constantly reminding us that all truth is God's truth and is therefore universal, global, and permanent. God has revealed Himself both in the Scriptures and in the natural world. Therefore, if we find a seeming contradiction between the two, we have not understood correctly either the Scriptures or the natural world, or both.

Perhaps a few examples may demonstrate how important the rejection of "double truth" is. Since there are truths of reason as well as truths of faith—which can never contradict each other—it cannot be that the earth is flat according to faith and religion, but at the same time spherical according to reason and science, for that would create a contradiction. In a similar way, if science tells us that the earth circles the sun, it cannot be true that the sun circles the earth. In all such cases we are dealing with contradictions that cannot both be true at the same time, given the fact that there is no "double truth." When we detect a "double truth," either one or both must have been claimed in error and must be reevaluated.

One word of caution, though. Sometimes we might think we have a "double truth" when, in fact, we do not. For instance, creation as understood by faith versus the big bang theory as understood by science do not contradict each other. The big bang is about the *beginning* of the universe—about how physical interactions came about—whereas faith in creation is about the *origin* of the universe—about how the universe is dependent on God (see chapter 32). Here is another example: creation, as understood by faith, versus evolution, as understood by science, do not contradict each other. Creation is about how natural causes are related to God, whereas evolution deals with how natural causes are related to each other through reproduction and natural selection (see chapter 33). The same can be said about randomness in science and providence in faith. Randomness is about how events can be related to each other, whereas providence is about how events can be related to God (see chapter 34). So we do not need to make a choice between two truths in these cases because there is no problem of "double truth" here.

The importance of the rejection of "double truth" can be seen when we weigh it against contrary views. Some believers—such as the Protestant Martin Luther in his more excitable moments—have held that faith at all times trumps reason. Others have held—especially so nowadays—that science must always trump faith if religion is to survive in the modern world. Contrary to these views, Thomas Aquinas and the Catholic Church claim that the truths of faith must agree with the truths of science, because God is author of both, and so any apparent conflict shows that we have failed to understand one or the other, or both. If something is true in philosophy or science, it must also be true in the Christian faith. Truth is truth, for all truth is God's truth. But we may not fully grasp the truth yet.

CONCLUSION

Catholics do *not* believe in "double truth." In Catholicism, there are no truths for Sunday and different truths for weekdays. Truths can never be in contradiction to each other. The truth is also that truth cannot be established by a majority vote. The idea of "many truths" is as detrimental to our cognitive health as the notion of "double truth." This is, in fact, a core principle of the Catholic religion, which sets it apart from practically all other religions. All truth comes from God, and therefore there can never be, ultimately, any conflict between the outcome of reason and the beliefs of faith, or between the data of the sciences and the facts of revelation, or between philosophical truths and theological truths.

30

CATHOLICS HAVE HELD SCIENCE BACK

THE LIE

The Catholic Church has been a constant hindrance to scientific development. For centuries, science had to wage a war against this old behemoth. Without the Catholic Church, science could have done much better.

No wonder some Catholics still adhere to the Bible in saying that the earth is flat and that the sun revolves around the earth. They let their faith decide what science should tell us.

THE TRUTH

First of all, the Catholic Church never made dogmatic statements about the shape of the earth or the position of the earth in the universe. It is not the Church's task to make scientific statements—that's not her expertise. She teaches how to go to Heaven, not how the heavens go. Our salvation does not depend on whether we believe in heliocentrism, evolution, man-made global warming, or any other scientific theory. Therefore, something like geocentrism was never and will never be declared a dogma, and the same holds true for other scientific theories. The Church can change her position on such issues, if need be, without affecting any dogma—for they are dogma-neutral (see chapter 29).

But it must also be stated that from the earliest times the Church always kept open the possibility that the earth is not flat or that the sun does not orbit the earth. As to a flat earth: anti-Catholic propaganda still has some of us believing that at the time of Galileo, the Catholic Church was of the opinion that the earth was flat (see chapter 31). Nothing is further from the truth. Hardly anyone at the time, and certainly not Church officials, believed the earth was flat. Pythagoras (500 B.C.), and others had already shown that the earth was a sphere, centuries earlier. Although St. Basil the Great declared it a matter of no interest to us whether the earth is a sphere or a cylinder or a disk, or concave in the middle like a fan, influential Christian thinkers such as St. Clement, Origen, St. Ambrose, St. Augustine, and St. Thomas Aquinas all accepted that the earth was a globe.

As to an orbiting earth: long before Galileo, some members of the Church had already suggested the earth was in motion. In the fourteenth century, Bishop Nicholas of Oresme showed that the apparent daily motion of the sun about the earth could be satisfactorily explained by rotation of the earth on its axis. And in the fifteenth century, Cardinal Nicolas of Cusa even speculated that all bodies, including both the earth and the sun, were in motion in an infinite universe that had no center. The Catholic Polish astronomer Nicolaus Copernicus (1473–1543) was the first one after the Middle Ages to publish the idea of a heliocentric model, suggesting that the earth orbited the sun.

Most notably, we should also mention what St. Thomas Aquinas thought about this problem some four centuries before

Galileo. He astutely noticed that the appearance of the visible motions of the celestial bodies "are produced either by the motion of the object seen or by the motion of the observer.... It makes no difference which one is moving." In other words, the sun could be moving, or we could be moving. Elsewhere, Aquinas says about the geocentric Ptolemaic astronomers of his time, "The suppositions that these men have invented need not necessarily be true." Apparently, Aquinas understood that the Ptolemaic theory was just that, a theory, and that there could be other theories. So some four centuries before Galileo, St. Thomas was ready to accept that Ptolemy's theory would one day be superseded by a simpler explanation, since all such theories are changeable and based on hypothetical reasoning.

So it is definitely a myth to make the sweeping claim that the Catholic Church has always obstructed science from doing its work. One could even make the opposite case: that the Catholic Church has made the rise of science actually possible.

How so?

The Catholic Church has always been very favorable to the enterprise that today we call science. The Church and the scientific community have a long-standing relationship with each other—actually, an existential relationship: without the Catholic Church, there would most likely not be any science. The case could be made that science, as we know it today, was born in the cradle of the Catholic Church, which might explain why it was not born anywhere else—not in China (with its sophisticated society), not in India (with its philosophical schools), not in Arabia (with its advanced mathematics), not in Japan (with its dedicated craftsmen and technologies), but on Judeo-Christian soil with Judeo-Christian roots (see chapter 28). Whereas almost every culture or religion has given rise to inventions and some form of technology—for one doesn't have to be a Christian to invent the wheel—science and scientific exploration of the world around us were nurtured in a culture with a distinct Judeo-Christian tradition.

The idea that Christianity gave rise to science might surprise many, as it did Alfred North Whitehead's Harvard audience in 1925, when this famous mathematician and philosopher told them that modern science was a product of Christianity. They were shocked, probably out of mere ignorance. But the idea was not new, and certainly not flimsy. As was said earlier, one of the first to be aware of the Catholic roots of science was Pierre Duhem (see chapter 28). No wonder then that many scientists have thanked the Catholic Church for her support. The nuclear physicist J. Robert Oppenheimer—not a Christian himself—had to acknowledge, "Christianity was needed to give birth to modern science."

Even someone like the philosopher of science Thomas Kuhn had to say about Europe—without identifying its Judeo-Christian heritage, though—"No other place and time has supported that very special community from which scientific productivity comes." But there are still many people who are not aware of these facts. The historian of science Edward Grant is probably right in stating that the gift from the Latin Middle Ages to the modern world "is a gift that may never be acknowledged. Perhaps it will always retain the status it has had for the past four centuries as the best-kept secret of Western civilization."

Why was the Catholic Church such a fertile hotbed for the emergence of science? In the Catholic mind-set, the universe is (1) the creation of a rational Intellect and (2) capable of being rationally interrogated. It is this very Judeo-Christian concept of a Creator God that makes science possible. Belief in a Creator

God entails that nature is not a divine but a created entity. Nature is not divine in itself; only its Maker is—which opens the door for scientific exploration. Without this belief, we would not be allowed to even "touch" the divine. A created world, by definition, is not divine in itself; it is other than God, and in that very otherness, scientists find their freedom to act. A rational God has created a universe that we can explore with our rational minds, made in the likeness of God's mind. The book of Wisdom (11:20) says about God, "Thou hast arranged all things by measure and number and weight." Hence, the only way to find out what the Creator has actually done is to go out, look, and measure—which opens the door for scientific exploration. It requires the "humility" of scientists to wait for and subject themselves to the outcome of their explorations.

It could also be argued that a tendency toward a different conception of divine causality, which distinguishes Judeo-Christian religion from other religions, is exactly what might explain why natural science improved in the West and weakened, or even was lacking, in the rest of the world. Because the Judeo-Christian God is a reliable God—not confined inside the Aristotelian box, not capricious like the Olympians in ancient Greece, and not entirely beyond human comprehension, as in Islam—the world depends on the laws that He has laid down in creation. Faith in this one God changes the universe, once inhabited with spirits, deities, and goddesses, into something "rational." In the Catholic view, only God is the source of the order as well as the intelligibility of the universe (see chapter 27).

The only way to find out what this order looks like is to "interrogate" the universe by investigation, exploration, and experiment. The door for science has been widely opened ever since. It is through scientific experiments that we can "read" God's mind, so to speak. It is this Catholic understanding that the world is both good and intelligible to us that laid the foundation for science and for Western society to pass on to successive generations the scientific discoveries that were made. Pagan cultures, on the other hand, hold a view of the world that inhibited scientific advancement, as they don't view the world as rational. They view things as being controlled by numerous, often whimsical, gods and magical powers. They don't view the world as something that is governed by laws of nature accessible to the human mind and waiting for discovery.

CONCLUSION

Catholics have *not* held science back. The Catholic Church is certainly not anti-science but has actually propelled the scientific enterprise. However, she does have a problem with the claim that science is all there is. Science may be everywhere, but science is not all there is—there is more to life than science. So the myth that the Catholic Church is anti-science is exactly that, a myth, a lie, and a fabrication. Science has religious, even Catholic roots; neither Catholicism nor science can ever sever those roots. All scientists are still living off Judeo-Christian capital, although many of them, sadly, may have lost awareness of this fact.

31

CATHOLICS LOST THE CASE AGAINST GALILEO

THE LIE

The Galileo affair nowadays is prima facie evidence that the free pursuit of truth became possible only after science had "liberated" itself from the theological and philosophical shackles of the Catholic Church.

The Catholic Church may have "won" the case by prosecuting, muzzling, incarcerating, and finally executing Galileo (1564–1642), but ultimately she was on the losing end. She ended up losing the case against Galileo, whereas Galileo himself still stands tall.

THE TRUTH

The Galileo case has spawned a whole conglomerate of myths, which obscure the facts about Galileo. Although conventional wisdom asserts that the controversy was simply a clash between Galileo's heliocentric theory and the traditional outdated view that the sun revolves around earth, there was a lot more going on than simply a disagreement about astronomy. Here is what is wrong with those myths.

1. Galileo did *not* discover that the earth is round. Many had done so long before Galileo was born. Columbus faced trouble going west not because his sailors thought they would sail off the edge of the world, but because they rightly thought that the distance between Europe and the East Indies was much greater than Columbus did. Even Aristotle had already come up with the following line of reasoning based on lunar eclipses: since it is the interposition of the earth that causes the eclipse, the form of this line will be caused by the form of the earth's surface, which is therefore spherical—and not flat. Aristotle did not have to wait for Galileo to come to this conclusion.

2. Galileo did *not* invent the telescope. When he heard about the invention of the "telescope" in Holland—called a "spyglass" there—he immediately built one for himself, characteristically taking full credit for the invention. But his telescope was still rather primitive. Soon the Jesuit Christopher Clavius of the Roman College was using an improved telescope, until Fr. Christoph Grienberger (sometimes spelled Gruemberger) invented a telescope in 1620 that rotated on an axis parallel to the earth's. The rather primitive features of Galileo's telescope partially explain why even Galileo himself had to concede, in a letter to Johannes Kepler, that many people were unable to see what they were "supposed" to see through his telescope. When Galileo demonstrated his simple telescope to a group of professors in Bologna in 1610, all admitted that the instrument seemed to deceive, with some fixed stars actually seen double. Of course, this raises also the question of how reliable Galileo's observations were. Optical illusions are not uncommon in science. Percival Lowell, founder of the Lowell Observatory, believed, on the basis

of "careful scientific observation," that there were Martian-made canals on Mars.

3. Galileo was *not* the first to advance heliocentrism. Nicolas Copernicus (1473–1543) was in fact the first astronomer after the Middle Ages to publish the idea of a heliocentric model, suggesting that the earth orbited the sun. In 1543, Copernicus had published *On the Revolution of the Celestial Orbs*, in which he supported heliocentricity—which was almost a century before Galileo "launched" his heliocentrism. So there was nothing really new "under the sun" with Galileo's claim. Actually, as early as the third century B.C., Aristarchus of Samos proposed a serious model of a heliocentric solar system.

4. Galileo did *not* prove heliocentrism. What he badly needed for his theory was what he could not provide—proof that his theory was true. The proof he came up with was actually nonsense. In his desperation, Galileo fabricated his theory of the tides, which purported to show that the tides are caused by the rotation of the earth. Even some of Galileo's friends could see that this was highly problematic, but Galileo plainly rejected the idea that the moon was a causal factor here.

On the other hand, Galileo could not solve the most serious problem heliocentrism was facing: an argument that had been made nearly two thousand years earlier by Aristotle himself. If the earth did orbit the sun, the philosopher wrote, then there would be a shift in the position of a star observed from the earth on one side of the sun, and then six months later from the other side—the so-called stellar parallaxes. Given the technology of Galileo's time, no such shifts in their positions could possibly be observed at the time, as it would require more sensitive measuring equipment that was not available until 1838. But the problem was still there.

5. Galileo was *not* an impartial scientist. He was consistent in ignoring the existence of alternative theories for what he tried to explain. He completely neglected the heliocentric model of Johannes Kepler, which had the planets move in ellipses instead of circles—which would turn out to be more accurate than Galileo's model. Second, there was also the geocentric model of Tycho Brahe. Brahe had the moon and the sun revolve around the earth (geocentrism), but the other planets (Mercury, Venus, Mars, Jupiter, and Saturn) revolve around the sun (heliocentrism); so he had the sun with those planets together revolve around the earth. Interestingly enough, Tycho's system did fit all the prevailing data and was mathematically identical to Galileo's system for all observations available at the time. Yet, all his life, Galileo ignored Tycho's system; he never mentioned it in any of his writings. But the Jesuits of the Roman College did not and could not ignore Tycho's model—they actually favored it as a halfway solution, which did not mean that they plainly rejected Galileo's model.

6. Galileo was *not* silenced by anti-scientists. Even his closest colleagues were not as convinced as he was about the validity of his heliocentrism. One can't even say that the Church condemned his theory. The Church and her Inquisition do not deal with disputes in science—only with controversies in theology, about matters of orthodoxy and heresy (see chapter 24). Because the inquisitors in the case were very aware that they were not competent to evaluate the scientific case, they decided in 1615 to consult their own experts for an opinion on the status of heliocentrism. They followed proper procedure by requesting expert opinions on the matter. Had the scientific experts been unanimous in their support of Galileo's model, perhaps the theologians would have bowed to their authority. But the scientific

community was divided herself — Tycho, Galileo, or Kepler? The scientific case was far from settled at the time.

7. Galileo did *not* have an open mind. We mentioned already how he kept silent about other astronomical theories, but he also was not willing to listen to wise advice. The main inquisitor, the Jesuit cardinal St. Robert Bellarmine, had pointed out to Galileo that it is perfectly acceptable to maintain Copernicanism, and thus Galileo's model, as a working hypothesis, but not necessarily as a theory about reality. But Galileo was not willing to accept Bellarmine's suggestion. He refused to present his theory as merely a hypothesis instead of established truth. He refused the reasonable third alternative, that heliocentrism might be considered a hypothesis until further proof could be given. Instead Galileo was intent on ramming heliocentrism down the throat of Christendom. And when Galileo deliberately ventured into theological territory, he was asking for more trouble. His friend Cardinal Dini had already warned him that he could write freely so long as he "kept out of the sacristy." But Galileo had his mind set.

8. Galileo did *not* mutter, "And yet it moves" — referring to a revolving earth — after he was sentenced by the Inquisition to keep silent on the subject for the rest of his life. This one-liner is a complete fabrication that suddenly popped up in a book written by Giuseppe Baretti, more than 120 years after Galileo's death. It gave at least a dramatic twist to the Galileo case that would live on for centuries to come. Myths can live a long life.

9. Galileo was *not* burned at the stake, nor was he tortured or incarcerated. Voltaire's line that Galileo "groaned away his days in the dungeons of the Inquisition" is a complete fabrication made up by an anti-Catholic. In fact, Galileo was never tortured, sentenced to death, or imprisoned. After a period with

the friendly Ascanio Piccolomini, the archbishop of Siena, Galileo was allowed to return to his villa at Arcetri near Florence in 1634, where he spent the last eight years of his life under house arrest. As the late Harvard mathematician and philosopher Alfred North Whitehead put it, "In a generation which saw the Thirty Years' War and remembered Alva in the Netherlands, the worst that happened to men of science was that Galileo suffered an honorable detention and a mild reproof, before dying peacefully in his bed."

10. Galileo was condemned by the Church not for his astronomy but for promoting a theory that seemingly contradicts Scripture as being certain, true, and proven, while not offering sufficient scientific evidence or mentioning any alternatives. To paint him as a "martyr" for science requires quite some imagination. May we consider the case closed?

CONCLUSION

The Catholic Church did not really lose the case against Galileo. A cloud of myths and lies obscures the facts about Galileo: he did not discover that the earth is round; he did not invent the telescope; he was not the first to advance heliocentrism; he did not prove heliocentrism; he was not silenced by anti-scientists; he was not tortured by the Inquisition; he was not incarcerated by the Inquisition; he did not mutter, "And yet the earth moves." Instead, what was condemned by the Church was not so much Galileo's science but proclaiming himself an expert in theological matters and promoting a theory that seemingly contradicts Scripture as certain, true, and proven, but without sufficient scientific evidence.

32

CATHOLICS ARE TROUBLED BY THE BIG BANG

THE LIE

The big bang not only caused an "explosion" at the beginning of our universe, but it also "exploded" what Catholics had thought for centuries about creation.

The idea of "creation out of nothing" (*creatio ex nihilo*) — taught in 1215 by the Fourth Lateran Council — is no longer a religious or philosophical concept that requires a Creator. We know now that cosmology has come up with a better present-day replacement of the "old" creation story. There is only one conclusion left: the big bang has left nothing for a creator to do. It has made the Catholic idea of a creator obsolete.

THE TRUTH

All the evidence available today seems to indicate that the universe has not always existed, but that it had a beginning, called the big bang, about fourteen billion years ago. That in itself is quite amazing, for there is no logical contradiction in the notion of an *eternal* but created universe. An eternal universe would be no less dependent on God the Creator than a universe that has a beginning in time. Even if there had always been a universe that never "began," it could exist at any moment in time only because the Creator was causing it to. It could be possible, for instance, that explosions and collapses follow each other in an endless sequence of expanding and contracting. If that were the case, then the universe might have never had a beginning. Aristotle, for one, did not believe in a beginning of the universe.

But in 1215, the Fourth Lateran Council did teach that the universe was created "out of nothing at the beginning of time"—an idea that would have scandalized most ancient Greeks as well as most nineteenth-century scientists, but which is now a commonplace of modern cosmology. It is amazing that the Church, without any scientific input, knew long ago that the world has not only an ending but also a beginning.

What is it then that the big bang theory tells us about the beginning of the universe? Edwin Hubble discovered in 1929 that the distances to faraway galaxies were generally proportional to their redshifts. "Redshift" is a term used to describe situations in which an astronomical object is observed moving away from the observer, such that emission or absorption features in the object's spectrum are seen to have shifted toward longer (red) wavelengths. Hubble's observation was taken to indicate that all very distant galaxies and clusters have an apparent velocity directly away from our vantage point, and the farther away, the higher their apparent velocity. This phenomenon had already been suggested in 1927 by the Belgian priest, astronomer, and physicist George Lemaître of the Catholic University of Louvain. In 1931, Fr. Lemaître went even further and suggested that the evident expansion of the universe, if projected back in time, meant that the further in the past, the smaller the universe was, until at some finite time in the past all the mass of the universe was concentrated in a single point—a "primeval atom," in Lemaître's own words—where and when the fabric of time and space must have started.

It is partially thanks to the big bang theory that we can now raise the question of the beginning of time. According to science today, time is something that *began* at one point. How did it begin? That's where the confusion sets in. Did it begin "by spontaneous creation," as some scientists say, or "by creation out of nothing," as Catholics would say? We will never be able to settle this discussion if we don't make some clear distinctions first: What do we mean by "creation" and what do we mean by "nothing"?

Let's start with "nothing" first. The concept of "nothing" (*nihil*) is used very differently in physics from in philosophy and theology. "Nothing" in philosophy refers literally to "no thing," whereas in physics it is in fact something. When an electron and a positron collide, they can "annihilate" and thus change into "nothing" (*nihil*). What really happens when they annihilate is that they emit a burst of energetic photons—which is certainly not "nothing" in a metaphysical sense. On the other hand, the reverse can occur too; this happens when an "empty" space is filled with an electric field, but no particles. In that situation, there is a certain probability that suddenly an electron-positron pair will pop out of "empty" space. It happens by a process called "quantum tunneling," which causes a "system" to change from one "state" (an electric field without particles) into another "state" (a changed electric field with two particles). These are different "states," but of the same "system." However, it should be stressed that a pair of particles does not suddenly appear out of "nothing," but actually out of an electric field of an existing "system"—which, again, is not "nothing" in a philosophical sense.

So when some physicists say that a universe could suddenly pop into existence from "nothing" by a quantum fluctuation—a fluctuation of a primal vacuum—we should really question their terminology. William E. Carroll characterizes a primal vacuum succinctly when he says, "It is still something—how else could 'it' fluctuate?" We are dealing here again with a "system" that has a set of possible "states." There is here, for instance, a "no-universe state" that precedes a "one-universe state," so to speak. Obviously a state is a state, not "nothing." It is a specific "state" of a specific, complicated quantum "system" governed by definite laws. Stephen Barr uses the analogy of having a bank account with no money in it; even if we have "nothing" in the bank, we still have a bank, with all that comes with it, but it happens to be in a "no-money state" for us. This kind of "nothing" is different from having no bank account at all. Let's leave it at that.

In philosophy and theology, on the other hand, "nothing" is literally "no thing." Whenever something changes in the material world, there must be something that changes, for nothing comes from nothing. Plenty of nothing is still nothing—you can have "plenty" of it, but it is still nothing. When God creates something out of nothing, this "nothingness" in philosophy is not a highly unusual kind of exotic "stuff" that is more difficult to observe or measure than other things; it is not some kind of element that has not found a position yet on the periodic table; it is in no way a material thing at all that can change into something else, but it is actually the absence of anything—and therefore, in philosophy and theology, we cannot treat no thing (*nihil*) as a some thing.

To think that no thing can change itself into some thing would be sheer philosophical magic. No thing can possibly do so on its own. The idea that matter can cause itself and explain itself has rightly been caricatured by Boston College philosopher Peter Kreeft as a magical "pop theory," which has things pop into existence without any cause. Nothing can just pop itself into existence; it must have a cause, because it does not and cannot have the power to make itself exist. For something to create itself, or produce itself, it would have to exist before it came into existence—which is logically and philosophically impossible. In other words, the concept of "nothing" in philosophy is very different from the concept of "nothing" in science.

Let's tackle next the concept of "creation." Aquinas makes an important distinction between producing (*facere*) and creating (*creare*). Most people use these two terms interchangeably, but Aquinas advises us clearly to separate them. Science is about "producing" something from something else—it is about changes taking place in this universe. Creation, on the other hand, is about "creating" something out of nothing—which is not a change at all; certainly not a change from "nothing" to "something." In other words, God the Creator doesn't just take preexisting stuff and fashion it, as does the Demiurge in Plato's *Timaeus*. Nor does the Creator use some something called "nothing" and then create the universe out of that. Rather, God calls the universe into existence without using preexisting space, matter, time, or anything else.

Therefore, *creating* something "out of nothing" is not *producing* something out of nothing—which would be a conceptual mistake, for it treats "nothing" as some kind of something. In contrast, the Christian doctrine of creation "out of nothing" (*ex nihilo*) claims that God made the universe without making it out of anything. Creation has everything to do with the philosophical and theological question as to why things exist at all, before they can even undergo change. Consequently, creation—but certainly not the big bang—is the reason there is something rather than nothing (including something such as the law of gravity). Science is about producing something from *something* else; religion is about creating something out of *nothing*. Creation is not a change; it's a cause, but of a very different, indeed unique, kind—which St. Thomas called a Primary Cause (see chapter 34). The book of Wisdom (11:25) puts it this way, "How would anything have endured if thou hadst not willed it? Or how would anything not called forth by thee have been preserved?" To paraphrase Shakespeare, creation is about "to be or not to be."

Once we have clarified these two important concepts—"nothing" and "creation"—the late Stephen Hawking's idea of a "spontaneous creation" turns out to be sheer philosophical magic. How could the universe "create itself" out of nothing—not to mention cause itself? The law of gravity cannot do the trick, for before the universe could ever create itself, if even possible, we would have to have laws of physics—which are ultimately the set of laws that govern the existing, created universe. So the astrophysicist Hawking and his followers are actually saying that laws that govern an existing universe can generate that universe and bring it into existence, along with its laws of nature, all by themselves before either exists—which makes for a logical contradiction.

In other words, scientists such as Stephen Hawking and the physical chemist Peter Atkins use the magical pop-theory without blinking an eye when they promote, in their own words, the "emergence of everything from absolutely nothing." St. Thomas Aquinas would keep hammering on the distinction between producing and creating, or between changing and creating, or between something and nothing. Creation does not mean changing a "no thing" into a "some thing," or changing something into something else — as chemists change water into hydrogen and oxygen; it means bringing everything into being and existence. To be or not to be: that is indeed the question.

This disagreement between theologians and physicists is caused by terminological confusion. Those who claim that a "vacuum" can mathematically be described with a wave function — which they consider the quantum gravity equivalent of the quantum vacuum in quantum field theory — seem entirely to miss the point that such a wave function also is something rather than nothing. A vacuum is a physical "state," which is not "nothing" — but more like an empty bank account. So what we have here is a conceptual mix-up. A "vacuum" in physics is not "nothing," and "nothing" in philosophy is not a "vacuum"; these two terms are not the same but belong to very different vocabularies.

This leads us to a related issue. Obviously, the unfolding of the universe, starting with the big bang, is a process that plays in time and can be studied by the physical sciences. Creation, on the other hand, cannot follow a timeline, as time itself is a product of creation as well. Even Augustine knew this long ago, "There can be no time without creation." Albert Einstein basically confirmed this from a scientific perspective when he showed us that both time and space are aspects of the physical world, just as much as matter and energy. In point of fact, time can be manipulated in the laboratory. The presence of mass (and, more generally, energy) causes space-time to curve. Time and space are part of the *physical* world.

In this specific sense, creation must come "first" before any events, even a big bang, can follow. However, creation in itself is not an event at all, so it cannot literally come "first" in time. Creation concerns the *origin* of the universe—its source of being—not its *beginning* in time. Creation is not some distant event; instead it is the complete causing of the existence of everything that is—in the past, now, and in the future. So creation must come "first" in the order of primacy, not in the order of time.

Therefore, we cannot place creation at the beginning of time, since there is no time until time has been created. Creating time "at a certain time" is just tough to do! God Himself is timeless. Creation is not something that happened long ago in time, and neither is the Creator someone who did something in the distant past, because the Creator does something "at all times"—by keeping a contingent world in existence, continually and faithfully.

Whereas the universe may have a beginning and a timeline, creation itself does not have a beginning or a timeline; creation makes the beginning of the universe and its timeline possible. Creation creates chronology, but it is not a part of chronology. Therefore, if time started with the big bang, it does not make sense to ask what happened "before" the big bang, because there was no time until time had been created. William E. Carroll is right when he stresses that we should never confuse temporal *beginnings* with metaphysical *origins*.

If rightly understood, creation is not a "one-time deal," but instead it copes with the question as to where this universe ultimately comes from, how it came into being, and how it stays in existence. The answer is that it does not come from the big bang but may have started with the big bang. Without creation, there could not be anything—no big bang, no gravity, no evolution, not even a timeline. Creation sets the "stage" for all of these things to happen, and it keeps this world in existence.

CONCLUSION

Catholics do *not* feel troubled by the big bang theory—one of them actually launched the idea. Catholics know that the big bang did not "create" time, any more than it "created" gravity, let alone the law of gravity. Only creation *ex nihilo* does! Without a Creator there would literally be nothing. That's an insight the Catholic Church had already reached long ago—long before we knew anything about the big bang. She also knew that the universe had a beginning long before scientists were willing to accept that idea.

33

CATHOLICS BELIEVE IN A
SIX-DAY CREATION

THE LIE

The Catholic idea of a creation in six days is absurd. A creation done in six days rejects evolution and means that dinosaurs and humans had to live next to each other. If so, Noah must have had dinosaurs in his ark, making the ark more crowded than a sardine can, and it would have to be of the proportions of an ocean liner to harbor those huge dinosaurs as well.

This primitive idea led James Ussher, the archbishop of Armagh in the Church of Ireland, to calculate a chronology of the history of the world. Based on a literal reading of the Old Testament, Ussher deduced that the first day of creation began at nightfall on Saturday, October 22, 4004 B.C. How primitive!

THE TRUTH

Maybe some Catholics do believe in a six-day creation, but they are not *required* to do so by Catholic doctrine and are even discouraged from doing so. Nowhere and never has the Church officially declared that the world cannot be more than six millennia old—or any other number of years that some Christians have calculated.

First of all, the Catholic Church never did and never will declare dogmas regarding a particular scientific theory. There is no dogma of heliocentrism, nor a dogma of the big bang, nor a dogma of biological evolution: that's not her expertise. She has always been very mindful of St. Augustine's warning that it is "dangerous to have an infidel hear a Christian ... talking nonsense." This might also apply to something like biological evolution. Whether there is some form of biological evolution of the body is not the Church's key concern. She allows evolution but does not impose it.

The Catholic Church does not enforce a literal reading of all parts of the Bible. The Scriptures have many types of texts: prayers (Psalms), visions (Revelation), debates (Job), parables (parts of the Gospels), letters (St. Paul), and, of course, historical reports (Acts). But not everything in the Bible is a historical report. Writing more than a century ago, Pope Leo XIII (1878–1903) used a quote of St. Augustine when he said:

> The sacred writers, or to speak more accurately, the Holy Ghost "Who spoke by them, did not intend to teach men these things (that is to say, the essential nature of the things of the visible universe), things in no way profitable unto salvation." Hence they did not seek to penetrate the secrets of nature, but rather described and dealt with things in more or less figurative language, or in terms which were commonly used at the time, and which in many instances are in daily use at this day, even by the most eminent men of science.

So why do a number of Catholics still have a serious problem with evolution? Most likely, some Protestant groups have

Catholics believe in a six-day creation

persuaded them that they should have a problem. When Scripture is the one and only authority—*sola Scriptura* (see chapter 3)—then Scripture is seen to be completely infallible if taken literally. Years ago, many Catholics in the pews understood that evolution of the human body was somehow acceptable in Church teaching. What has changed recently is not Church teaching, nor science, but the fact that non-Catholic fundamentalists and Evangelicals now have an enormous impact on our culture, especially in North America—and so has their rejection of evolution, making Catholics feel as if they must be suspicious of evolution if they want to be "faithful" in their religion.

As a result of this, the theory of evolution has become highly suspect, even among some Catholics. Lost in this debate is the profound Catholic truth, affirmed by popes and theologians from the earliest Church until today, that science can never conflict with the truths of faith—not even evolution (see chapter 29). There is just no room in modern society for a "King James Version" of science textbooks. In schools, we should teach science, not preach it! Pope John Paul II said it right: "Scientific culture today requires Christians to have a mature faith."

The Catholic Church has always seen this quite clearly, because from very early on she accepted Augustine's insight that God speaks to us in two ways: through the Book of Scripture as well as through the Book of Nature—both coming from the same source, God. In Augustine's own words, "It is the divine page that you must listen to; it is the book of the universe that you must observe." This conviction was shared in the past by many other Catholic thinkers: from early apologists and Fathers to St. Basil; from St. Gregory of Nyssa to St. Augustine; from St. Albert the Great to St. Thomas Aquinas. But there is an important caveat: we should never read the Book of Scripture as

265

if it were the Book of Nature, or vice versa. We should not turn science into a semi-religion, or turn religion into a semi-science.

So the question is: What does the Book of Nature tell us about the beginning and the development of our world—at least for now? Put in a nutshell, astrophysics estimates that the big bang happened approximately 13.8 billion years ago, which is now considered the age of the Universe. Astronomy tells us the age of the earth is 4.5 billion years, based on evidence from radiometric age dating of meteorites and other material. Geology adds to this that ancient rocks exceeding 3.5 billion years in age are found on all of the earth's continents. (The earth's oldest rocks have been recycled and destroyed by the process of plate tectonics.) And paleontology shows us that fossils range enormously in age and can even be as old as 4.1 billion years. It is tremendously difficult to harmonize this with Ussher's calculation based on Scripture, if we accept there is no such thing as "double truth" (see chapter 29).

So the question becomes even more pressing: What is it then that the Book of Scripture tells us about the beginning and the development of this world? To find answers, we must turn to the first chapters of the book of Genesis. Genesis has *two* creation accounts—one in chapter 1 and another in chapter 2. After the six-day creation account in Genesis 1, followed by a day of rest, there is the creation account from Genesis 2. It is almost as if the Bible starts all over again in this second chapter, but now with roles reversed.

Genesis 1, on the one hand, paints an immense world with abundant water, carrying an insignificant human being who appears at the eleventh hour—Day 6—while everything is waiting for him. Genesis 2, on the other hand, describes a mirror image: a small world with a shortage of water, in which an immensely significant human being stalks about like a giant and nothing starts working until this being is around. In other words, Genesis 2 keeps everything on hold until mankind arrives; all the earth is thirsty until a human being begins to cultivate it; the animals do not have names until he gives them names. Obviously, a literal interpretation is out of the question, for there are serious contradictions between these two accounts. We cannot read Genesis 1 and 2 as if they were modern, scientific reports. This is the Book of Scripture, not of Nature.

Yet, many Christians like to see in chapter 1 a *chronological* account of creation, done in six days. But even that is hard to believe. According to this reading, the six days of creation followed one another in strict chronological order. However, there are several indications that this account cannot be taken literally. First, there is the fact that the creation of the sun happens three days after the day-and-night cycle is established. In addition, the plants were created one day before the sun was created. This is especially troublesome if a creation "day" is interpreted as a longer period, since plants need sunlight. So we can draw the provisional conclusion that Genesis 1 is not meant to be understood as a literal chronological account.

This takes us to the second possibility: Genesis 1 is to be given a nonchronological, *structural* reading. Advocates of this view point out that ancient literature commonly placed historical material in a sequential order according to a particular structure or framework, rather than in strict chronological order. The *Catechism* explains that "Scripture presents the work of the Creator symbolically as a succession of six days of divine 'work,' concluded by the 'rest' of the seventh day" (337). The structural interpretation holds that the seven days of creation are not to be taken literally as a chronology of how God made the world.

Instead, the structural interpretation stresses that Genesis 1 tells us *what* God did, without attempting to tell us in a literal fashion *when* and *how* God did it. It tells us *that* God created the world—God is the origin of everything—whereas science tells us *how* He did it.

The structural approach is not a new, modern idea. For many centuries, it has been recognized that the six days of creation are divided into two sets of three. In the first set, God separates one thing from another: on day 1, He separates the light and the darkness (thus giving rise to day and night); on day 2, He separates the waters above from the waters below (thus giving rise to the sky and the sea); and on day 3, He separates the waters below from each other (thus giving rise to dry land in between the waters). Classically, this section is known as describing the work of *division*.

In the second set of three days, God goes back over the realms He produced by division during the first three days and then populates, or "adorns," them. On day 4, He adorns the day and the night with the sun, the moon, and the stars. On day 5, He populates the sky and sea with birds and fish. And on day 6, he populates the land (between the divided waters) with animals and man. Classically, this is known as describing the work of *adornment*.

That this twofold process does indeed represent the ordering principle of Genesis 1 is also indicated at the beginning and end of the account. At the beginning, we are told that "the earth was without form and void" (Gen. 1:2). The work of *division* cures the formless problem, whereas the work of *adornment* fixes the void problem. Likewise, at the end of the account we are told "the heavens and the earth were finished [i.e., by division], and all the host of them [i.e., by adornment]" (Gen. 2:1). Biblical scholars have recognized for centuries that these are the ordering principles at work in Genesis 1. So this is not something modern Bible scholars have come up with; we find this idea, for instance, in the writings of St. Thomas Aquinas many centuries ago.

It is through this structure that Genesis 1 proclaims its core message: a radical and imperative affirmation of *monotheism* against pagan beliefs. Each day dismisses an additional cluster of pagan deities: on the first day, the gods of light and darkness; on the second day, the gods of sky and sea; on the third day, earth gods and gods of vegetation; on the fourth day, sun, moon, and star gods (including astrology); on the fifth and sixth days, gods from the animal kingdom (such as sacred falcons, lions, serpents, and golden calves). Finally, even humans are emptied of any intrinsic divinity, although they are granted a divine likeness.

So each day of creation shows us how another set of idols is being smashed. Nothing on earth is a god, but everything comes from God. Obviously, the issue at stake in Genesis 1 is idolatry, not science; mythology, not natural history; theology, not chronology. Genesis proclaims monotheism, not a scientific theory of origin. It concludes that creation is good, very good, but it is certainly not divine. The main message is this: God is the Creator of everything, and there are no other gods or deities besides Him.

One question remains: How can the Book of Nature and the Book of Scripture be harmonized? We discovered already that each book has its own message. As we noted earlier, the difference between the two is basically simple: The Book of Scripture shows us how to go to Heaven, and the Book of Nature shows us how the heavens go. Science tries to explain how everything develops; religion tries to explain where everything ultimately comes from.

Creating an unbridgeable chasm between these two books would be detrimental, for the truth is that they both have the same goal of explaining *reality*—either the material part of reality or the immaterial part of reality. It remains the very same world that we live in—whether we look at it from a religious or a scientific viewpoint. Seeing the world from both the perspective of science and the perspective of religion is something the English theoretical physicist and Anglican priest John Polkinghorne describes as seeing the world with "two eyes instead of one." As he explains, "Seeing the world with two eyes—having binocular vision—enables me to understand more than I could with either eye on its own."

Does this mean that creation and evolution offer us two different ways of looking at the world? It certainly does not mean that Catholics are forced to believe in evolution, although they do have to believe in creation. At least, it means there is no conflict between the idea of creation and the idea of evolution. It is for this reason that Pope Benedict XVI called it an *absurdity* that "whoever believes in the creator could not believe in evolution, and whoever asserts belief in evolution would have to disbelieve in God." The pontiff certainly did not say that we as Catholics are required to believe in evolution, but if we do, then this does not imply that we are rejecting God and our Catholic Faith by doing so.

In other words, there may be creation without evolution, but there cannot be any evolution without creation. Take the analogy of a novel: the *beginning* of the novel consists of its first words or sentences; but the *origin* of the novel is what the author of the novel has come up with. No matter what the first lines of the novel are, there must be an author. No matter how the world and everything in it came along, there must be a divine Author.

Therefore, unlike their fellow Christians—the Protestant fundamentalists—Catholics do not have to reject evolution as long as they put it in the proper context. William E. Carroll applied this to science education: "Rather than excluding Darwin from the curriculum, the schools should add Aquinas."

CONCLUSION

Catholics do *not* believe in a six-day creation, or at least do not have to. It is not a dogma. The Catholic Church has a much more mature understanding of the difference between creation and evolution. She has a centuries-old nonchronological reading of what the six-day creation account tells us. Catholics do not read the Book of Scripture as if it were the Book of Nature.

34

CATHOLICS MAKE GOD A MAGICIAN

THE LIE

Catholics portray God as a miracle-worker who constantly needs to make sure things in this universe run the right way, and they make Him the magician who makes miraculous things happen in each person's life.

They have a very primitive, childlike image of God—an image that modern science can't support.

THE TRUTH

Modern science does indeed seem to leave little room for God in this universe. At best, it allows God to be the Creator of the world, but only like a watchmaker who makes a watch, winds it up, and then abandons it to itself, taking the hands-off approach, so to speak, of an absentee landlord.

This portrayal of God is a distortion of the Catholic view of creation, for it leaves no room for God in our daily lives. But it does have a kernel of truth, for the Catholic Church takes the "sovereignty" of the universe very seriously. The universe has its own laws of nature. They work on their own accord, without direct interference from outside. Nature is bound to "obey" its God-given laws of nature. One simple example of this is that God made a universe in which material objects are attracted to each other, which we call the force of gravity. We do not have to wonder about God's will every time a stone falls to the ground, even if it strikes us on the head. God has given us the force of gravity, which is the direct cause of each stone's earthly plummet. It is not His direct, but His indirect, doing.

This way, we live in a world that we can trust and count on because it follows some God-given laws of nature in a predictable way. The evolutionary biologist Francisco Ayala rightly places this in a much wider context: "As floods and drought were a necessary consequence of the fabric of the physical world, predators and parasites, dysfunctions and diseases were a consequence of the evolution of life." Causes like these explain what happens in this world, but without making God directly responsible for the outcome.

If this is the way the universe works—somehow "independently" of God—then we cannot accept that God needs to direct or redirect his own God-given laws of nature. Yet it seems to be a timeless temptation for Christians to have God constantly interfere in what He created. Even the famous physicist Isaac Newton fell for this temptation of having God keep a "divine foot" in the door, when he called upon God's active intervention to reform the solar system periodically from increasing irregularities and to prevent the stars from falling in on each other, and perhaps even in preventing the amount of motion in the universe from decaying due to viscosity and friction. However, we should ask why God would have to make such interventions if there are laws of nature that are supposed to take care of all of this. As a matter of fact, what Newton could not yet explain

Catholics make God a magician

science would soon be able to explain, by coming up with better laws—which are God's laws anyway. In that sense, the universe has its own "sovereignty."

On the other hand, how can the Catholic Church substantiate her position on the world's "sovereignty" without taking anything away from God's sovereignty? St. Thomas Aquinas has provided the framework for solving this problem. He makes a vital distinction between the Primary Cause (First Cause) and secondary causes, as he calls them. All creatures are real causes of the wide array of changes that occur in the world, but they are only secondary causes. God alone is the Cause of *being as such*—He is the Primary Cause of all other causes. God's causality is so different from the causality of creatures that there is no competition between the two—that is, we do not need to limit God's causality, as it were, to make room for the causality of creatures. God, the Primary Cause, causes creatures to be causes of their own—secondary causes, that is. That's *their* "sovereignty."

It is the secondary causes that we are all familiar with: "like causes having like effects." Science, for instance, deals with this kind of causality. It is the causality that reigns "inside" the universe, linking causes together in a chain of secondary causes—a chain of causes and effects. However, any part of the chain can do any causing only if it first exists. The need for causes must come to an end: there must be a cause that is not itself in need of a cause—a Primary Cause. When Aquinas describes God as the First Cause, what he means is not merely "first" in the sense of being before the second cause in time, and not "first" in the sense of coming before the second cause in a sequence, but rather "first" in the sense of being the *source* of all secondary causes—a power from which all other causes derive their being and their causal powers. It is God, the Primary Cause of all creation, who ordains that the universe will be governed by a series of secondary causes through the laws of nature.

Does all of this mean God cannot perform miracles anymore? Certainly not. To explain how miracles are still possible within the seemingly "rigid" setting of secondary causes, we need to reflect a bit on our own doings first. We ourselves are constantly performing the role of miracle-workers. Think of the numerous "miracles" we have created: cars, planes, computers, surgery, antibiotics—and the list keeps growing. What we have to realize, though, is that in creating such "miracles," we do not change the laws of nature, but we use them to reach our own purposes and intentions. Our minds have the capacity to employ the laws of nature to achieve the specific goals we have in mind.

This is also what happens constantly in games—to use another down-to-earth example. When watching a game on the golf course or on the pool table, we see balls following precisely determined courses of cause and effect; they follow rigid, physical laws. Yet there is one element that does not fit into this predetermined picture, into this cascade of causes and effects: the players of the game. Although there is a cascade of physical causes and effects in each of these games, there is much more going on in each process—the players of the game have a very specific intention in mind, which eludes and transcends the laws of science. They don't go *against* the laws of nature, but they do go freely *beyond* those laws. People who are unable to look beyond these physical laws and causes are completely missing out on what the game is all about. In their freedom, the players fall outside the realm of physics; they themselves can steer the course of the laws of nature from "outside." They work their own "miracles."

These are just simple and trivial examples, of course. Yet, somehow the direction of balls on the pool table or on the golf course is ruled not only by laws of nature but also by something as "enigmatic" as the human mind and will—that is, by players who have a certain goal in mind.

Why is this so enigmatic?

Because the mind is part of the body without being a physical part of it. Yes, the *brain* is a physical part of the body, but the *mind* is not identical to the brain. The physical brain is as much responsible for thinking as the hand is for grasping or the leg for kicking, yet the brain does not do the thinking—the mind does, albeit with the help of the brain. This explains why the brain cannot study itself; we need a mind to study the brain. Therefore, if humans can perform miracle work, it is because their minds are able to do miraculous work.

Now, the point is this: if we can be miracle-workers ourselves, why would God not be able to do the same—in an analogous way, of course? Perhaps the analogy of the working of the human mind can help us better understand the "working" of God's mind in this world. He is actively present in this world, not by going against the laws of nature and its secondary causes, or by supplementing or replacing them, but rather by letting them be the way they are and yet steering them in a certain direction without overstepping the autonomy of secondary causes. Of course, that is not all there is to it, but perhaps this analogy opens the door for us to understand better what God's presence is like in this world.

In other words, God does not violate the laws of nature, but He can manipulate them for His own purposes. That's called God's *providence*. Just as builders are not a physical part of their buildings yet are an active part of every part of them, so God is not a part of what He created, yet He is actively involved with each and every part of it. God is the First Cause who operates in and through secondary causes. This analogy of the relationship between mind and body may help us see how God is the "soul" and "spirit" that pervades all of creation and is thus part of everything in creation, but without becoming a physical part of it. God is not one of the players on the world scene, but He is the Author and Director of this cosmic play. That's how God works miracles in our world.

Back to the main question: Do Catholics see God as some kind of magician? Yes and no. They know God cannot do the impossible, cannot perform what is contradictory, and cannot go against His own laws of nature, but He does have "magic" and "miraculous" power, similar to the way He gave that power also to us, who were made in His image and likeness. He is as much at work in the world as we can be at work at the pool table or on the golf course. As Cardinal Avery Dulles put it, "Why should God be capable of creating the world from nothing but incapable of acting within the world He has made?"

CONCLUSION

Catholics do *not* make God a magician. They take the sovereignty of the world and its laws of nature very seriously. Yet, at the same time they acknowledge that God works actively and constantly in the world and in each person's life without violating the laws of nature. He is not a magician but rather a miracle-worker similar to the way each one of us can be a miracle-worker. The mystery of the human mind translates into the mystery of God's mind. That's how God works miracles in our world, no matter what science tells us. There is nothing primitive or child-like about that belief.

PART 7

CATHOLICISM AND SOCIETY

.

35

CATHOLICS REJECT MODERN IDEAS

THE LIE

One of the darkest periods in the history of Catholicism is her rejection of modernism, or modernity—a rejection of innovative ideas in society such as materialism, rationalism, humanism, relativism, secularism, and scientism.

The Anti-Modernist Oath issued by Pope Pius X in 1910 was a direct attack on modern developments in society. That's when the Catholic Church closed her doors and windows to the surrounding world.

THE TRUTH

The Catholic Church does not reject modern ideas or new movements per se, but she does reject them when they come with *monopolistic* claims. She rejects the claim of *materialism* that there is only matter, and nothing spiritual or supernatural. She rejects the claim of *rationalism* that everything must be judged by reason alone, without faith. She rejects the claim of *relativism* that there is no truth, but only opinions about what is true, depending on one's point of view. She rejects the claim of *liberalism* that all our choices in life must be free of any restrictions. She rejects the claim of *secularism* that all religions have to bend to the demands of a nonreligious government. She rejects the claim of *scientism* that there can only be scientific answers to all our questions.

All the above claims and developments are basically doctrines or ideologies. Where did they come from? They can basically be traced back to the period of the Enlightenment — although some of them have a much longer history. Somehow, they have affected each one of us nowadays, Catholic or not. We have been bombarded with them in school and through the mass media — they have virtually become endemic.

Especially during the eighteenth century, Enlightenment thinkers, particularly in Britain and France, embraced the notion that humanity could be enormously improved through exclusively rational change. Rationalism became associated with "free thought" as the only possible intellectual attitude of a reasoning and reasonable person. The central idea of the Enlightenment was that the Age of Faith had to be replaced by the Age of Reason, and eventually by the Age of Science, so that humanity could move from a state of ignorant superstition to one of sweeping development and scientific progress. It did not take the Catholic Church long to discover how destructive these "enlightened" ideas would be to the Catholic Faith. So the Church soon started her "campaign" against what she called *modernism*, or more recently *modernity*. Etymologically, "modernism" means an exaggerated love of what is modern and an obsession with modern ideas.

Not surprisingly, in the eyes of the Church, modernism and Catholicism cannot possibly live in the same religious house. Catholicism acknowledges that what was true in Church doctrine yesterday cannot be false today or tomorrow, and what was immoral yesterday cannot be moral today or tomorrow. Therefore, modernism has been condemned by the Church on several occasions for trying to transform Catholicism from the inside. In his encyclical *Pascendi Dominici Gregis* (1907), Pope Pius X, in no uncertain terms, denounced modernism as "the synthesis of all heresies."

To counteract the false philosophies behind the ideas of modernism, the Church began to reemphasize the role of the very sound philosophy of Thomas Aquinas, in the form of Thomism and neo-Thomism. This revival had already been instigated by Pope Leo XIII through his encyclical *Aeterni Patris* (1879). More recently, Pope John Paul II would explain this move as follows: "A renewed insistence upon the thought of the Angelic Doctor seemed to Pope Leo XIII the best way to recover the practice of a philosophy consonant with the demands of faith." Pope John Paul II would later praise that development with these words, "The Magisterium's intention has always been to show how Saint Thomas is an authentic model for all who seek the truth."

This new emphasis on Thomistic philosophy came to be particularly pronounced in the early twentieth century, as exemplified by the issuing of the Anti-Modernist Oath by Pope Pius X in 1910, and the publication in 1914 of twenty-four Thomistic propositions that had to be taught in all colleges and seminaries as fundamental elements of theology. The oath mandated that "all clergy, pastors, confessors, preachers, religious superiors, and professors in philosophical-theological seminaries" of the Catholic Church swear to it. The oath continued to be taken until July 1967, when the Congregation for the Doctrine of the Faith rescinded it. Nowadays, no one is compelled to take the oath, nor is anyone prohibited from taking it. But more and more Catholic colleges feel they need something akin to it.

Forty Anti-Catholic Lies

As is to be expected, this response of the Church — especially her mandate of the Anti-Modernist Oath — has been ridiculed by modernists. Modernism's leading figure, the Scripture scholar Alfred Loisy, complained that Pius X not only had condemned modernism but had actually "invent[ed] the system" that he condemned. However, there is a certain irony here: modernists accuse the Catholic Church of being authoritarian, but they themselves are at least as authoritarian as the Church, for they allow no room for anything but their own doctrine of modernism. If the Catholic Church is against modernist ideas, it is not because they are new, but because they are false in making monopolistic claims. What the Church rejects is not progression but regression — that is, the loss of vital elements of life, society, and tradition.

This raises the question then of what is wrong with the ideologies modernists promote. G. K. Chesterton said, "Nine out of ten of what we call new ideas are simply old mistakes."

Which ones?

Relativism: this doctrine tells us that all that we have left in matters of truth is our own personal opinion — the freedom to believe what we like. In the eyes of relativists, religious beliefs (see chapter 20) and moral values (see chapter 39) are merely a matter of personal taste. What's wrong with that? Well, if the world is round, someone's opinion will not make it flat. Opinions don't trump truths. Besides, the statement "all truth is relative" leads to a contradiction. Denying that there is objective truth means you are insisting in your denial that what you say is objectively true, which by its own verdict cannot be true.

Nevertheless, relativism is on the rise, in spite of the fact that science is currently one of the (perhaps last?) strongholds where truth is still respected in our culture. If truth were at the mercy of some individuals, science would have to abandon all its truth claims. Contrary to what relativists believe, we are dealing in science with truth and reason, not sentiment and habit. To cross a river, we need a bridge built by engineers with the right knowledge, not with better habits or opinions; and to get into Heaven, we need faith based on the right knowledge, not on better sentiments. Chesterton once firmly asserted that "truth exists whether we like it or not, and it is for us to accommodate ourselves to it."

Rationalism: this doctrine glorifies the power of reason. However, at the same time, it curtails its power by putting it in competition with faith and religion. The reasoning behind it goes as follows: if you accept faith, you can do so only by neglecting reason; if you choose reason, you must abandon faith, in spite of the fact that rationalism itself is based on faith—faith in the power of reason (see chapter 27). There is a leap of faith required in putting all of one's intellectual reliance on the pedestal of reason.

Secularism: this doctrine seeks to eliminate religion, or at the very least to privatize and thus marginalize it in everyone's life and in society at large. It promotes not merely "freedom *of* religion," but more specifically "freedom *from* religion" (see chapter 36). It has been given an antireligious overtone—a vision of the future as devoid of religion, instead of separated from religion.

Secularists make us believe that we are fully self-made, in full control of our own history and destination. They declare humanity to be the measure of all things by pronouncing that all our problems can be entirely solved by using the right human knowledge, technology, reasoning, and judgment.

Liberalism: this is often called "humanism without God"—or secular humanism. It is a vision of the human person that is incomplete—it no longer has a religious dimension. This kind of humanism declares human beings to be fully sufficient in themselves, fully self-made, and in complete control of their own history. It is a philosophy of life that views man as the "supreme being" on earth, so there is no need for, or no space left for, a Supreme Being in Heaven. It pretends that all our problems—personal, social, technological, and what have you—can be entirely solved by using the right human knowledge, technology, reasoning, and judgment. We are supposed to be in full control of ourselves and should further free ourselves through economic, technological, and social liberation—free from any moral restraints. From then on, not Heaven but the sky is the limit. The slogan is: We do not need God; we do not even want God because such a God undermines the power of man, the power of "me, myself, and I."

Scientism: this doctrine equates reasoning with scientific reasoning and identifies reason with the way scientists use reason. Supporters of scientism claim that science provides the one and only valid way of finding truth. They hold that all our questions have a scientific answer phrased in terms of particles, quantities, and equations. They maintain that there is no other point of view than the "scientific" worldview. They believe that there is no corner of the universe, no dimension of reality, no feature of human existence beyond science's reach. In other words, they have an unshakable belief in the omnicompetence of science—giving it the status of a know-all and cure-all (see chapter 29). In that sense, scientism may sound very compelling, but there are many reasons the Church challenges what scientism claims. Here are a few of them.

First of all, those who defend scientism seem to be unaware that the truth of the statement "No statements are true unless they can be proven scientifically" cannot itself be proven scientifically. It is not a scientific discovery but at best a philosophical stance—and a poor one at that.

Second, the astonishing successes of science have not been gained by answering every kind of question, but precisely by refusing to do so. There are many more truths than scientific truths—truths about beauty, love, morality, and God.

Third, an instrument or technique can detect only what it is designed to detect. So instead of letting reality determine the techniques that are appropriate for its various parts, scientism lets its favorite scientific technique dictate what is considered "real" in life, thus declaring everything else illusionary.

Fourth, we cannot use the scientific method to prove that the scientific method is the only way of proving anything. Using the scientific method to evaluate the scientific method is a form of circular reasoning.

Fifth, scientists have made the decision to limit themselves to what is material and can be dissected, counted, measured, and quantified. From there, everything that cannot be dissected, measured, counted, or quantified is off-limits for science—in spite of the fact that scientism claims there is nothing else in this world than what is material and can be examined in terms of particles, quantities, and equations. However, this verdict itself is not material and therefore cannot be dissected, counted, measured, or quantified—which makes scientism more like a boomerang that comes back to hit its own truth claims.

All of this leaves us with the question: How should we assess the antimodernist approach of the Church? The previous objections against modernism and its doctrines are based on sound philosophy, especially the seemingly timeless philosophy of St. Thomas Aquinas that has survived more than seven centuries—a beacon of safety in times of uncertainty, confusion, and tribulations. Neo-Thomism was, and still is, the Church's way to bridge the Catholic Faith and modern science in a time of attacks by modernists, who still maintain that everything is in a flux and subject to evolution. Interestingly enough, it was thanks to neo-Thomism, rather than modernism, that the Church was able to come to terms with scientific issues such as cosmology and evolution. That fact may also explain why evolution is less controversial nowadays among Catholics than among Evangelicals.

However, some still see Vatican II as a reversal of the Church's antimodernist stand. True, Vatican II made an attempt to present the Church's age-old doctrines and moral outlook in a new way that would be intelligible to the minds of modern men and women. Instead of conforming the Church to modernity, though, the council's goal was to modernize the Church in order to evangelize the world, to proclaim the perennial truths of revelation in a way that modern ears can hear and understand. In her efforts, the Church changed no doctrine and abandoned not one of her perennial moral laws. The council affirmed all. It did not try to sell us *new* truths; it merely presented *old* truths in contemporary terms.

CONCLUSION

Catholics do *not* reject modern ideas. The Catholic Church is not afraid of new ideas, as long as they don't demand exclusivity. She does not close her doors and windows to the surrounding world, but instead uses reason and faith—not fear—to evaluate what is new. That's what the Anti-Modernist Oath issued by Pope Pius X tried to achieve. As Chesterton once said, "The Catholic Church is the only thing which saves man from the degrading slavery of being a child of his age."

36

CATHOLICS ARE
AGAINST FREE SPEECH

THE LIE

Catholics don't allow free speech. The fact that there was a Catholic *Index of Forbidden Books* (*Index Librorum Prohibitorum*) demonstrates there is no freedom of speech in the Catholic Church. Although the *Index* itself has not existed since 1966, the idea behind it still does. The Church has always been very suspicious of new ideas.

This means the era of the Inquisition is not over. Catholics are told to be constantly on their guard against certain ideas, authors, and books. The Vatican still has an Oath of Fidelity to Church teachings, and some Catholic colleges ask all faculty members to take the oath. Others require the oath from their theology professors. The oath is actually prescribed in canon 833 of the *Code of Canon Law*.

THE TRUTH

To someone living in the twenty-first century, it must be horrifying to hear about the *Index of Forbidden Books*. The truth is that the Catholic Church did have such an index. But having said that, we must acknowledge there are different ways of looking at this issue. Here are at least six perspectives to consider.

1. The *Index* serves as a protection tool. If you want to protect yourself during the flu season, you must avoid crowded places, public restrooms, close bodily contact, and so on. In a similar way, if you want to remain Catholic, you must avoid anti-Catholic propaganda, or at least learn how to counter anti-Catholic attacks. That's what the *Index of Forbidden Books* tried to achieve, and that's what we are trying to do in this book.

Self-protection and self-defense are very basic human responses. When the Protestant Reformation, soon followed by the Enlightenment, began to attack everything Catholic, the Catholic Church had to defend herself in response. The first list of forbidden books was not published in Rome, but in the then-Catholic Netherlands (1529). Soon the first Roman Index was printed in 1557 under the direction of Pope Paul IV. By mid-century, in the tense atmosphere of wars of religion in Germany and France, both Protestant and Catholic authorities reasoned that only control of the press, including a catalog of prohibited works coordinated by ecclesiastical and governmental authorities, could prevent the spread of heresy (see chapter 24). However, the *Index* was not simply a confrontational work. Roman Catholic authors also had the opportunity to defend their writings and could prepare a new edition with necessary corrections or deletions, either to avoid or to limit a ban on their works.

The ultimate aim of the *Index* was to protect the faith and morals of the faithful by preventing exposure to heretical and immoral books—ranging from heretical treatises to pornography. The twentieth and final edition of the *Index* appeared in 1948, but the *Index* was formally abolished in 1966 by Pope Paul VI. Catholic canon law still recommends that works concerning sacred Scripture, theology, canon law, Church history, and any writings that specifically concern religion or morals be submitted to the judgment of the local bishop, who then consults someone whom he considers competent to give a judgment. If that person gives the *nihil obstat* (nothing forbids), the local bishop grants the *imprimatur* (let it be printed). These terms are still being used, but more recently, they are often replaced by the expression "published with ecclesiastical approval."

2. It is not just a Catholic thing to have something like an index — other institutions have had similar reasons for making their own index. A "hidden index" is much more common than usually thought — as a way to protect morals and beliefs from hostile attacks and unwanted intrusion. The United States, for instance, had one for a while to protect its Constitution from attacks by communists and anarchists. China still bans certain information from its Internet services. More in general, we protect our children from harmful information by using filters on television, computers, and cell phones. We even protect adult citizens from unwanted intrusions and spam by implementing certain regulations. Most societies officially tag movies and videos, and sometimes add warnings to them. To uphold the dignity of women, we need to ban pornography on the Internet. Why would religions not be allowed to do something similar?

3. Having an index of forbidden books is far less destructive than *burning* books. Although Catholics did burn anti-Catholic books, book burnings are certainly not an exclusively Catholic phenomenon. There is a long history of book burnings. Examples include the burning of books and burying of scholars under China's Qin Dynasty, the destruction of Aztec codices by

Itzcoatl, and of course, the infamous Nazi book burnings. Book burnings were also very popular among Protestant Reformers. The Calvinist-dominated City Council of Geneva in 1553 ordered that Michael Servetus be burned at the stake along with his manuscript, in conjunction with a copy of a printed book tied to his waist. During the violence of the anti-Catholic French Revolution, there were public burnings of breviaries, missals, and copies of the Old and New Testaments. As a matter of fact, most revolutions are known for their book burnings. During the Cultural Revolution in China, many copies of the Buddhist, Taoist, and Confucian books were destroyed, as they were thought to be promoting the "old" way of thinking.

Even the United States—a country known for its freedom of speech—had its book burnings. William Pynchon's book *The Meritorious Price of Our Redemption* was banned in 1651 for criticizing the Puritans, and all known copies were publicly burned. Book burning became institutionalized in the late nineteenth century after Anthony Comstock persuaded Congress to adopt a federal obscenity law in 1873. In the 1950s, over six tons of books by psychiatrist William Reich were burned in the United States under judicial orders. But even as recently as 2001, University of California–Berkeley students burned copies of Daniel J. Flynn's book on political activist Mumia Abu-Jamal after verbally shouting the author down during his scheduled speech. How much nicer would an index have been!

4. There are other ways of protecting the identity of Catholic institutions. What the *Index of Forbidden Books* used to do—shaping Catholic identity and protecting it from losing that identity—can also be achieved with other methods. A clear example is using an oath instead of an index to protect the identity of Catholic colleges.

Many great North American universities were once clearly and openly religious and began under religious auspices and for religious purposes — Harvard, Yale, Princeton, the University of Chicago, and Boston University, to name just a few. They have since become purely secular, or even secularist institutions — indistinguishable from their nonreligious counterparts, except for their spacious and now largely unused chapels. Catholic colleges and universities have mostly run the same course. The institutions that should be educating Catholics to examine critically the values of the culture they live in have instead become the main vehicle by which Catholics are indoctrinated into the secularist "values" of their surroundings. What secularists call their "values" are typically pro-abortion, pro-euthanasia, and pro-homosexual activity. Again, conformity with the surrounding culture of secularism ranks higher at these institutions than supporting a culture steeped in religious beliefs and moral values. The philosopher Peter Kreeft, for instance, who has taught for many years at Boston College, is known to say, "BC is a Jesuit College, not a Catholic College."

In response to such developments, Pope John Paul II stated in his 1990 apostolic constitution *Ex Corde Ecclesiae* (From the Heart of the Church), "Catholic members of the university community are also called to a personal fidelity to the Church with all that this implies. Non-Catholic members are required to respect the Catholic character of the University, while the University in turn respects their religious liberty." Further efforts by the Vatican and U.S. bishops to implement the *Proposed Ordinances for Catholic Colleges and Universities in the United States* led, among other things, to what the bishops worded as follows: "The attestation or declaration of the professor that he or she will teach in communion with the Church can be expressed by the profession of faith and oath of fidelity or in any other reasonable manner."

In spite of strong opposition—an oath might carry the American Catholic colleges and universities back to the 1950s, many critics said—some Catholic colleges accepted this challenge, perhaps also because they might otherwise lose their official accreditation as Catholic. Since then, several more positive statements have been uttered. Here are a few: "If you are going to call yourself a Catholic school, then you should really be faithful to Catholic teaching"; "Students—whether faithful Catholics or non-Catholics of good will—should have confidence that their theology classes will be conducted as advertised"; "When professors take the Oath, the students know exactly what to expect, namely, the teachings of the Church, and not the creative theological theories of their professors or anyone else." Mean what you say and say what you mean.

5. There continues to be a strong opposition against an index or an oath, because these violate the idea of free speech. However, objecting to an index or oath on grounds of free-speech violation might easily obscure the fact that the relationship between the Catholic Church and freedom of speech is much closer and more existential than many realize.

First of all, freedom of speech—and specifically, religious freedom—is ultimately rooted in religious belief. Robert Royal, who considers that secularism, like communism, is a system that cannot endure, rightly remarked that "without a belief in human dignity as rooted in the Creator, as our Declaration of Independence proclaims, there's no rational basis for a free society except a limp 'live and let live' mentality." The concept of religious freedom is not rooted in a belief that all religions have the same value or truth, but in the conviction that religious truth is so important that the state has the duty to cherish the search for it (see chapter 39).

Second, the rule of freedom of speech cannot be an absolute rule that rejects any exceptions, for then it would also have to allow for hate speech and the like. And it would even have to accept the rejection of freedom of speech based on the rule of freedom of speech—which means it could actually annihilate itself, similar to Hitler's use of democracy in order to abolish democracy. In other words, freedom of speech is not unlimited. When it becomes hate speech or speech against freedom of speech, for instance, limits have obviously been reached.

But there is a more serious problem. Popular current ideologies such as materialism and scientism (see chapter 35) make us believe that there is no such thing as human freedom. They make it look as if all our "free" actions are completely ruled and determined by genes, hormones, and neural circuitry. If that were true, then there could not be anything "free" in our speech, not even in claiming "freedom" of speech.

The Church tells us differently.

In contrast to such ideologies, the Catholic Church has always been a staunch defender of human freedom. Why single out the Catholic Church? you might ask. Isn't this a common view in all of Christianity? Not really. Certain groups of Christians have made this issue into an either-or dilemma by opposing human sovereignty in making free choices to God's sovereignty over the world: Either, they argue, we win and God loses all, or we lose and God wins all (see chapter 8). How could such a serious contradiction ever arise in Christianity?

On the one hand, there is the heretic Pelagius (354–420), who held that we alone are in charge of our own actions. In his view, claiming differently would be an offense to human sovereignty.

If God were in control of our decisions, then we would just be marionettes in God's hands, as He would orchestrate every movement, directing every choice and decision so they would create the music of His choice. That's one side of the debate: *we* are in charge.

On the other hand, there is the Protestant Reformer John Calvin in particular, who argued the opposite: God alone is in charge of what we "decide" to do. Theologians such as Calvin keep maintaining that our capability of choosing would be a direct violation of God's sovereignty. They claim that if human beings were able to frustrate God's decisions, then God's will would not be all powerful. Human beings would be more powerful than God, as they have the power to frustrate God's power. Therefore, these theologians made God the absolute and only cause of all our doings. All our acts are supposedly really God's acts.

In contrast, the Catholic Church maintains against both views that this is a false dilemma, which makes either God alone responsible for our choices or us alone responsible for our choices. According to the Catholic Church, leaving either one out does great injustice to divine sovereignty as well as to human sovereignty. God does not lose His sovereignty when we use the human freedom He gave us.

The fact that we do have freedom points to a Creator after whose image we were made. For how could we be *free* if there were no God who has *freely* created us after His image? Of course, human freedom is an imperfect reflection of the perfect freedom God has in His divine sovereignty. Yet God does not rob us of any decisions we make ourselves. He is, in fact, the one who gives us decision-making power; He allows us to become causes of our own acts. Phrased in the terminology we introduced earlier (see chapter 34), without a Primary Cause, we could not even be secondary causes of our own. That would surely be the end of free speech.

CONCLUSION

Catholics are *not* against free speech as such. As a matter of fact, it is the Catholic Church that strongly upholds and defends the idea that free speech and making free decisions is, in fact, possible (see chapter 8). She actually proclaims that human freedom is rooted in God. The *Index* does not stop free speech, for we still have the freedom to reject the *Index* and ultimately the Catholic Faith. The *Index* acknowledges that people do have the freedom to sway the religious convictions of others exactly because they have freedom of speech. Freedom of speech means we can say whatever we want, but we cannot mandate as true whatever we want.

37

CATHOLICS ARE AGAINST WOMEN

THE LIE

In the hierarchy of the Catholic Church there is no space or role for women. There will never be equality in the Catholic Church until women can be ordained. Men, as controllers of the Church, are keeping women at bay and preventing them from fulfilling their potential as priests and leaders.

That's also why the Catholic Church rejects the claims of feminism. The Church hierarchy consists of male celibates who cannot understand women's issues, such as reproductive rights and the like.

THE TRUTH

Is the Church against women? The simple answer is no. Unlike the situation in their surrounding culture, Jesus affirmed the dignity of women by treating them the same as He treated His male disciples. Who stood at the foot of the Cross? The women disciples! Who were the first individuals to witness Jesus risen from the dead? Women!

St. Paul preaches what Jesus told His disciples and speaks of a radical equality of all in Christ, including an equality of the sexes: "There is neither Jew nor Greek, there is neither slave nor free person, *there is not male and female*; for you are all one in Christ Jesus" (Gal. 3:28, emphasis added). But this does not mean that Jews are Greeks, nor that men are women. There is a difference between men and women; yet, beyond their different "natures," there is a spiritual unity. Paul addresses women as well as men as his "fellow workers" (*synergoi*). At the end of his letter to the Romans, Paul acknowledges twenty-nine leading Christians in the Roman community to whom he sends greetings—ten of them are women.

Did the Church keep honoring the position of women later in history? Yes, she did—at least most of the time. From the very beginning, the Church made women and men equal in an unprecedented way, when compared with Jewish and Roman society. A remarkable accomplishment of the early Church was to gain wide acceptance of the ideal of permanent monogamy in cultures where polygamy was common and men were permitted to put aside their wives. That's why St. Paul proclaims, "Husbands should love their wives as their own bodies" (Eph. 5:28).

Also the Church Fathers taught in unison—counter to then-current opinions—that a woman has the right to consent to marriage; otherwise the marriage will be invalid. St. Ambrose insisted that the dowry system was unjust because it treated women as property. St. Augustine exhorted wives not to tolerate their husband's infidelity. Later, the Council of Trent stood firm against marriages arranged without the consent of both spouses. Besides, the Church opened the consecrated life as a vocation for women and also canonized numerous women, some of whom have become Doctors of the Church: Teresa of Ávila, Catherine of

Siena, Thérèse of Lisieux, and Hildegard of Bingen. The American Catholic novelist Flannery O'Connor was right when she said, "The Church would just as soon canonize a woman as a man and I suppose has done more than any other force in history to *free women*" (emphasis added).

Education is the major force of change in traditional sex-role patterns. The Catholic Church has always, from the very beginning of the school system in Europe, placed major emphasis on the education of girls and women. Today, the Church is one of the foremost educators in the developing world. Catholic women, both religious and lay, are superintendents, principals, and trustees in the world's largest provider of private elementary and secondary education. Something similar can be said about the Church's health-care system, the second largest in the world. Its leadership roles are managed almost entirely by Catholic women.

Is the Church against *ordained* women?

If this means ordaining women to the sacramental priesthood, the answer is yes. Church teaching on the ordination of only men to the priesthood finds its origins in what Christ taught us. While He was on earth, Jesus chose only men to be His apostles — excluding even His holy Mother — and He passed on authority to these men to carry out his work of preaching (Luke 9:1–2) and forgiving sins (John 20:23).

This is not culturally conditioned, for there were priestesses all over the Roman world; Jesus never followed cultural fashions. Because Jesus came to us on earth in the form of a man, He determined that the ones who represent Him and stand in for Him are to be men as well. The *Catechism* explains, "The Church recognizes herself to be bound by this choice made by the Lord himself. For this reason the ordination of women is not possible" (1577). Furthermore, it informs us that "no one has a right to receive the sacrament of Holy Orders. Indeed no one claims this office for himself; he is called to it by God" (1578). It is a gift, not a right — it can't be both.

Although we cannot always know exactly why Christ made some of the choices He made, we do know that He did not view women as inferior to men. Christ simply made clear that this particular vocation — the sacramental priesthood — would be reserved for men. In obedience to the will of God, the Catholic Church has and will continue to follow this practice of ordaining only men to the priesthood. In the words of Stephen J. Kovacs, "Women do possess authority in the Church, but not in the same manner as ordained priests, who, by virtue of their masculinity, act *in persona Christi*." But, again, this does not mean the Catholic Church is against women. Saying that the Church is against women because women cannot become priests is as silly as saying that the Church is against marriage because priests cannot get married.

So why has the issue of female priests become so contentious? Harvard law professor Mary Ann Glendon, former U.S. ambassador to the Holy See, has some clarifying thoughts on this issue. She speaks of "a confusion about the nature of the Church and the priesthood — leading to inapposite analogies from the secular realm. The Church is neither a business corporation nor a government. Its province is neither profit nor power, but the care of souls. Obviously, the Church cannot be run on the same principles as General Motors or city hall." Then she adds that the ordination question has been further clouded by a widespread failure to distinguish between the sacramental roles that are reserved to priests and the vastly broader range of pastoral and ministerial roles for nonordained persons.

Pastoral and ministerial roles today are more open than ever to women.

So this leaves us with the question: Is the Church perhaps against *feminists*? The answer depends on what "feminism" means. There are at least two versions of feminism: a radical version and a Christian version. It is to be expected that the Church is against radical feminists, but not necessarily against Christian feminists. So what is the difference?

Radical feminism resents what it calls the tendency of churches and families to base their vision of women's roles upon assumptions about female nature, most notably female sexuality. Thus, radical feminists frequently link their campaign for women's sexual freedom to their campaign against family and religion, arguing that to survive in the Christian churches, women must reclaim their sexuality from the male domination that Christianity has foisted upon them, especially when it comes to exercising their autonomy in matters of abortion. Hence, a woman supposedly has the "right" to do with her body whatever she wants.

Radical feminists think they can defend their pro-choice position by speaking of "reproductive rights"—which is a very deceiving label, to say the least, for it's not about a woman's right to reproduce, but at best about her "right" either to continue or discontinue a pregnancy. However, even if a woman were allowed to do with her body whatever she wants, we need to admit that the unborn baby is not *her* body. The baby is *in* her body, yes, but not a *part* of her body—it is a genetically distinct being. So abortion affects not only her own body, but also someone else's body—the unborn baby's. Why would a pregnant woman not allow the baby a right to his own body, when this is a right she claims so insistently for herself as a woman? Does the unborn baby not have the same right to say: "This is my body, and not yours"?

Forty Anti-Catholic Lies

What often unites radical feminists is their visceral hostility toward Catholicism, particularly the Church's opposition to abortion. Their opinions are more anti-Church than pro-woman. They detest the very idea that the capacity for or experience of motherhood might in any way distinguish women from men—out of fear that the acknowledgment of this difference might in some way compromise their chances for success. However, the Church's stand against abortion is to protect human life, not to demean women. Women's bodies do bear children, which places on women the greater portion of the task of living in accordance with the Church's teaching on life. Let's recall that Eve's punishment, for her part in the Fall, was not to bear children, but to bring them forth in pain.

The historian Elizabeth Ann Fox-Genovese puts this in the right context: "Increasingly, feminists seem to be insisting that women's equality with men requires that women be liberated from the consequences of their bodies, notably the ability to bear children." The radical feminist paradigm still focuses on a vision of sexual equality that prizes autonomy above all—the autonomy of "self-determination," even in matters of the life and death of others. It is this radical form of feminism that the Church rejects. Pope Benedict XVI said, "What feminism promotes in its radical form is no longer the Christianity that we know; it is another religion." That's what the Church is against. Being against radical feminists is not the same as being against women.

There is some irony in the stand of radical feminism: discrimination occurs not only when like entities are treated in unequal ways, but also when unlike entities are treated as equal. Women and men are different, and women must therefore not be treated as if they were men. Contemporary policies for men and women's roles often treat men and women in exactly the same manner. In this case, "equality" means that women must be allowed to imitate and become men. The point here is that women should not have to imitate men, because they are not men — they should be themselves. Furthermore, there is no reason to single out women and create an ideology called feminism just for them alone.

On the other hand, there is another form of feminism that the Church is not opposed to. As a matter of fact, Pope John Paul II aligned himself with women's quest for freedom and adopted much of the language of the women's movement, even calling for a "new feminism" in his encyclical *Evangelium Vitae*.

Apparently, he was talking about a different kind of feminism. Unlike radical feminism, *true feminism* is about equality for both genders, while encouraging individuality and respect for gender differences. The *Catechism* speaks of it this way: "By creating human beings man and woman, God gives personal dignity equally to the one and to the other. Masculinity and femininity are complementary — different but equal expressions of what it is to be human. Each of them, man and woman, should acknowledge and accept his sexual identity" (2393).

In other words, women are not equal to men apart from the equality of their personhood. They are different from men in more ways than simple biology. Women's identities are complex and irreducible to the single feature of sex or gender. Their identities are constituted as much by race, nation, and other categories of identity as they are by sex or gender. Peter Kreeft makes an acute diagnosis of the problem: "The main fault in the old stereotypes was their too-tight connection between sexual being and social doing, their tying of sexual identity to social roles, especially for women: the feeling that it was somehow unfeminine to be a doctor, lawyer, or politician. But the antidote to this illness is not confusing sexual identities but locating them in our being rather than in our doing."

For this reason, St. Edith Stein could express some appreciation for true feminism with the words, "Every profession in which woman's soul comes into its own and which can be formed by woman's soul is an authentic woman's profession." And she added, "Christ embodies the ideal of human perfection.... That is why we see in holy men a tenderness and a truly maternal solicitude for the souls entrusted to them while in holy women there is manly boldness, proficiency, and determination."

A person who nicely fits into this feminist mode is St. Catherine of Siena (1347–1380). It is not so difficult to understand why some feminists wish to claim her patronage. After all, a version of her life goes like this: At seven years of age she determines never to marry. When she is pressured by her parents to submit to an arranged marriage, at age twelve, she defiantly cuts off her hair and neglects her appearance. Later, she develops quite a following in her town. Men and women alike seek her counsel. Soon she is bringing influence to bear in political circles then unknown to women. She arbitrates family feuds. She brokers peace within and between the city-states of Tuscany. Bankers, generals, princes, dukes, kings, and queens, as well as scholars and abbots seek her counsel. Catherine's greatest political success is also a spiritual triumph—convincing Pope Gregory XI to return the papacy from France to Rome. Christopher Check, president of Catholic Answers, summarizes her life this way: "A real glass-ceiling breaker, Catherine made it big in a man's world."

But here is the kicker. In marked contrast to radical feminism, St. Catherine never understood herself as a pioneer for women's rights, much less a model for narcissistic self-fulfillment. On the contrary, she put into practice the truth her Holy Bridegroom had revealed to her: "I am that which is; you are that which is not." As Christopher Check remarks, "Because she commanded the actions of the pope, it is doubtless this action which most excites the feminists. Alas, they entirely miss the point. At no time ever in her correspondence with Pope Gregory, which is indeed direct, does she question his authority. On the contrary she tells him 'Esto vir!' Be a man! Use your authority."

CONCLUSION

Catholics are *not* against women. Women play important roles in the Church and in her history, except when it comes to the priestly hierarchy. As a matter of fact, from the beginning, the Catholic Church made women and men equal in an unprecedented way. Therefore, she does not reject the view of feminism, provided it is a Christian form of feminism, not a radical version that centers exclusively on sexual freedom and so-called reproductive rights. One could even make the case that the Church prepared the way for feminism in society by changing traditional sex-role patterns.

38

CATHOLICS IMPOSE THEIR OWN SHARIA LAW

THE LIE

The Catholic Church rejects Islamic Sharia law, but at the same time she enforces her own law, which she calls the natural law. How inconsistent can one be? You cannot reject what others do if they do something similar to what you do.

THE TRUTH

It must be admitted that the Catholic Church does promote natural law in a way that might look like the way Islam promotes Sharia law. But, in fact, they are very different.

Sharia law is derived from the religious precepts of Islam, particularly the Qur'an and the Hadith. It deals with many topics, including crime, politics, marriage contracts, trade regulations, religious prescriptions, and economics, as well as personal matters, such as sexual intercourse, hygiene, diet, prayer, everyday etiquette, and fasting. It is a law that regulates everything in life from A to Z.

An explanation of the natural law, on the other hand, needs a bit more time and space. It is based on the reality of human *nature* — nature seen as something that is distinct from God (yet ultimately dependent on God). Therefore, the natural law can be understood by everyone, even without reference to God. It is the reflection of God's eternal law "written" into human nature. That is how we can know that certain actions are good and others bad, just by the use of reason, even without any input from religious faith. As St. Thomas Aquinas put it, we know the natural law through *reasoning*, which is accessible to *all* human beings as human beings, regardless of their religion.

Natural law holds that we live in a universe of things that have a nature to themselves and that we shall get the best out of these things if we act in accord with the nature that is written into each of them. When we act rationally, we act in accord with our own nature and reality and in accord with the nature and reality of other things. This holds also for morality.

The philosopher Peter Kreeft puts it this way: the laws of morality are not rules that we invent but principles that we discover, like the laws of a science such as physiology; they are based on human nature, and human nature is essentially unchanging; therefore, the laws of morality are also essentially unchanging, just like the laws of physiology. Just as our physiological nature makes it necessary for us to eat certain foods and to breathe oxygen for our bodies to be healthy, so our moral nature makes certain moral rules and values necessary for our souls to be healthy. There is not only a physical order in nature but also a moral order that is beyond our control.

Once we know this, we can compare natural law with Sharia law. For many reasons, their similarity is very dubious. It is hard to see how they could live next to each other in the same society, let alone substitute each other.

The first reason is that Sharia law is much more invasive into societal life than natural law is. Sharia law governs nearly every facet of life, from the great affairs of state and diplomacy to the smallest concerns of the average person. It permeates the entire society. Enforcement of Sharia law is done by the government or its ruler, and punishments are severe. Unlike our separation of church and state, there is no separation of mosque and state. In a way, the Qur'an serves as the constitution of the state.

Natural law is very different. It is not directly controlled by the society or its government. Even during the time of the Inquisition, there was no court system to enforce natural law. Markedly, Thomas Aquinas made a clear distinction between the universal natural law and the local (legal, civil, or positive) laws made and upheld by local governments. These two sides are not always in agreement with each other. Civil laws can very well be "unjust" when seen in the context of natural law. As Martin Luther King Jr. said, the law of the land is not always a reflection of the moral law.

The second reason for rejecting the equivalence between Sharia law and natural law is that the Catholic Church makes a strong distinction between state and religion, or between church and state—which Islam does not. What we call nowadays the separation of church and state is actually Jesus' "invention." When Pope Benedict XVI discussed the separation of religion and politics—church and state, if you will—he wrote in his book *Jesus of Nazareth*, "In his teaching and in his whole ministry, Jesus had inaugurated a non-political Messianic kingdom and had begun to detach these two hitherto inseparable realities from one another." In other words—actually in Jesus' words—we should render to Caesar what is Caesar's, but never should render to Caesar what is God's. On the one hand, the Church benefits from the state to

keep and enforce justice. On the other hand, the state benefits
from religious beliefs, which help people respond to each other
in a moral and respectful way. But we should never confuse them
with each other.

Unfortunately, in the history of Christianity, this rule got
lost for a while when religious conflicts were mitigated as part
of the Peace of Augsburg in 1555 by the principle that the religion of the ruler, either Catholic or Protestant, is that of the
people (*cuius regio, eius religio*). But gradually the rule of separation would be brought back again as being more Christlike.
Therefore, we can reject the myth that the Catholic Church
takes over control of society with its natural law in a way similar
to what Sharia law does. Christians would fight Islam if it were
trying to impose its Sharia law on them. But Christianity has
no intention of taking over society's life, for it gives to Caesar
what is Caesar's.

The third reason for rejecting the identification of natural
law and Sharia law is that the latter is tightly connected with
Islam, whereas natural law is not tied to any specific religion
but to reason in general, shared by all of humanity. Because the
moral directives of natural law are common to all humans, every
culture in history has had some version of the Ten Commandments, or at least of the last seven of them. There is hardly anything religious, let alone Catholic, about "Don't steal" or "Don't
kill." Perhaps the best-known universal moral principle is the
so-called Golden Rule: "Do unto others what you would have
done unto yourself." The Golden Rule can be found in Christian,
Jewish, Islamic, Buddhist, and Confucian texts, among others.
As St. Paul says about the Gentiles, "What the law requires is
written on their hearts" (Rom. 2:15)—that is, on the hearts of
all people.

Catholics impose their own Sharia law

Everyone who is not "morally blind" is able to see this. As a matter of fact, there is not a great deal of difference between many elements in Christian morality, Jewish morality, Hindu morality, Muslim morality, and Buddhist morality—although there's a great difference in these religions. C. S. Lewis tells us they all have some version of what he calls the "Tao," the natural moral law. As Peter Kreeft puts it, "We find similar morals, beneath different mores." In other words, what the Catholic Church has to offer is not some outlandish faith, but a faith that comes with reason. Most of all, she has the natural law to offer, which has always focused on the common good of society and is ingrained in human nature. Whoever refuses to accept this proposition is missing out on something very essential—the common sense of the natural law. Although the natural law is not universally obeyed, or even universally admitted, it is still universally binding and authoritative.

If anyone objects that the Ten Commandments are very "religious" because God is explicitly mentioned in the First Commandment, then the best retort would be: If God is not the ultimate Lawgiver, how could any moral rule be obligatory? Neither the state nor social pressure can make anything intrinsically wrong. No one has the right to demand our absolute obedience but God. Morality is based not on human authority but on God's authority.

The fourth reason for rejecting the identification of natural law and Sharia law is that Sharia law *imposes* moral directives, whereas natural law *proposes* them. The distinction between imposing and proposing was emphasized by Pope John Paul II, who famously said, "The Church proposes; she imposes nothing." The Catholic Church does not impose do's and don'ts on society, but she does offer society a moral compass based on reason and natural law.

As said before, just as our physiological nature makes it necessary for us to eat certain foods, so our moral nature makes certain moral rules and values necessary for our souls to be healthy. Just as it is plainly evident that there is order in this world and that *like causes* produce *like effects*, so it is equally evident that human beings must act in accordance with the natural law. Reason tells us there is a moral order in nature. You don't have to be a Catholic or Muslim to see this—unless you are just not willing to.

CONCLUSION

Catholics do *not* impose natural law as their version of Sharia law. These two kinds of law are very different. Unlike Sharia law, the natural law is not dependent on a specific religion but is a universal law; it is not imposed by humans of a particular religion; it is not imposed by governments or rulers; it is written in everyone's heart; it is proposed by the Catholic Church, not imposed.

39

CATHOLICS USE RELIGION TO DISCRIMINATE

THE LIE

Catholic individuals and Catholic institutions think they have a right to discriminate based on religious objections—for instance, by refusing to provide certain services to women and to lesbian, gay, bisexual, and transgender (LGBT) persons.

Catholics use their religion as an excuse to discriminate against and harm others. The American Civil Liberties Union (ACLU) puts it this way: religious freedom in America means that we all have a right to our religious beliefs, but this does not give us the right to use our religion to discriminate against and impose those beliefs on others who do not share them.

THE TRUTH

Like freedom of speech (see chapter 36), freedom of religion has become a very contentious issue.

Pope John Paul II used to make a distinction between secularism and secularity. Unlike secularism, secularity merely draws a dividing line between religion and state, or between religious institutions and governmental institutions (see chapter 38). However, times have changed. Secularism has gone much further in the minds of most secularists. It has shifted from freedom *of* religion to freedom *from* religion. Whereas secularity merely separates the nonreligious realm from the religious realm, secularism is intolerant of religion and imposes its own totally secular standards on everything else, including religion.

Modern secularism rejects the impact not so much of any beliefs—for secularism itself is a belief—but of *religious* beliefs in particular. We see Western secularization crossing the line here from neutrality to outright hostility toward religion in general, and toward Catholicism in particular. Bishop Barron of Los Angeles puts it this way: "The secularist state recognizes that its principle enemy is the Church Catholic. Accordingly, it wants Catholicism off the public stage and relegated to a private realm where it cannot interfere with secularism's totalitarian agenda."

This makes Iain T. Benson, a Scottish legal philosopher, question the secularists' agenda as follows: "Are we only to allow all kinds of influence as long as they do not come from religion? Why, for example, ought the beliefs of a politician that originate in materialism be acceptable but a critique of materialism animated by religious convictions be unacceptable?" Secularism wants you to give up your *religious* values, and replace them with *secular* values, which are far from neutral—they are usually pro-abortion, pro-euthanasia, and pro-homosexual activity. However, we should ask ourselves: If religion cannot impose its values on secular society, why should secular society have the right to impose its values on religion?

However, there is a much more serious problem with the secularist view of "religious liberty." The ACLU, for instance, constantly speaks about religious liberty in terms of *beliefs*, as do almost all secularists. Catholics, for instance, are seen as discriminating against others based on their moral and religious convictions—which the ACLU and its proponents consistently call *beliefs*. They insist that religion and moral directives should be reduced to a body of mere "beliefs" with no claim to truth; and hence no claim should be taken seriously by anyone who does not share those beliefs. If this were true, that would indeed weaken the position of those religious individuals and religious institutions who are finding themselves forced, through civil laws and mandates, to take part in performing activities they morally object to. All they would have left is to claim an *exemption* from the laws imposed on them, while leaving those laws in place—for laws trump "beliefs."

This makes it very tempting to speak here of a "moral conflict." Take, for example, the LGBT discussion. In the eyes of many people, there is a moral conflict here, often portrayed as the "rights" of LGBT people versus the "beliefs" of certain religious groups. But that's exactly where the problem lies. They portray their own beliefs as "rights," but the rights of their opponents as mere "beliefs." You cannot reject the rights of others by labeling them as mere beliefs, while refusing to do the same for yourself.

However, as said earlier (see chapter 38), a "moral code" is not just a religious belief but is a directive based on natural law, and natural law is by its very nature accessible to any human being by the mere power of reason, without the input of any religion. It is based on human nature, on the way we *are* and were made by our Creator. Since morality is a function of human nature, *reason* can discover valid moral principles by looking at the nature of humanity and society. Therefore, a "moral" judgment moves beyond statements of merely private *beliefs*; it speaks to the things that are right or wrong, just or unjust, generally or universally—*for others as well as ourselves.* Morality is about the common good—and thus indirectly also about the personal good, since we are social beings by nature. The *Catechism* says, "In keeping with the social nature of man, the good of each individual is necessarily related to the common good, which in turn can be defined only in reference to the human person" (1905).

The natural law comes with natural rights and natural duties. It tells us what we owe others—our natural *duties*—and what others owe us—our natural *rights.* In fact, for every moral right there is a corresponding responsibility, and vice versa. Moral duties and rights go hand in hand and have a natural reciprocity. The duty of self-preservation comes with the right of self-preservation; the duty to seek the truth matches the right to seek it; the duty to work for justice comes with the right to pursue it; the duty to protect life goes with the right of life's protection; the right of receiving religious freedom corresponds with the duty to respect religious freedom; the duty to acknowledge human dignity implies also the right to claim it.

Once we uncouple moral rights from duties, fake new "rights" can pop up like mushrooms. They are invented and claimed on the spot, but the question of duty is utterly lost. At best they can become *entitlements,* or privileges, enforced by a legal system—the laws of the land, so to speak. Entitlements are at best something the government owes us, but not something we owe the government. We gain entitlements and privileges as we age; in the United States, for instance, we can drive a car at sixteen, vote at eighteen, and buy alcohol at twenty-one. But we cannot apply this kind of reasoning to moral rights. Rights are not gained with age. We have rights because we are all human beings subjected to the natural law; but entitlements we only have because we belong to a certain society. Rights we cannot invent

womb. Once again, there is no appeal to faith or beliefs. One doesn't have to be Catholic or religious in order to understand this argument—and that has been precisely the argument of the Church, that this is a matter that turns on the moral reasoning of the Natural Law.

Needless to say, this puts certain discussions in the legislative branch of government in a completely different light.

Let's go back to our original question: Can religion be an excuse for discrimination? The answer is yes and no. On the one hand, the answer is yes, depending on what discrimination means. If it just means "making a distinction," then those who say Catholics discriminate are themselves discriminating against Catholics as well. But if discrimination is seen as something morally good or bad, then we need to face the fact that Catholics have *valid* reasons to discriminate, for their reasons are based on the natural law that we all share—Catholics and non-Catholics alike.

On the other hand, the answer can also be no. It all depends on what "religion" means. Not all religions are of the same "quality" (see chapter 20). Just search the Internet, and you will find the weirdest kinds of so-called religions. Once we reduce "religion" to a mere set of beliefs and opinions, *untested by reason*, anything can go under that banner—even white-supremacist beliefs would qualify as "religion." In other words, not everything that calls itself religion should be regarded as a legitimate religion. Given such a diversity, not all "religions"—ranging from legitimate to illegitimate —can be used as an excuse to discriminate. What we need instead is something that transcends and unites all religions—which is the natural law, based on reason.

CONCLUSION

Catholics do *not* use religion to discriminate. What they really use is the natural law, not just their religious beliefs. Religion is seen by many as a body of mere "beliefs" with no claim to truth; and hence no claim should be taken seriously by anyone who does not share those beliefs. A moral code, on the other hand, is not just a belief but a directive based on natural law, and natural law is by its very nature accessible to any human being by the mere power of reason. When Catholics refuse to provide certain services to women and to other particular groups, they do so by virtue of the natural law, but their opponents claim that Catholics discriminate against their "rights." Ironically, these opponents portray their own beliefs as "rights," but the rights of their opponents as mere "beliefs." So they really are asking Catholics to give up their own fundamental rights.

CATHOLICS ARE HIGHLY SELECTIVE IN MORALITY

THE LIE

Catholics are very inconsistent. They say, for instance, "You shall not kill," but then they apply this rule according to circumstances. It doesn't hold in what they call a "just war." It doesn't hold when it comes to "gun control." For some Catholics, it doesn't even apply to abortion or euthanasia. Being smug is a characteristic once defined by Mark Twain as best exemplified by "a Christian with five aces."

Catholic morality is full of inconsistencies: life in the womb is sacred, but life on the battlefield is not; telling untruths is forbidden, but telling half-truths is not; stealing is forbidden, but promoting equal distribution of wealth is a form of "fair stealing." Each time they choose whatever fits best.

THE TRUTH

There are some strong resemblances between scientific laws (laws of nature) and moral laws (the natural law). They both are universal (applicable to everyone everywhere), absolute (without exceptions), timeless (even if we do not know the underlying law yet), and objective (given, independent of us and of any human authority). In other words, they are objective, universal, timeless, absolute standards — no matter whether we are talking laws of nature in terms of true and false, or moral laws in terms of right and wrong. Just as "truths are true," even when we do not know yet that they are true, so "rights are right," even though we may not realize yet they are morally right.

Because moral rights, laws, and values are universal, absolute, timeless, objective, and nonnegotiable standards of human behavior, we cannot just pick whatever we want when it comes to morality. We cannot just vote to decide whether we are anti-slavery and anti-abortion. In other words, there is no "pro-choice" in morality. Morality obliges us to choose, unconditionally, what is morally good and right. This raises at least two important questions: (1) Does this mean moral rights, laws, and values can never change? (2) Does this mean that there are never situations when killing or lying can be morally right?

The answer to the first question is that, indeed, moral values can never change. Morality is not a function of the clock. Some people might object to this idea, saying that moral values clearly have been subject to change during the course of human history — slavery, for instance, was only recently considered morally wrong; had the slaveholders won the Civil War, so they say, we might see it today as an admirable institution. Well, did our moral values, moral laws, and moral rules change over time? Not really. We have a mix-up here between moral *values* and moral *evaluations*. Moral evaluations are our personal feelings or discernments regarding moral values.

Some people think that, in making moral evaluations, we create moral values in accordance with these evaluations. So when evaluations change, the moral values and moral laws are said to change as well. If that were true, our moral values would indeed be subject to various cultural and historical fluctuations; morality would just be a matter of emotions, personal preferences, private beliefs, cultural trends, political powers, and majority votes. As a result, moral correctness would just be a matter of political correctness.

In response to this, the Catholic Church emphasizes that evaluations are merely a reflection of the way we discern absolute moral values and react to them for the time being. Whereas moral evaluations may be volatile and fluctuating, moral values and moral laws are timeless, universal, objective, and absolute. Think of the following comparison. Our current understanding of physical or biological laws needs revision each time science reaches a better understanding of those laws as they really are. In the meantime, we assume there are absolute and universal laws of nature, although we may not yet have fully captured them in our current understanding and in our existing evaluations.

Something similar holds for moral values. As C. S. Lewis once put it, "The human mind has no more power of inventing a new value than of imagining a new primary color." To use a more specific example, we could ask about Nazi death camps: Were they really morally wrong, or were they just wrong in the eyes of nations other than Germany after World War II? Almost everyone would agree they were morally wrong and will always be wrong, although some may have adjusted their moral evaluations to their own personal outlook, because people can be morally blind—blinded by upbringing, character, personality, or self-interest. Moral blindness can even spread like an infectious disease.

The answer to question 2 is that, indeed, murder or lying can never be morally right. Since moral rights, moral laws, and moral values are universal, absolute, timeless, objective, and nonnegotiable standards of human behavior, they are essentially without any exceptions. Murder is always morally wrong; stealing is always morally wrong; lying is always morally wrong—that is, no matter who you are and where you are, regardless of your status in society, and regardless of any particular circumstances.

But does this stand really exclude any exemptions? Perhaps killing is not murder when war is necessary for peace. Perhaps stealing is not theft when taking a weapon away from a terrorist. If so, does this not reek of relativism? Not really, for this does not mean that morality is relative. It is flawed to argue that if morality is determined by situations, and situations are relative, then morality must be relative. The fact that the same moral principles must be applied differently to different situations presupposes the absolute validity of those principles. Situations may vary, but the moral principles do not. If the standard were as flexible as the situation, then it would be no standard at all. Yardsticks have to be rigid. In other words, murder is always wrong, even in a just war; stealing is always wrong, even when disarming a killer. Yet, there may be situations in which killing is permissible. Killing for self-defense does not automatically change killing into murder.

How can the Catholic Church defend this seeming ambiguity of both rejecting exceptions and accepting exceptions? On the one hand, the *Catechism* says, "Circumstances of themselves cannot change the moral quality of acts themselves; they can make neither good nor right an action that is in itself evil" (1754). On the other hand, it also acknowledges that "application of the natural law varies greatly; it can demand reflection that takes account of various conditions of life according to places, times, and circumstances" (1957). How can these two statements go together, without contradicting each other?

Catholics are highly selective in morality

Whenever an exception is made to a moral law, there is always a more general moral law that justifies the exception. The more general law we are speaking of here is the so-called law, or principle, of *double effect*. A clear example of this principle is self-defense. In the words of the *Catechism*: "The act of self-defense can have a double effect: the preservation of one's own life; and the killing of the aggressor.... The one is intended, the other is not" (2263).

Apparently, this principle invokes the distinction between the good effect one intends and the evil effect one does not intend. This principle does not make Catholic morality highly selective, as some think, but it gives morality a more solid foundation. According to this principle, it may be morally permissible to perform an act with double effect, but only if all of the following criteria are fulfilled: (1) the act is not intrinsically evil; (2) the bad effect is not directly intended; (3) the bad effect is not the means for attaining the good effect; (4) and the good effect outweighs the bad effect.

Based on this principle, self-defense or waging war may be morally justified for the following reason: one may use violence against another to save one's own life, even if a consequence of self-defense will be the death of the aggressor. There is a clear difference here between the good effect one intends and the evil effect one does *not* intend. The moral law forbids murder — in which a bad effect is directly intended and a good effect is missing — but not necessarily killing, if there is an intended good effect that offsets the not-intended bad effect. So not all killing is murder; what does make it murder is the intended bad effect. Obviously, the principle of double effect can play an important role in making moral decisions, especially during crisis situations. Here are two more brief examples of situations where we can apply this principle: abortion and euthanasia.

How could this principle apply to abortion? Let us state first that medical considerations can never overrule moral considerations. Medical rules should always comply with the moral rule of preserving life, for morality is not a calculus of consequences, depending on circumstances or the end in view. Sometimes abortion may be medically recommended, but that does not automatically make it also morally right. Every obstetrician should always take care of *two* patients—both the mother and her unborn baby. However, abortion can be considered for medical reasons—such as saving the life of the pregnant mother when it is endangered by the pregnancy—and those reasons need to be taken into moral consideration.

Let us analyze the principle of double effect a bit further for cases in which a woman has a rather serious pathological condition during her pregnancy. Operations, treatments, and medications that will result in the death of the unborn baby might be morally permissible if, and only if, they have as their direct purpose to cure the pregnant woman, and if they cannot be safely postponed until the unborn baby is viable. In other words, actions that may result in the death of an unborn baby *might* be morally permitted, but only if all of the following conditions are met: (1) the act is not intrinsically evil; (2) the bad effect is not directly intended; (3) the bad effect is not the means for attaining the good effect; (4) and the good effect outweighs the bad effect.

This principle can also be applied to situations in which euthanasia is considered. There are several questions that need to be addressed here. First, there is the question of giving pain-relief treatment to terminally ill or near-death patients. Such treatment is morally permissible, provided it is given with the primary intention to relieve pain. The principle makes intention in the mind of the doctor a crucial factor in judging the moral correctness of the doctor's action. Providing necessary pain relief, even if it shortens life, fulfills all four conditions of the principle of double effect. "Active" euthanasia, on the other hand, fulfills none of them. It would be morally wrong to hasten death intentionally in order to cut short the suffering of a terminally ill patient.

A second question is this: What about prolonging life when death is near? The *Catechism* is very explicit on this issue: "Discontinuing medical procedures that are burdensome, dangerous, extraordinary, or disproportionate to the expected outcome can be legitimate; it is the refusal of 'over-zealous' treatment. Here one does not will to cause death; one's inability to impede it is merely accepted" (2278). Again, death is not a directly intended effect here; the bad effect is foreseen but not intended.

A third question to address is this one: What about stopping artificial nutrition and hydration of a near-death patient? There is no moral obligation to provide nutrition and hydration in the last hours if a sick person's body is no longer able to process food and water. These patients will die of their disease or their organ failure before starvation or dehydration could kill them.

A fourth question to address is the following: What about providing pain relief to near-death patients or terminally ill patients? This is known as palliative care—medical care for patients with terminal illness in need of pain relief by administering opioid drugs. Physicians and researchers have insisted repeatedly that it is a myth that opioids administered for pain relief can be expected to hasten death. If that argument is correct, that would mean there is nothing morally wrong with administering pain relief, for it is not even a form of passive euthanasia.

However, the situation would be different if or when it turns out that opioid drugs do in fact hasten death. But even then, administering pain relief can be morally permissible. Giving pain-relief treatment that also hastens death would be justified if the main intention is to relieve the pain, not deliberately to cause the death. In other words, providing necessary pain relief, even if it shortens life, is not active euthanasia unless the explicit intent was to kill. The *Catechism* is very explicit on this too: "The use of painkillers to alleviate the sufferings of the dying, even at the risk of shortening their days, can be morally in conformity with human dignity if death is not willed as either an end or a means, but only foreseen and tolerated as inevitable" (2279).

An added problem with moral issues is that some people legitimize their violations of moral rules by adjusting their vocabulary. They redefine euthanasia as "mercy killing," or abortion as a "health care" issue. Usually, verbal engineering comes before social engineering. But the moral issue doesn't disappear.

What all the above considerations show is that the Catholic Church is highly consistent in matters of morality, but certainly not highly selective — the ones who redefine terms are. Yet the Church also knows that each one of us is highly selective as to whether we really want to do what is right. As Fr. James V. Schall, S.J., puts it, "We are not asked to save the world, but to save our souls in a world mostly at odds with what it means to save our souls."

CONCLUSION

Catholics are *not* highly selective in morality. They are actually highly consistent in their moral evaluations. Murder, stealing, and lying are *always* morally wrong. If there seems to be any

Catholics are highly selective in morality

inconsistency, we might be dealing with an exception. Whenever an exception is made to a moral law, there is always a more general moral law that justifies the exception—for instance, the law of *double effect*.

AFTERWORD

As the previous chapters show, there is a large spectrum of misperceptions, prejudices, fabrications, and even patent lies regarding what Catholics believe—or more accurately what the Catholic Church teaches. They cover a wide array of religious matters—ranging from biblical foundations and historical events, to social and moral questions. In each case, the Catholic Church is supposed to have it wrong. Unfortunately, there is much misinformation in our culture about Catholicism. It has been spread through books, newspapers, television, the Internet, and other mass media. But it turns out to be fabricated information based on an antireligion bias, and more specifically an anti-Catholic prejudice in media and academia.

This book was written to set the record straight. As we showed and argued in the previous chapters, these accusations are untruths and fabrications. They are distortions made up by people who want to legitimize why they wanted to separate themselves from the one, holy, catholic, and apostolic Church.

They claim that present Catholic teachings are deviations from the original Christian message that Jesus preached. However, as we've now seen, those teachings are deeply rooted in what Jesus taught us, what the apostles told us, and what the early Church Fathers handed down to us. They all trace their origin back to Jesus Himself.

When some people say that the Catholic Church is no longer Christian, or that the core of Christianity has never been Catholic, they are denying a profound truth. As the earliest records of Christianity demonstrate, Christians were Catholic, and Catholics were Christians. Catholics didn't grow away from their Christian origin.

If many Protestants still think that the history of the Church ended with the closure of the New Testament and picked up again with the sixteenth-century Protestant Reformation, this book has news for them. The Catholic Church never broke with the early Church; instead it was the Protestant Church that broke away and separated itself from our common Christian, Catholic roots. Catholics are Christians, and Christians should be Catholics.

ABOUT THE AUTHOR

Gerard M. Verschuuren is a human biologist, specialized in human genetics. He also earned a doctorate in the philosophy of science. He has studied and worked at universities in Europe and in the United States. Currently semi-retired, he spends most of his time as a writer, speaker, and consultant on the interface of science and religion, faith and reason.

Some of his most recent books are *God and Evolution?: Science Meets Faith* (Pauline Books, 2012); *The Destiny of the Universe: In Pursuit of the Great Unknown* (Paragon House, 2014); *Five Anti-Catholic Myths: Slavery, Crusades, Inquisition, Galileo, Holocaust* (Angelico Press, 2015); *Life's Journey: A Guide from Conception to Growing Up, Growing Old, and Natural Death* (Angelico Press, 2016); *Aquinas and Modern Science: A New Synthesis of Faith and Reason* (Angelico Press, 2016); *Faith and Reason: The Cradle of Truth* (EnRoute Books, 2017); *The Myth of an Anti-Science Church: Galileo, Darwin, Teilhard, Hawking, Dawkins* (Angelico Press, 2018); *The First Christians: Keeping the Faith in Times of Trouble* (EnRoute Books, 2018); and *The Eclipse of God: Is Religion on the Way Out?* (EnRoute Books, 2018).

Dr. Verschuuren can be contacted at www.where-do-we-come-from.com.

INDEX

Cornwell, John, 209, 211
creation, 239, 253, 257, 263, 266
Crick, Francis, 236
Cronin, Frank, 234
crucifix, 125
crusades, 181
Cusa, Nicolas of, 242
Cyprian, 145

D

Dachau, 201, 205
Dark Ages, 6, 182, 223, 227
Decalogue. See Ten
   Commandments
deuterocanonical, 14, 16
Didache, 43, 56, 68, 87, 120
dogma, 242
Donatism, 80
Douay-Rheims Bible, 11, 23
double effect, 327, 328
double truth, 238
Duhem, Pierre, 226, 244

E

Easter, 174
Einstein, Albert, 259
Eliot, T. S., 188
Enlightenment, 182, 223–224,
   282, 290
entitlements, 318
Eucharist, 35, 37, 39, 74, 81, 120,
   122, 131–133, 136
eugenics, 205
euthanasia, 201, 328
evolution, 264

F

faith and reason, 218, 234
falsification, 226

Father, 77
feminism, 303
Feyerabend, Paul, 235
First Cause. *See* Primary Cause
Fox-Genovese, Elizabeth Ann, 304
freedom, 50, 63, 65, 147, 220,
   285, 295, 303, 316
freedom of expression, 191
free speech, 294

G

Gamaliel, 30
Glendon, Mary Ann, 302
Gnosticism, 165
grace, 63
Grant, Edward, 244
Groeschel, Benedict, 48, 132
Grosseteste, Robert, 226
Guardini, Romano, 122

H

Hahn, Scott, 107, 120, 135
Heaven, 50, 114
heliocentrism, 242
Hell, 50, 52, 147
heresy, 191, 290
hierarchy, 164
Hildegard of Bingen, 226
Himmler, Heinrich, 200
Hitler, Adolf, 199
Hochhuth, Rolf, 213–214
Holocaust, 205–206, 209, 211
Hubble, Edwin, 254
humanism, 285
human rights, 319

I

idolatry, 31, 40, 109, 111–112,
   115, 117, 269

Index

Index

St. Thomas Aquinas, 10, 22, 73,
133, 135, 138, 220, 242, 271,
275, 287
St. Thomas More, 10, 25
statue, 109, 116
stellar parallaxes, 249
Steno, Nicolas, 230
Sylvester II, 225

T

Ten Commandments, 29–32,
312–313
Tertullian, 45, 126, 135
Theotokos, 102, 103
Thomas. *See* St. Thomas
Aquinas
Thurien, Max, 106
Torquemada, Tomás, 195
Tradition, 15, 19, 24, 26, 167
transubstantiation, 131, 133–134
truth, 238, 284
Tyndale, William, 10, 72, 177

U

Urban II, 183

V

values vs. evaluations, 324
Vatican II, 12, 121, 122, 148, 149,
288
Virgin Mary, 102–105
virtuality, 229
Vulgate, 7, 11, 14, 16, 23, 45

W

Weigel, George, 9
Whitehead, Alfred North, 244,
252
worship, 117
Wycliffe, John, 10, 24, 72

Z

Zolli, Israel, 160, 213

Sophia Institute

Sophia Institute is a nonprofit institution that seeks to nurture the spiritual, moral, and cultural life of souls and to spread the Gospel of Christ in conformity with the authentic teachings of the Roman Catholic Church.

Sophia Institute Press fulfills this mission by offering translations, reprints, and new publications that afford readers a rich source of the enduring wisdom of mankind.

Sophia Institute also operates two popular online Catholic resources: CrisisMagazine.com and CatholicExchange.com.

Crisis Magazine provides insightful cultural analysis that arms readers with the arguments necessary for navigating the ideological and theological minefields of the day. *Catholic Exchange* provides world news from a Catholic perspective as well as daily devotionals and articles that will help you to grow in holiness and live a life consistent with the teachings of the Church.

In 2013, Sophia Institute launched Sophia Institute for Teachers to renew and rebuild Catholic culture through service to Catholic education. With the goal of nurturing the spiritual, moral, and cultural life of souls, and an abiding respect for the role and work of teachers, we strive to provide materials and programs that are at once enlightening to the mind and ennobling to the heart; faithful and complete, as well as useful and practical.

Sophia Institute gratefully recognizes the Solidarity Association for preserving and encouraging the growth of our apostolate over the course of many years. Without their generous and timely support, this book would not be in your hands.

www.SophiaInstitute.com
www.CatholicExchange.com
www.CrisisMagazine.com
www.SophiaInstituteforTeachers.org

Sophia Institute Press® is a registered trademark of Sophia Institute.
Sophia Institute is a tax-exempt institution as defined by the
Internal Revenue Code, Section 501(c)(3). Tax I.D. 22-2548708.